Cinematic Thinking

Cinematic Thinking

Philosophical Approaches to the New Cinema

EDITED BY **James Phillips**

Stanford University Press

Stanford, California

Stanford University Press
Stanford, California

Printed in the United States of America on acid-free, archival-quality paper

Library of Congress Cataloging-in-Publication Data

Cinematic thinking : philosophical approaches to the new cinema / edited by
James Phillips.
    p. cm.
Includes bibliographical references and index.
    ISBN 978-0-8047-5800-0 (cloth : alk. paper)--ISBN 978-0-8047-5801-7 (pbk. :
alk. paper)
    1. Motion pictures--Philosophy. I. Phillips, James, 1970-
PN1995.C5352 2008
791.4301--dc22   2008004784

Designed by Bruce Lundquist
Typeset at Stanford University Press in 11/13.5 Adobe Garamond

Contents

Contributors

ALEXANDER GARCÍA DÜTTMANN is professor of philosophy and visual culture at Goldsmiths College, University of London. Recent publications include *Philosophy of Exaggeration* (London: Continuum, 2007); *Visconti: Einsichten in Fleisch und Blut* (Berlin: Kadmos, 2006); and *So ist es: Ein philosophischer Kommentar zu Adornos "Minima Moralia"* (Frankfurt am Main: Suhrkamp, 2004).

JEFF MALPAS is professor of philosophy at the University of Tasmania, in Hobart, Tasmania. He is the author of many books and essays on a wide range of philosophical topics ranging from the history of philosophy to applied ethics. He is perhaps best known for his work on the philosophy of Donald Davidson and Martin Heidegger and on the philosophy of space and place. His most recent book is *Heidegger's Topology* (Cambridge, MA: MIT Press, 2006).

ANDREW J. MITCHELL is assistant professor of philosophy at Emory University. His research interests include materiality, mediation, and the philosophy of literature. He is the author of a number of essays on Heidegger, Nietzsche, Derrida, and James Joyce. Andrew Mitchell is the cotranslator of *Heidegger's Four Seminars* (Bloomington: Indiana University Press, 2003); and coeditor of *Community, Communication, Communism: The Thought of Georges Bataille* (Albany: State University of New York Press, forthcoming). He is currently completing revisions to a book-length study entitled *The Fourfold: Thing and World in Late Heidegger*.

JEAN-LUC NANCY is professor of philosophy at the Université Marc Bloch, Strasbourg. Among his many books, he is the author of the following titles published by Stanford University Press: *Multiple Arts* (2006); *A Finite Thinking* (2003); *The Speculative Remark* (2001); *Being Singular Plural* (2000); *The Muses* (1996); *The Birth to Presence* (1993); and *The Experience of Freedom* (1993).

KELLY OLIVER is W. Alton Jones Chair and professor of philosophy at Vanderbilt University. She is the author of more than fifty articles and fifteen books, including *The Colonization of Psychic Space: A Psychoanalytic Theory of Oppression* (Minneapolis: University of Minnesota Press, 2004); *Noir Anxiety: Race, Sex, and Maternity in Film Noir* (Minneapolis: University of Minnesota Press, 2002); *Witnessing: Beyond Recognition* (Minneapolis: University of Minnesota Press, 2001); *Subjectivity Without Subjects: From Abject Fathers to Desiring Mothers* (Lanham, MD: Rowman and Littlefield, 1998); *Family Values: Subjects Between Nature and Culture* (New York: Routledge, 1997); *Womanizing Nietzsche: Philosophy's Relation to "the Feminine"* (New York: Routledge, 1995); and *Reading Kristeva: Unraveling the Double-Bind* (Bloomington: Indiana University Press, 1993).

JAMES PHILLIPS is an ARC Australian research fellow in the School of Philosophy and History at the University of New South Wales. He is the author of *The Equivocation of Reason: Kleist Reading Kant* (Stanford, CA: Stanford University Press, 2007); and *Heidegger's Volk: Between National Socialism and Poetry* (Stanford, CA: Stanford University Press, 2005).

ALISON ROSS teaches in the Centre for Comparative Literature and Cultural Studies at Monash University, Melbourne. She is the author of *The Aesthetic Paths of Philosophy: Presentation in Kant, Heidegger, Lacoue-Labarthe, and Nancy* (Stanford, CA: Stanford University Press, 2007).

MICHAEL J. SHAPIRO is professor of political science at the University of Hawaii. Among his recent publications are *Methods and Nations: Cultural Governance and the Indigenous Subject* (New York: Routledge, 2004); and *Deforming American Political Thought: Ethnicity, Facticity, and Genre* (Lexington: University Press of Kentucky, 2006). He is currently completing a manuscript entitled *Cinematic Geopolitics*.

CECILIA SJÖHOLM is associate professor in the Program of Aesthetics at South Stockholm University College and the author of *The Antigone Complex* (Stanford, CA: Stanford University Press, 2004).

KRZYSZTOF ZIAREK is professor of comparative literature at the State University of New York at Buffalo. He is the author of *Inflected Language: Toward a Hermeneutics of Nearness* (Albany: State University of New York Press, 1994); *The Historicity of Experience: Modernity, the Avant-Garde, and the Event* (Evanston, IL: Northwestern University Press, 2001); and *The Force of Art* (Stanford, CA: Stanford University Press, 2004). He has also published numerous essays on Coolidge, Stein, Stevens, Heidegger, Benjamin, Irigaray, and Levinas, and he has coedited two collections of essays: *Future Crossings: Literature Between Philosophy and Cultural Studies* (Evanston, IL: Northwestern University Press, 2000); and *Adorno and Heidegger* (Stanford, CA: Stanford University Press, 2007). He is the author of two books of poetry in Polish, *Zaimejlowane z Polski* and *Sąd dostateczny*.

Cinematic Thinking

Introduction
What Can Cinema Do?

JAMES PHILLIPS

ONE WAY A BOOK of philosophical essays on film might begin
is with an attempt to justify bringing philosophy and cinema together.
Something could be made of the fact that the two share a constitutive and
ambiguous relation to the past. The reality now projected on the screen,
before which the present of its technological projection effaces itself, is
no longer real. And by arriving after the event, as Hegel intimates in the
preface to the *Philosophy of Right*, thinking opens up the difference from
actuality in which it can lay claim to being the truth of what is.[1] Notwithstanding the physical exertions, managerial vigilance, and, for want of a
nicer if not better term, power politics that are seemingly prerequisites of
the cinematic profession, the filmmaker is the contemplative among the
artists. The specificity of the cinematic art is the passivity of the technological apparatus of reproduction before a given scene: to put it a little too
pompously but not, for that matter, inaccurately, cinema is the contemplative eye of the storm of the technological manipulation of beings. The myth
common to philosophy and cinema is that they acquiesce in front of the
spectacle of what is. This myth does not so much inform philosophy's title
to truth as ground the very understanding of truth. Cinema, which to begin with could not be acknowledged as art by the terms of late nineteenth-
century aesthetics because a realistic art is an oxymoron, perhaps should
not have found a place so quickly among the traditional arts. This is not to
suggest that cinema should have been assimilated to philosophy; an analogy, and nothing further, exists between the disingenuousness with which
Hegel writes of philosophy's resignation with respect to actuality and the

1

alleged passivity of the cinematic reproduction of phenomena. But it is to suggest that there is something peculiar about cinema. It is more realistic than the arts, but because it lacks their comparative self-subsistence, because its realism consists in pointing to what is no longer, in even being what is no longer, it is also less real, less actual.

Another way a book of philosophical essays on film might begin is with a statement of the irreconcilability of cinema and metaphysics. In the brute positivity of its reproductions of what is, cinema remains immersed in the singularity of phenomena and forgoes a claim to the universality in which metaphysical knowledge has its element. Even when cinema falters before the singular, it aligns itself with the cliché rather than the concept. If Hitchcock is a great director, if his recognition as an artist of genius was long resisted, it is arguably because his domain is the specifically cinematic space of nonideal, animistic, and conspiratorial singular objects. Cinema's gift for horror lies in its passivity and its attendant, paradoxically technological, invention of the experience of the pretechnological exposure to the tyranny of things. But the singularities with which cinema is populated can also be the occasion for a declaration of faith in the world: this is something that unites Cavell's and Deleuze's texts on film, just as it is something that could only properly be borne out by a profusion of at once exacting and eccentric observations (another shared feature of their texts). Cinema, whose passivity before what is slips all too easily over into a cynical complacency in the face of clichés, can by its receptiveness to the unassimilable recall metaphysics to its foundation in wonder.

Each of the essays in this collection addresses a single director from what, very broadly understood, may be called the New Cinema. Defined in purely historical terms, the New Cinema names the resurgence of various national film industries after the devastation wrought by World War II and the commercial dominance of the American sound film. But the Italian neorealism of the 1940s and 1950s, the French *nouvelle vague* (new wave) of the 1960s, the *Neuer Deutscher Film* (new German cinema) of the 1970s, along with other national and international styles and movements, resemble one another in more than their historical conditions. As the newness of the New Cinema is inextricable from a renewal of the very question of cinema, from a search for ways to open up the medium, it is one-sided to define the movement by its works rather than by its principle of an interrogation and rejection of the habits of cinema. If a case can be made for including *Psycho* and *The Birds*, it is because these films take advantage of the cracks in the crumbling studio system against which the New Cinema was a reaction. The big-budget B-grade movies that in the 1970s restored Hollywood's fortunes were not committed to Hitchcock's insight into the horror of the everyday but sought in the supernatural and the extraterrestrial new resources for illusionist cinema. And the recent work of Claire Denis, the last director covered here, inasmuch as it eschews the marketable conventions of Hollywood and its foreign aspirants, as well as the hermetism of so-called experimental film, participates in the New Cinema's desire to extricate a medium of mass appeal from the clutches of cliché.

The philosophical interest of the New Cinema is its simultaneously material and political interest. Siegfried Kracauer clarifies this conjunction of the material and the political when he sets out the dilemma by whose refusal the New Cinema might be defined: "Average theatrical films and certain high-level avant-garde films must be lumped together in spite of all that separates them. Films of this kind exploit, not explore, the material phenomena they insert; they insert them not in their own interest but for the purpose of establishing a significant whole; and in pointing up some such whole, they refer us from the material dimension back to that of ideology."[2] Kracauer regrets these two paths of cinema because they betray cinema's specific innovation of a passivity before phenomena.[3] What the New Cinema advances against ideology, in the wake of fascism and Stalinism, in the context of Algeria, Vietnam, and military dictatorships in Latin America and elsewhere, is the *longueur*. To the extent that boredom breaks open the ideological whole, it is an avatar of the wonder of the Greeks (the decadence with which Heidegger, Duchamp, and Beckett, for instance, espouse boredom is also their originarity). What is at stake is the proximity of the New Cinema to philosophy and the redefinition of art, politics, and their relationship that is the corollary of this proximity. The generality of such a statement, offered as it is in the introduction to an anthology, is not so much the articulation of the program of the collection as its problem: the point of indifference that an introduction might extract from the individual contributions is either so general as to be indifferent in the bad sense or at risk of being taken for true on no better grounds than consensus. It is not an issue of posing *the* question of cinema but of searching for new ways to pursue the debate around the phenomenon.

As each essay in this collection revolves around the work of a single director, it might appear that a decision on the nature of the phenomenon of cinema has been presupposed. Is it not the case that even if one bears in mind that the proper name of a director denotes a constellation of collaborators, rather than a lone individual given over to the expression of his or her personal artistic vision, the specificity that Kracauer ascribes to cinema on the basis of its engagement with the material dimension has been exchanged for the understanding of the arts in general as the stamping of material with an overarching message (the message of the collaborators)? This question, however, is a little unfair. The cinematic proper name invariably escapes the interiority of an individual or a collective to invoke the historical and perceptual thickness of a given place: it becomes a path into that very concreteness of the cinematic image that remains unattainable for a general discussion of cinema.

In another sense, however, as Walter Benjamin contends in his essay "The Work of Art in the Age of Its Technical Reproducibility" (Das Kunstwerk im Zeitalter seiner technischen Reproduzierbarkeit), cinema amounts to a break with the concrete: the here and now of the work of art, as constitutive of its "aura," yield to the nondeterminant locality and temporality of the multiple copies of a film. Whatever pretensions Kracauer may put forward in the name of the superior material engagement of cinema have to be set against the dissolution of the material singularity of the cinematic work itself. Reproductions of a work of the visual arts testify, as copies, to the privileged here and now of the original, whereas the performances of a theatrical text or a musical score, inasmuch as they first endow their sources with the singularity of a here and now, are their realization more than their reproduction. In cinema there is no such relation between original and copy. Benjamin, who wishes to ascribe a revolutionary potential to simulacra, writes off the here and now of the work of art as vestiges of the cult object. But in this regard Benjamin's Marxism remains too metaphysical. Political activism, which is by necessity a confrontation with, as well as enactment of, the here and now, cannot be given its due in an account that defines *authenticity* (*aura*) by the here and now and undertakes its liquidation.

The political hopes that Benjamin was not alone in placing in the "democratic" medium of cinema appear ill-founded so far as the disavowal of the here and now of the public at a given screening is concerned. By virtue of the possibility / threat / prohibition of participation, the one-off aesthetic space of a theatrical performance is much closer in nature to the volatile political space of a party meeting or mass rally than the lightless, abstract realm where individuals gather for the private consumption of the interchangeable commodity of a film. The cinema presents its audience with a fait accompli. What is shown is already past, and although it opens itself up to the populations of the world through distribution and low entry prices, the cinema excludes its public by means of the fatalism with which a film plays itself out in being screened (even if audience members stop the projection, they are too late to influence the film). In the epilogue to his text Benjamin warns that fascism is turning politics into a theatrical performance.[4] Yet were one to base one's judgment solely—and with no doubt an inexcusable degree of historical irresponsibility, but here that is not to the point—on their structural similarities, one might await a reconversion of the theatrical into the political. From this perspective Cavell's diagnosis of the politics of cinema in *The World Viewed* seems much more desperate. The past that film restores to us is not myth (the continuity of culture and the vitality of traditions) but the raw fact of a here and now from which we are excluded:

On film, the past which is present is pastness or presentness itself, time itself, visually preserved in endless repetition, an eternal return, but thereby removed from the power to preserve us; in particular, powerless to bring us together. The myth of movies replaces the myth according to which obedience to law, being obedience to laws I have consented to and thus established, is obedience to the best of myself, hence constitutes my freedom—the myth of democracy. In replacing this myth, it suggests that democracy itself, the sacred image of secular politics, is unliveable.[5]

Film is illusionist not simply in certain of its themes; it is in itself an opiate because it gives us a here and now in which we cannot do anything.

It is specifically as cinema that cinema intervenes against the myth of the accommodating openness of democracy. A greater danger to democratic openness lies in this specificity than in what may have seemed to favor early conceptions of cinema as a *Gesamtkunstwerk*. Each component that is brought into play in the significant whole of a Wagnerian opera is an art. In cinema, however, the passivity of the recording apparatus is a mechanical intruder on the literary, musical, histrionic, and other artistic components. Given the disparity between its artistic and mechanical constituents, film may attain a degree of internal dissent incompatible with the notion of a *Gesamtkunstwerk*. But this dissent, as much as it works against the totalizing procedures of ideology that Kracauer deplores, does not suffice to establish cinema's democratic credentials. Cinema effects its own kind of closure: in place of the closed world of ideology, it presents the closed world of the past. That the means of playing audiovisual material can be employed to show, rather than what was, that which is occurring simultaneously—as in the case of live feeds on the Internet or the now customary giant screens that magnify the proceedings at a concert or political rally—is an argument not so much against defining cinema by a relation to the past as for excluding such uses from the class of phenomena to be discussed. Where recordings survive their immediate relay, their subsequent appearance in television schedules and screening programs, alongside what has come to be known as cinema, reconfigures their content as what is past.

Cinema is not incidentally but essentially a mass medium. It creates a mass mentality as much as it caters to it. Claiming that the presence of the actors in a theater stands in the way of the oneiric stupor in which a film screening takes its course, André Bazin ascribes to theater an insistence on an "active individual consciousness."[6] Even if this insistence is intellectual in what it demands of the audience, it is grounded in the lived experience of a body among bodies. Cinema may appeal to what are called the lowest instincts, but the circumstances of its reception, when contrasted with the shared physical space of a theatrical performance, are further removed from the pheromone-filled air of prehistoric life on the savannah. Cinema cheats itself and its audience of an engagement with the present insofar as its technological means of recording what is can only put forward reproductions of what is past. The price of the realism of its reproduction is an unreality in the circumstances of its reception. The realism that is the automatic achievement of the technology of cinema reformulates rather than solves the problem in the visual arts of the relation to what is: its deviations in the representation of what is have to do not with fantasy and inaccuracy but with pastness. Technological proficiency in the replication of phenomena is the starting point of cinema, whereas in the visual arts it is a goal. As this technological proficiency does not allow itself to be appropriated by the individual filmmaker, the exhaustiveness of its reality can however be called into question. The supplementary reality that is not a technological given in the reception of cinema (precisely because of the technological nature of this reception) is also not an achievement of the mimetic technique (or naturalist commitments) of the individual filmmaker. It is the reality that certain politicized filmmakers in the New Cinema will conceive as the outcome of breaking the technological spell in which the masses are held—cinema is to leap out of the hermetically sealed abstract space of its reception into the here and now of the political.

The struggle against the intrinsic unreality of cinema is invariably tied up with the struggle against the illusionism that is the prevailing possibility of film, in other words, with the struggle against Hollywood. Campaigns in defense of small national film industries often claim too much and too little politically for local productions, since substituting familiar accents, scenery, and so forth is incapable of annulling the cinemagoer's entrenched alienation, just as framing the debate around the notion of "cultural products" needlessly preempts the decision regarding the relation of these works to the (other) arts, the political, and truth. The extraordinary appeal of cinematic illusionism is due, not in small part, to the plausibility that the cinema's technological exactitude of reproduction lends to the fantastic: the cinema offers not so much fantasies as documents of fantasies. The truthfulness of cinema, its forensic admissibility (Hitchcock's films, for instance, are films of information), distinguishes it from a cultural product (nonetheless, this distinction, never absolute, is in the process of being corroded by the incursion of computer-generated images). Hence what the flourishing of national film industries in the 1960s and 1970s could set forth in self-defense was, above and beyond an upsurge of non-American perspectives, the works' truthfulness.

Yet the culturally and regionally specific truthfulness of what the image presents is rarely in accord with its conditions of possibility in the imported technology. In this way, as well, realism in cinema is both a given and a problem. Illusionist cinema, which could long be recognized by its disavowal of the problem, has of late applied itself, by means of a saturation with special effects, to erasing realism even as a given of the cinematic image. Such films stage the bankruptcy of the skeptical tradition of Anglo-Saxon culture. It is the essential absurdity of abusing film to advance the thesis of the unknowability of reality that makes *The Truman Show*, *Fight Club*, and *The Matrix* suffocating exercises. The New Cinema's suspicion of the image is taken up, but its "exaggeration" to the point of a hackneyed metaphysical position amounts to the vitiation of the properly political critique of illusionism. As in the days when Jack Valenti, head of the Motion Picture Association of America, crisscrossed the world bullying heads of state into rescinding support for local film industries, illusionist cinema knows when to put aside its doubts concerning its relation to reality and to pursue a policy of formidable pragmatism and opportunism, securing and increasing its lion's share of the global market.

Cinema, which was seen to situate itself on the threshold between art and reality, between the expressiveness of manipulated material and the impassivity of bare fact, is prone to an alienation from the here and now, to a hermetism from which traditional works of art are exempt. Cinema is life itself and an unprecedented parody of life. To be sure, the life that the projector brings to the lifeless photographic stills of which a film is composed requires the participation of its immediate audience, since the cinematic golem of movement owes its appearance of animation to the memory traces in the perceptual apparatus of those viewing it. The specificity of cinema is nothing technological: cinema differentiates itself from photography by a negation of the individual frames that are the sum of its actuality, coming into its difference from photography between the frames, in the caesura where its nonmaterial essence colludes with the synthetic prejudices of human perception. The romanticism of cinema is this setting to work of what is not there. In this respect at least, cinema precludes totalization, since it comes about less by putting images together than by preserving the intervals that hold images apart. A film does not begin and end as cinema but rather as photography: the film is reclaimed by the still in the same way that poetry yields to prose after the final enjambment. But the aesthetic engagement whereby cinema comes into its element in the immediacy of an audience's sensory processes does not resolve the ambiguity in which cinema is at once life and a parody of life because the mere immediacy of life is a shadow of life. Ontologically, the essence of cinema belongs more to the transcendental structures of experience than to the phenomenal realm, yet this intimacy that characterizes our relation to cinema goes hand in hand with the disengagement that marks our reception of the interchangeable copies of a film.

· · ·

Whatever negative appraisal might be made of cinema through comparing it with the traditional arts is risible in the face of the contemporary pervasiveness of film: the judgment's pretensions to critical negativity dissolve into nostalgia. It is not just that cinema now has a one-hundred-year history; the history of the last one hundred years has itself become cinematic for us—the nature of the technology of film in a given period reaches into the period to define it for us and to date it so that our sense of the historical continuum of events is inextricable from our understanding of the developments in the technology with which those events were filmed. But if cinema cannot be dislodged by criticism, it can at least be better understood. This involves, in part, thinking through the way in which the sense of the here and the now of the political has been irrevocably transformed by cinema. Cinema was always destined to leave the planet, to rediscover Earth as the reality of the miraculous. Since everything has been reinscribed on the shed skin of light that may or may not be spooled on a reel of film, the question of cinema can no longer be posed from outside of cinema. There is no authoritative vantage ground from which a normative judgment could be passed concerning cinema as such. The question, because it now belongs to cinema, asks, "What can cinema do?"

1

Alfred Hitchcock
Fowl Play and the Domestication of Horror

KELLY OLIVER

ALFRED HITCHCOCK'S *PSYCHO,* arguably the most shocking and groundbreaking Hollywood film of 1960, ushered in a new era of American film.[1] With its opening scene suggesting illicit sex in a cheap hotel, the first look at a toilet in American cinema, heartthrob Anthony Perkins playing a peeping tom, and the stunning shower scene in which the heroine (Janet Leigh as Marion Crane) is brutally murdered early on, *Psycho* flirted with censorship from beginning to end; however, what the censors found most objectionable was the use of the word *transvestite* applied to Norman in the penultimate scene.[2] With the corpse of Norman's mother, which Norman stuffed like one of his birds, *Psycho* also plays at the boundary between thriller and horror.

Before *Psycho* the horror genre was dominated by Britain's Hammer Studios and Hollywood's Roger Corman and their formula for box-office success, B creature features with human-cum-animal, sexy women, supernatural monsters, and mad scientists. Hitchcock was inspired by these low-budget moneymakers to show what a "master" could do with such restrictions.[3] And, with *Psycho* and then *The Birds* (1963), Hitchcock not only transformed the horror genre but also made it respectable by moving horror out of the realm of the fantastic and into the realm of the everyday. By suggesting that horror lies within the mundane rather than the supernatural, that it haunts rural landscapes and picturesque homes rather than cemeteries and laboratories, Hitchcock's mixture of suspense and horror hit home. What have become formulaic elements of contemporary horror films began with *Psycho* and *The Birds* in the early 1960s.

In *Terror and Everyday Life: Singular Moments in the History of the Horror Film,* Jonathan Lake Crane sets out three key elements of contemporary horror, which he claims originate with *Night of the Living Dead* (1968) and *Halloween* (1978): "all collective action will fail; knowledge and experience have no value when one is engaged with the horrible; and the destruction of the menace (should it occur) carries no guarantee that the future will be safe"; in fact the most popular horror films are those in which the monster is not killed but returns over and over again in sequels.[4] Crane also maintains that what is horrific in these films is their connection to everyday life, which separates them from earlier horror films that no longer seem scary at all. Given Crane's description of the contemporary horror genre, Hitchcock's turn to horror in the early 1960s seems definitive.

In neither *Psycho* nor *The Birds* is the "monster" killed; in fact, *The Birds* ends with thousands of birds covering the landscape and the suggestion that they may be moving into more urban areas; and *Psycho* spawned several sequels in which "mother" continues to terrorize. Although terror in *The Birds* acts as a form of "family therapy" that brings Mitch and Melanie together and gives Melanie the mother that she never had, it comes at the price of the continued threat of the birds and Melanie's catatonia. This type of melancholy "resolution" that leaves open the threat of the "monster" continues to be popular today in films such as *Alien* (1979, 1992), *Aliens* (1986), and *War of the Worlds* (2005). In addition, the film never reveals why the birds attack. And although *Psycho* ends with the psychiatrist explaining Norman's psychosis, this is the most disappointing scene in the film—even Hitchcock told his screenwriter that it was "a hat grabber," meaning that viewers would grab their hats and leave the theater.[5] In the end it is "mother" who has the last word when we see Norman in his cell and hear mother's voice saying that she wouldn't hurt a fly, while her skull is superimposed on Norman's face. The last scene, of Marion's car being pulled from the swamp, suggests just the beginning of the process of dredging the swamp for others. *Psycho* and *The Birds* prefigure the contemporary horror genre's lack of resolution and the failure of knowledge and action to prevent horror, but most shocking of all, they locate horror in the everyday.

Hitchcock moves the animal, whose supernatural threat dominated earlier horror films, into the realm of the natural and everyday and replaces earlier literal transformations of humans into monstrous animals with allegorical and metaphorical associations between humans and animals.[6] Birds in particular, associated with women and with the deadly gaze of the camera, play a central role in both *Psycho* and *The Birds*. And *Marnie* (1964) revolves around the association of woman and animal that drives Mark Rutland (Sean Connery) wild. Rather than give us mad scientists or science gone wrong, Hitchcock gives us cool-headed lawyers and zoologists who interrogate and study nature / woman in their attempts to domesticate her. In his films from the early 1960s Hitchcock makes sexual perversion and illicit sex the mundane triggers for gruesome horror that shocks precisely because it domesticates the monstrous. In this chapter I will explore the association of women and animals as horrific in what Michele Piso calls Hitchcock's "trilogy of modern despair":[7] *Psycho, The Birds*, and *Marnie*.

In her analysis of Hitchcock's *Frenzy* (1972), with its grisly rape and murder scenes and connections between cooked animal parts and women's corpses, Tania Modleski argues that the film's graphic violence should be considered "not simply as the reflection of the dirty mind of a frustrated old man nor even of a new 'freedom' in sexual mores, but rather as a cultural response to women's demands for sexual and social liberation."[8] The same can be said of Hitchcock's trilogy from the early 1960s. Throughout the 1950s and 1960s birth control advocates were going to court to legalize birth control; and in 1960, the same year that *Psycho* was released, the Food and Drug Administration approved birth control pills, which gave women more sexual freedom. In 1963, the same year that *The Birds* was released, the first report of the President's Commission on the Status of Women indicated that women were discriminated against in the workforce; and *The Feminine Mystique*, Betty Friedan's commentary on white middle-class housewives' dissatisfaction with domestic life, was published. In the context of this history it is noteworthy that women have been called "birds" and "chicks." In 1964, the year that *Marnie* was released, Title VII of the Civil Rights Act, which bars discrimination in employment on the basis of race or sex, was passed; and the Equal Employment Opportunity Commission was established—Marion Crane, Marnie Edgar, and her mother, Bernice Edgar, are, after all, working girls.

In *Psycho, The Birds*, and *Marnie* the association between women and animals becomes explicit, and the mother comes to occupy an especially significant and threatening position. Although the mother is a liminal figure throughout Hitchcock's work, especially in films such as *The*

Lady Vanishes (1938), *Rebecca* (1940), *Notorious* (1946), *Strangers on a Train* (1951), *Vertigo* (1958), and even *North by Northwest* (1959), she dominates plot motivation in the films from the early 1960s. Perhaps not coincidently, at this same time Hitchcock introduces animals, particularly birds, and turns from thrillers to horror. The most dramatic invocation of the association of the mother with horror is *Psycho*, where Norman Bates dresses up as his mother and takes on her persona to murder young women to whom he is attracted. The film suggests that Norman's relationship with his mother motivates his psychotic homicidal violence, which is triggered by animal lust and executed in the famous shower scene in the bathroom, sandwiched between scenes of Marion eating and a toilet flushing that also evoke animality.

The threat of the animal and attempts to contain it are more obvious with Norman's hobby, taxidermy: his parlor is filled with stuffed birds of prey; and it is there that he tells Marion that she "eats like a bird" and informs her that "birds eat a tremendous lot." After the shower scene Marion is again compared to a bird, this time visually, when the picture of a bird falls off of the hotel-room wall when Norman recoils from Marion's dead body; the bird stares up at Norman from the floor just as Marion's lifeless eye stares into the camera from the bathroom floor after her murder. In this context it is noteworthy that like a crane, a bird of prey who eats fish, Marion Crane ends up in the swamp. Several times in the film, Norman also compares his mother to a bird. He tells Marion that his mother is as harmless as one of his stuffed birds; and in the final scene Norman-as-mother tells the audience in voice-over that "she" is as harmless as one of her son's stuffed birds. Of course, Norman has stuffed her like one of his birds. And like a bird of prey, "she" preys on the young women to whom Norman is attracted. This association between mother and the stuffed birds in Norman's parlor adds to the creepiness of the film and of the horrible revelation that he keeps her stuffed corpse in the house.

In her analysis of *Psycho*, Barbara Creed argues that "woman as monstrous is associated with bodily appetites, cruel eyes, a pecking beak."[9] She catalogues the many ways that both Marion and mother are associated with birds, including the birdlike screeching on the sound track whenever "mother" enters with a knife and the way that the knife pecks like a beak at its victims; before Norman tells Marion that she eats like a bird, in voice-over "mother" reprimands Norman that she won't have women satisfying their "ugly appetites" with her food or her son. Raymond Bellour also comments on the association between Marion, Norman-mother, and birds not only in the dialogue but also in the imagery of the film, wherein Norman visually comes to occupy the position of the stuffed owl with outstretched beak and widespread wings while Marion occupies the place of winged angels in a painting above her head in the parlor scene, a painting that is "penetrated" by "the menacing shadow of a crow . . . like a knifeblade or penis."[10] For Bellour the menacing phallic bird of prey is associated with Norman as mother, ultimately with the mother, while Marion is associated with the angel bird that becomes the phallic mother's prey. If Bellour reads Mrs. Bates as a phallic mother (this is also suggested by Hitchcock in the preview when he identifies the mother as domineering), Creed argues that she is not so much phallic as castrating; in fact, Creed makes a point of distinguishing the phallic from the castrating mother in order to motivate Norman's urge to identify with the mother to castrate rather than be castrated.

Thinking about *Psycho* in the context of the cultural transitions playing out from the 1950s to the 1960s, especially in terms of the women's movement and calls for sexual liberation, it is useful to think of Mrs. Bates—along with Mrs. Brenner of *The Birds* and Mrs. Edgar of *Marnie*—as representing maternal authority at odds with the supposed paternal authority of patriarchal culture. In all of these cases maternal authority challenges paternal authority at the same time that it lays down the law in relation to the daughters' sexuality. In both *Psycho* and *The Birds* this maternal authority is associated with vengeful animality, particularly with birds of prey that attack daughters who exhibit sexual agency reserved within a patriarchal economy for men. These mothers, then, become the surrogates for the punishing paternal superego. In both *Psycho* and *The Birds*, mothers take the place of the father after he is dead and because their sons are not man enough (especially Nor-man) to take the paternal position.[11] In *Marnie* the paternal position is vacant (Marnie's mother, Bernice Edgar, was impregnated at fifteen by a boy named Billy in exchange for his sweater), and Mrs. Edgar and Marnie resist any man's attempt to fill it, to the point that Marnie won't let men touch her (because her mother raised her to be "decent"). But at the same time that these mothers are enforcing patriarchal prohibitions against women's sexual liberation and sexual agency, they are themselves displacing paternal authority and assimilating it as their own.

Modleski argues that "fear of the devouring, voracious mother is central in much of Hitchcock's work" and that in this regard *Psycho* is not only "paradigmatic of the fear haunting many Hitchcock films" but also "the quintessential horror film."[12] In her commentary on *Frenzy* Modleski uses Julia Kristeva's theory of abjection to formulate a connection between women and impure animals; discussing the scene in which the serial rapist and murderer Bob Rusk (Barry Foster) returns to the corpse of one of his victims, whom he has stuffed into a potato sack, Modleski says that "the feeling is very much one of violating an ultimate taboo, of being placed in close contact with the most 'impure' of 'impure animals': the carcass of the decaying female."[13] Modleski invokes Kristeva's analysis of phobia in *Powers of Horror*, in which Kristeva identifies the source of all phobia, particularly dietary prohibitions against eating certain animals and fear of contamination by carcasses of impure animals, with the mother, whose body is made abject by the male child and by patriarchal culture generally.[14]

In *Powers of Horror* Kristeva proposes that within patriarchal culture the mother's body and her authority must be contained. Kristeva maintains that various rituals, particularly religious rituals, serve that function. The threat of the maternal body is one of abjection or contamination that threatens the very identity of the child, especially the male child, who must distinguish his identity from the maternal / female. Kristeva defines the abject as what calls into question boundaries; the abject, then, is anything that threatens identity. On the level of individual development, the infant's own identity is threatened by its identification with its mother. It must "abject" its mother, turn away from her, to become an individual. On the level of social development, families, groups, and nations are also defined against what has been made abject or jettisoned from the group's identity, which are parts of itself that it imagines as unclean or impure. On both levels the figure that poses the greatest threat to identity is the maternal body or the female body insofar as it conjures maternity. This is because we were all once part of that body; and on both the individual and social levels we continue to struggle to distinguish ourselves from it, especially insofar as the maternal is associated with the natural and the animal.

Certainly, Kristeva's analysis seems to fit Norman Bates, who cannot distinguish himself from his mother and as a result finds his own sexual desires and their objects abject and therefore becomes abject himself. The film forces the viewer to identify with Norman, thereby challenging the viewer's identity and putting him or her into the position of the abject as well as the position of one abjecting both the mother and Norman's victims. In this regard it is important to note that for Kristeva the abject is not only horrifying but also fascinating; we are drawn to it even while it repulses us. This is why Kristeva's theory of abjection has been popular among feminist film critics who discuss the horror genre, which both fascinates and terrifies viewers who are drawn to horror.[15]

Kristeva's theory also links the threat of the maternal and the feminine with the threat of the animal and animality:

[T]he abject confronts us, on the one hand, with those fragile states where man strays on the territories of *animal*. Thus, by way of abjection, primitive societies have marked out a precise area of their culture in order to remove it from the threatening world of animals and animalism, which were imagined as representatives of sex and murder. The abject confronts us, on the other hand, and this time within our personal archeology, with our earliest attempts to release the hold of *maternal* entity.[16]

Within this analysis the animal and the maternal are the original threats to our identities as human and as individuals; and the animal and maternal are linked in their relation to the threat of the natural world, the threat of sex, birth, and death that makes them abject. But what makes the mother's body abject is also what gives her authority, an authority that comes from her connection with the natural world, particularly her power to give birth and the infant's dependence on her body for its life. The women in Hitchcock's films, particularly the films from the early 1960s, are mothers and daughters who represent the power and threat of maternal authority and the power and threat of feminine sexuality unchecked by that authority. These women are presented as abject in the double sense of horrifying and yet fascinating, especially in their association with the animal and animality. And the struggle between these two aspects of the maternal / feminine—horrifying and fascinating—is represented in the tension between mothers and daughters in these films.

It is noteworthy that the "daughters" in these films are associated with the mother at the same time that they are punished by her. Their names all begin with *M*, as if for "mother": Marion, Melanie, Marnie. And all of Marnie's names are versions of *Mary*, as in the Virgin Mary: Margaret, Mary, Marion (an echo of *Psycho*).[17] If we trace the trajectory of mother-daughter relations from *Psycho* to *Marnie*, we see first Marion Crane, who mentions her mother in the opening scene with her lover in the hotel room in Phoenix when she tells him that she would like to meet him "respectably," with her "mother's picture on the mantel." Soon after, she is brutally murdered, seemingly for her sexual freedom and the freedom of movement that allows her to check into a hotel room alone on the way to find her lover and give him the money she has stolen. Marion's mother represents respectability while Marion compromises respectability to meet her lover for lunchtime trysts in cheap hotels, steals money to be with her lover, and checks into another cheap roadside motel alone using an alias. Norman's mother also represents a type of maternal superego, only now dominating her son (at least within his imaginary since it is only through Norman that we know his mother). We also find out that Norman killed his mother and her lover, according to the psychiatrist because he was jealous of the lover. Norman has internalized maternal prohibitions to the point that his persona is split between the dutiful son and the threatening and vengeful mother. The mother herself was murdered for her own outlaw desire, for taking a lover after the death of Norman's father. And maternal authority is represented in the film by the person of the "transvestite" and feminine son.

In *The Birds*, after Mitch Brenner (Rod Taylor) tells Melanie Daniels (Tippi Hedren) that she needs "a mother's care," she replies that her mother ran off with a "hotel man" when she was young. Perhaps the "hotel man" is an allusion to Norman Bates, who within the narrative of *Psycho* is a seemingly potential lover for sexually available Marion.[18] Unlike *Psycho*, in *The Birds* there is an actual mother character, Mitch's mother, Lydia Brenner (Jessica Tandy). Melanie is warned by Mitch's former girlfriend, Annie (Suzanne Pleshette), that his mother controls his relationships with women and that she broke up her own relationship with Mitch. As Jacqueline Rose points out, Mitch is a lawyer and represents the paternal law, which does not hold sway at his mother's house, where her authority is at odds with the law.[19] Melanie is seen as transgressing both the paternal law (Mitch first meets her in court because of her practical jokes that led to the destruction of property) and the maternal authority (she is represented as competing with the mother for Mitch's attention). While in San Francisco, the realm of paternal law, all of the birds are in cages and therefore harmless; but in Bodega Bay, the realm of maternal authority, the birds are wild and hostile and seem to act as surrogate mothers who punish Melanie (and those around her) for her sexual advances toward Mitch. After all, Melanie is the one pursuing Mitch to the point of finding out where his mother lives and making a surprise visit. The birds attack whenever Melanie is near; and as her desire for Mitch becomes more obvious, so does the intensity of the attacks.

At the beginning of the film, Melanie is presented as confident of her own agency. In the first scene, she plays the part of a saleswoman in a pet store to fool Mitch. Soon we find out that she is a rich playgirl used to having her own way, who has been in the society papers for her antics, including breaking a plate-glass window and jumping into a fountain in Rome, nude. But in the opening scene she is also put in her place by Mitch (representative of paternal law). He catches the bird that Melanie accidentally freed, saying, "Back in your gilded cage Melanie Daniels," indicating that he is the true agent in control not only of the situation but also of Melanie, whom he compares to the bird that he catches and cages. Later in the film, Melanie is shown in a phone booth under attack by birds; in an interview Hitchcock describes this scene as a reinforcement of the comparison between Melanie and the caged bird; only now her cage is not gilded but dangerous.[20] Melanie is also associated with the birds that are breaking the glass of the phone booth and windows throughout the movie in that like the birds she has broken a plate-glass window, which is why she went to court.

The most haunting scene of the film comes at the same time as Melanie and Mitch apparently consummate their desire: Melanie is shown in her nightgown, brushing her hair and putting on lipstick, as Lydia drives off to talk to her neighbor about the chickens not eating their feed. When Lydia returns, after seeing her neighbor with his eyes pecked out, she catches Mitch and Melanie (still in her nightgown under her coat with her hair down) in a romantic pose; when they approach her to see what is wrong, she violently pushes them both out of her way and runs into the house. She was composed enough to leave the scene of the gory bird attack and drive the truck back home, but when she sees Mitch and Melanie after they have perhaps consummated their desire, she becomes violent. Next Lydia is in bed, telling Melanie, who brings her tea, that she cannot stand to be alone and that she wishes she were stronger—a phrase she repeats several times. Although she has just witnessed the horrors at the chicken farm, her only fear is being abandoned and losing Mitch to Melanie, whom, as she says, she doesn't even know if she likes. In the end the mother-surrogates, the birds or Mother Nature, render Melanie delusional and catatonic after a brutal bird attack in the attic. It is only after Melanie's agency is taken away completely that Lydia can embrace her. By the end of the film, the sexually active "playgirl" is both punished for her sexual agency and rendered passive.

Given that *The Birds* was released during the cold war and just one year after the Cuban missile crisis, when the threat of nuclear destruction hung in the collective imagination like an ominous cloud, combined with rising concerns over capitalism's wanton destruction of the environment, the birds also represent the revenge of Mother Nature.[21] As Mrs. Bundy (Ethel Griffies), an ornithologist, tells the people gathered in the restaurant, birds are not by nature aggressive creatures; rather, man is. Birds, she says, have no reason to start a war with man. At this same moment the waitress yells out "two fried chickens!" A little boy, who has been eating chicken, asks his mother, "Are the birds going to eat us, Mommy?" And a man at the bar rants about birds being messy animals that should be wiped off the face of the earth. In this scene Mrs. Bundy suggests that whereas birds are by nature passive and peaceful creatures, humanity deserves to be attacked by them as recompense for what humans have done to nature; if the birds have become aggressive, then humanity is responsible. If humans eat birds, then why shouldn't birds eat humans? In an interview, in his own tongue-in-cheek way, Hitchcock expresses sympathy for the birds against humans:

I can look at a corpse chopped to bits without batting an eyelid, but I can't bear the sight of a dead bird. Too heartrending. I can't even bear to see them suffer, birds, or get tired. During the making of my movie, in which I used fifteen hundred trained crows, there was a representative of the Royal Society for the Prevention of Cruelty to Animals on the scene at all times, and whenever he said, "That's enough now, Mr. Hitchcock, I think the birds are getting tired," I would stop at once. I have the highest consideration for birds, and, quite apart from the movie, I think it very right they should take their revenge on men that way. For hundreds of centuries birds have been persecuted by men, killed, put in the pot, in the oven, on the spit, used for writing pens, feathers for hats, turned into bloodcurdling stuffed ornaments. . . . Such infamy deserves exemplary punishment.[22]

In his films Hitchcock gives us birds carved and eaten in scene after scene, worn in hats along with other animals (in those beautiful Edith Head costumes), and turned into bloodcurdling stuffed ornaments in *Psycho*. Should it surprise us that Hitchcock's father was a poultry dealer in London? When asked why he didn't use wild birds instead of trained ones in *The Birds*, Hitchcock replied, "I don't trust them."[23] And while he says that "blood is jolly, red," he claims to be frightened of eggs because the yolks spill "revolting yellow liquid."[24] If "man's infamy deserves exemplary punishment," Hitchcock's films deliver; yet more often they punish woman, man's victim, for her association with the abject threat of Mother Nature's revenge. His films are littered with female corpses, associated with animality, food, and death. Just as food is served in nearly every film, women are served up as dishes (in *Marnie*, Mark's sister-in-law, Lil, asks him, "Who's the dish?" in reference to Marnie): Janet Leigh is covered in chocolate sauce "blood" for her black-and-white demise in the shower; the sound of the knife being plunged into her naked body is the sound of a knife being plunged into a melon; and as Tania Modleski points out, the grotesque associations between women and food in *Frenzy* are the basis of the so-called black humor of the film.[25] More specifically, in *Frenzy* women's corpses are compared to the animal parts that the inspector's wife feeds him: fish heads and pigs' feet. In these films from the 1960s and early 1970s, through both visual and narrative conceits, women's bodies, particularly women's dead bodies, are compared to dead animals or animal parts: Marion Crane and the stuffed and painted birds from *Psycho*; Melanie Daniels and the evil and dead birds from *The Birds* (not to mention her fur coat that catches the attention of every man she passes); Marnie as the wild animal hunted, caught, and domesticated by Mark Rutland; Rusk's victims in *Frenzy*, one stuffed into a potato sack, whose bodies are interchangeable with dead cooked animal parts, suggesting cannibalism humor.

In *The Birds* it is the mother who had been eating chicken with her kids in the restaurant who blames Melanie for the bird attacks. After the birds attack the gas station across the street, the women, huddled in a hallway, stare at Melanie, and the mother becomes hysterical, accusing Melanie of being the cause of the attacks and calling her "evil." The mother screams at Melanie, "Who are you? *What* are you?" and Melanie slaps her face. The mother's "What are you?" suggests that Melanie is not human but some kind of monster or animal that incites the bird attacks. The connection throughout the film between Melanie and the birds, and Mrs. Bundy's lecture on how it isn't natural for birds to be aggressive, suggests that Melanie's aggressive behavior toward Mitch is not natural. She is not passive like a good "bird" should be; she has left her gilded cage, flown to Bodega Bay, and with the fury of Mother Nature herself, is wreaking havoc on even innocent children.

Perhaps the most troubling representation of mothers and daughters in Hitchcock's films, however, comes in *Marnie*, where the daughter is constantly compared to a wild animal, studied, hunted, trapped, raped, and "domesticated" by the male protagonist. And the mother is a crippled man-hating former prostitute who removes her daughter from their bed whenever one of her sailor johns knocks at the door. The daughter, Margaret Edgar or "Marnie," is traumatized by a repressed childhood memory of one of her mother's johns who kissed her and whom she killed. This episode with the john—"my accident," as Mrs. Edgar calls it—leaves Mrs. Edgar lame with pain in her leg and leaves Marnie psychologically scarred in a painful relationship to her mother. Marnie wants her mother's love but never receives it because, although as we find out in Mrs. Edgar's final confession, she loved Marnie more than anything and fought to keep her, apparently the "accident" tainted her love for her daughter; and it left Marnie unable to tolerate any man's touch, what within the patriarchal imaginary is considered frigidity. What the film and its male protagonist, Mark Rutland, identify as sexual aberrations are identified with Marnie's relationship to her mother.

Mark is the son of a wealthy man and a part-time zoologist who, as E. Ann Kaplan points out, is attracted to Marnie because "she represents the wild animal in the jungle that always threatens to overwhelm society."[26] Several critics have commented on the way that Mark hunts and traps Marnie like a wild animal,[27] a reading that is made explicit in the dialogue of the film, particularly in the scene where Mark finds Marnie after she has robbed Rutland's safe and blackmails her into marrying him. She tells Mark that she is "just some animal" that he has caught; and he replies that he caught a "wild one" this time. Like Sophie, the wild Jaguarondi whose picture he keeps in his office, whom he claims to have "trained to trust" him, Mark proceeds to try to "train" Marnie throughout the rest of the film. *Marnie* is filled with allusions to animals, animal lust, and animal instincts. As Mary Lucretia Knapp points out, from the beginning of the film Marnie is associated with the girls' jump-rope song about the lady with the alligator purse. Marnie's yellow purse dominates the screen in one of the first scenes of the film. After her first robbery she visits her mother's apartment in Baltimore, where the girls are jumping rope outside; they are singing the same song at the end of the film when Mark and Marnie leave her mother's apartment after the revelation that Marnie killed the sailor. Robin Wood argues that the giant ship looming on the painted set behind the street on which her mother lives suggests a trap, the trap of false memory and unreality from which the truth will set Marnie free.[28]

But the association between Marnie and trapped animals goes beyond the visual connections to alligator purses or claustrophobic fake sets. Marnie's most satisfying relationship is with her horse, Forio, whom she shoots near the end of the film; the only being with whom she is free is Forio, and her whole personality changes when she is riding. The first time that we see her riding, it looks as if she rides her horse right up the street in front of her mother's apartment; the perspective is hers (or the horse's) as we ride through the trees and then up the street toward the fake ship, riding into the trap of her childhood. This "trap" is the supposed cause of her "illness," an illness foretold in the girls' jump-rope song:

Mother, Mother, I am ill.
Call for the doctor over the hill.
Call for the doctor. Call for the nurse.
Call for the lady with the alligator purse.
"Mumps," said the doctor. "Measles," said the nurse.
Nothing said the lady with the alligator purse.

Marnie repeatedly gives the response "nothing" throughout the film when asked what is wrong. She insists that nothing is wrong; like the lady with the alligator purse, she says "nothing."

When she arrives at her mother's apartment, she is hurt to see the little neighbor girl "roosting" there and receiving her mother's attention. She presents her mother with a fur collar (another dead animal), and we first realize that the color red is the catalyst for her seeing red, the color of blood. Shortly after, we see Marnie (in "drag" as a mild-mannered secretary) at Rutland's office, where Mark insists that the office manager hire her. In the first scene between Mark and Marnie, we learn that Mark is a zoologist who studies predatory behavior, especially in female animals. He tells Marnie that he studies instinctual behavior in animals, and she asks if he studies human beings and "lady animals." Mark answers that he studies the criminal class of the animal world in which "lady animals" figure largely as predators. All the while, the audience knows (and Mark suspects) that Marnie is herself a "lady criminal" preying on unsuspecting employers.

When Mark discovers that Marnie is interested in horses, he invites her to the horse races (where she has another attack of seeing red prompted by the jockey's jersey on a horse named "Telepathy"). It is there that Marnie tells Mark that she believes in *nothing* . . . horses maybe, but not people." When Telepathy wins the race after Marnie tells Mark not to bet on him because he is "wall-eyed," Mark says that she shouldn't have "chickened" out because her wall-eyed reject won. Taking Marnie to meet his father, Mark reassures Marnie (who didn't expect to be making the visit) that his father "goes by scent—if you smell anything like a horse, you're in." And when he introduces her to his father—who exclaims, "A girl!"—Mark says, "Not really a girl, a horse fancier." In the next scene Marnie is robbing the safe at Rutland's office, after which Mark tracks her down. And, as I mentioned earlier, the exchange between Mark and Marnie at this point revolves around the metaphor of Marnie as a trapped animal. Mark says that he can't just turn her "loose" after she accuses him of trapping her. And when Mark imagines his father's response to their sudden marriage, he says, "Dad admires wholesome animal lust." When Marnie is worried about the name that would appear on the marriage license (she has been using the alias Mary Taylor), Mark says that it doesn't matter if the license says "Minnie Q. Mouse"; it is still legal. And he says that he can easily explain why he is calling her Marnie rather than Mary, by saying that it is a "pet" name. On their honeymoon, when she screams for Mark to unhand her, she exclaims that she cannot "bear to be handled" as if she is a horse or an animal. Indeed, she says that marriage is degrading; "it's animal!" And when Mark suggests that she is sick because she won't let him touch her, she tells him, "Men, you say no thanks to one of them and you're a candidate for the funny farm," again an allusion to the animal.

During a conversation on their honeymoon, Mark is explaining how a certain coral-colored insect evades detection by birds by taking the shape of a flower; Marnie is likened to this insect insofar as she is a criminal evading detection by taking the shape of a beautiful mild-mannered widow. Later that evening, Mark leaves his book *Animals of the Seashore and Marine Life* behind to fulfill his uncontrollable animal lusts by raping Marnie; but the next morning, he finds her floating face-down in the swimming pool. When he asks her why she didn't just jump overboard (they are on a ship), she replies that she wanted to kill herself, "not feed the damned fishes." When they return home, she clandestinely calls her mother, explaining her absence by telling her that she had the flu and couldn't visit or call, saying, "I'm still a little hoarse," a homophone of "I'm still a little horse." Mark trades in his marine biology books for *Sexual Aberrations of the Criminal Female* and begins to interrogate Marnie about her childhood, to the point that Marnie says, "You Freud, me Jane," again pointing up Mark's (and the film's) linking of Marnie and the primitive.

Like so many detectives in Hitchcock's earlier films, Mark searches for clues to the mystery of Marnie's sexuality.[29] As he discovers, the key to the mystery of her sexual "aberration" lies with her mother. Raymond Bellour suggests that Marnie's horse, Forio, is one key to her sexuality insofar as the horse represents Marnie's desire for the phallus.[30] And Knapp argues that the horse is a lesbian fetish onto which the desire between Lil and Marnie is displaced.[31] But the film suggests a link between the horse and Marnie's mother. Marnie's love for her horse and, more significant, her love for her mother compete with Mark and seem to foreclose the possibility of her love for him. It is her mother who made her "decent" and taught her to hate men. But her mother's link to Marnie's beloved horse, Forio, goes beyond Marnie's love. It is also evidenced in the words that Marnie says to comfort the horse after she shoots him, suggesting that the horse's broken leg represents her mother's broken leg (suffered in her accident, when the sailor falls on top of her), the horse's pain becomes her mother's pain, and his screams are like her screams for help. After she shoots the horse, Marnie says, "There, there now," as if to comfort him. She hysterically insists on getting a gun to shoot him because he is "screaming" in pain, and she desperately wants to stop both his screaming and his pain. As we discover at the end of the film in flashback, when she was a small girl, her mother defended her against a drunken sailor who began to beat Mrs. Edgar. Marnie wanted the sailor to stop and when the sailor fell on her mother and her mother screamed for Marnie to help her, Marnie grabbed the fire-poker and hit the sailor on the head. After we see the sailor fall dead (in her flashback), Marnie says, "There, there now," as if comforting her mother. Finally, Marnie's mother is indirectly compared to the horse when Lil quips to Mark in reference to Marnie that she thought that "a girl's best friend is her mother." The adage is, of course, that man's best friend is his dog; and in Marnie's case her best friend is her horse.

In the end both Mark and the film hold Mrs. Edgar responsible for Marnie's criminal and sexual perversions, which is why Mark can reassure Marnie that after he tells the authorities what he has to tell, she won't go to jail. Mrs. Edgar, a loose woman herself, has ensured that her daughter will be "decent" to the point of hating men and "preying" on them for their money. Here, the mother, herself an outlaw who lives in a world of women (she plans to invite the little girl Jesse and her mother to live with her), has such a powerful hold on her daughter that its excess threatens patriarchal order in which men possess women. Although Mrs. Edgar has been exploited by men sexually, she was never possessed by them. Marnie is torn from this world of women—the world of her mother, to which she regularly returns with her plunder, and the women's world of secretaries—by Mark, who captures and possesses her like a wild animal. But in spite of his attempts to "train" her to trust him, he cannot train her to love or desire him. As they leave her mother's apartment, with the girls singing the jump-rope song in the background, Marnie tells Mark that she would rather stay with him than go to jail, which is hardly a declaration of love. As she reminds him (and us) throughout the film, he is as "ill" as she insofar as he has a "pathological" desire for a man-hating criminal who cannot stand his touch. Perhaps as Norman Bates tells Marion, we are all in our own private traps, and we "scratch and claw" at each other to escape.

In conclusion, Hitchcock's films from the early 1960s associate women, animals, and animality with an outlaw maternal authority at odds with paternal law and patriarchal order. Within the logic of his films, this authority has its source in the generative power of women and Mother Nature, and its aim is revenge against the animals who have, in Hitchcock's words, been persecuted by men for centuries. These films can be read as a response to the women's movement, particularly the struggle for greater sexual freedom and sexual agency. Hitchcock's films represent both the threat and the power of maternal authority, both the threat and the power of women's sexual agency, both the possibility of confident, strong women characters and the desire to reinscribe them within patriarchal order by domesticating them.

2

Luchino Visconti
Insights into Flesh and Blood

ALEXANDER GARCÍA DÜTTMANN

LUCHINO VISCONTI'S FILMS give expression to an insight of Adorno's from *Negative Dialectics*.[1] At the end of his introduction Adorno writes: "Utopia is blocked off by possibility, never by immediate reality."[2] As a declaration of my intent, such a claim raises a number of questions, questions regarding intellectual and historical links, questions regarding definitions, questions regarding the relationship between art and concept. Do I wish to understand Visconti's films as an emotive or vivid illustration of an insight that he and Adorno share but that the latter grasps conceptually? Perhaps there would be no objection to such a view or interpretation, at least not if one's starting point is that one can speak of an *insight* and that speaking of an insight does not imply a priority of the concept. Something can be understood as much by the means of the expression elevating the films above blind intuition as by the aphoristic sharpness issuing from the resources of the concept, even as it remains bound to experience. The exercises of the understanding and the respective intelligibility that they produce may, however, turn out to be scarcely comparable, perhaps even incomparable.

Here one might recall the following entry in Hans-Erich Nossack's diary: "Indeed, how could you then even want to share a thought that has passed into your flesh and blood? Such a thought can be expressed no longer in words, but only in an act."[3] Nossack is not saying that between thought and act a mediating authority intrudes, a reflection similar to his diary entry. Rather, the thought has shed its ties to reflection. Without ceasing to be a thought, it has thereby transformed itself, and, as an act, it maintains a grip on an insight and expresses it. A thought's understandability, which an act alone is able to furnish, is not simply identical with that intelligibility for which a meaningful linguistic utterance provides. Hence it is not simply the same whether one understands something through the expression of individual films, through the constellation that a series of films composes, or through conceptual means whereby one attempts to conceptualize an insight. There are many ways of understanding, and in all of them the faculty of understanding itself, the possibility of understanding something, has a part. Must, however, the insight—that which is understood—be so affected by this difference that in the end only in the case of the knowledge employing and indebted to conceptual means can one speak of an insight? Such a restriction seems arbitrary.

Is the insight therefore something preexisting, which the illustration as much as the concept can approach in order to give it expression? In the first scene of *Somnambula*, which Visconti together with Bernstein and Callas so successfully brought to the stage at La Scala, the overwhelmed Amina sings, "Ma la voce, o mio tesoro, / non risponde al mio pensier."[4] Can the incapacity of the voice to articulate explanatory words be separated from a pure thought whose service it quits? That one cannot differentiate between the pure thought, on the one hand, and the voice and its failure, on the other, means that nothing is able to express the thought more purely than that very failure of explanation that arises from being overwhelmed. The opera comes into existence. Amina's fiancé replies:

> Tutto, ah! Tutto in questo istante
> parla a me del foco ond'ardi:
> io lo leggo ne' tuoi sguardi,
> nel tuo vezzo lusinghier.[5]

Hence, instead of regarding the insight as something given, one could view it as something that first achieves an essential concreteness with the image, having no existence independent of it. The image: an eye that surveys the world and that is surveyed by the world. "In the eye the soul is concentrated and the soul does not merely see through it but is also seen in it," Hegel says in his lectures on aesthetics, immediately before describing the work of art as a "thousand-eyed Argus."[6] With each film Visconti contributes to the expression of an insight, to its discovery and development, to the illumination of an aspect. The significance of the insight measures itself against its very inseparability from its expression. The insight is not simply put forward as a thesis in a dialogue, since the enunciation of the thought in the form of a thesis itself belongs to a discovery and development overreaching such enunciation.

In this way the "cinematic circle" is formed of which, following hermeneutics, Stanley Cavell speaks. It rests on the "reciprocity of element and significance."[7] The "aesthetic possibilities" of the medium of film are not "givens";[8] each film must conquer them through their realization; the "medium" first needs to be created. The film is an actuality that does not presuppose any possibility. Of course, Cavell occasionally wavers between two arguments, between a historicist argument, which observes in modernity a loss of existing schemata or "automatisms" binding medium and instance, and a structural argument, which never grasps the instance as a mere actualization of the possibilities of an existing medium. The "cinematic circle" attests not only to the formal or logical possibility of that which is to be understood, given that the intuition of the "element" presupposes comprehension of the "significance," which in turn presupposes an intuition of the "element." The "cinematic circle" attests likewise to the sensuously and intellectually experienceable *transition* of the "element" to "significance," to a certain kind of utopia, if utopia can be understood as a removal of barriers. In a film that has turned out well, in a film that is art and precisely on that account cannot be included in the repellent genre of art films, no "element" is to be met for its own sake, as a mere thing so to speak, and no "significance" shoots beyond the "elements," as an abstract thought. Should one wish to use the concept of experience as a concept for a certain kind of resistance, one could also say that the "cinematic circle" demarcates the distance between thing, sign, and referent without the demarcation leaving behind a trace, the trace of an experience. The criterion for the success of a film is thus not the classical ideal of a complete mediation of form and content—this ideal is the accompaniment of a primacy of spirit and the end of art. The criterion is the shaping through and imaging of the work, for which the disruption of mediation, the thingliness of the "element" or "significance," is still not entirely arbitrary, as though a spiritless end of art were to appear beside the spiritual. The disruption of mediation, the experience, remains in a state of tension with respect to that shaping through of the work that aims at mediation, at the closure of the "cinematic circle." The failing voice, the voice as sound, is in the work of art not a free-floating effect.

In *Morte a Venezia*, a film in which Visconti is extremely sparing with dialogue, word and image drift apart. The words dominating the brief, inserted flashbacks, the arguments about the life and death of art, have something awkward and clumsy about them, something aesthetically vulgar that does not fit the image. Is Visconti trying to make a silent film, the silent film that, according to Cavell, has never been made?[9] Do the flashbacks therefore underline the helplessness and tedium of the words while the music pursues an investigation of the gestural as that which is the essence of cinema? The gestural composes the intensity of the image and thus does not include only iconic poses, the boy's upraised arm, but also the city itself, the elements, light, colors, moods. Intensive images are images at which one gazes to one's fill, insatiably, because they possess the power to awaken the dead, the power of a "That's how it is." The dead of the work of art are neither those who lived in the past nor the living who have died a death in life and to whom the work of art addresses itself.[10] To speak of the dead is, however, not on this account senseless, because the figures, even the landscapes that draw the figures into themselves and for their part turn into figures, are just as little fanciful concoctions. Something somnambulistic corresponds to them. Before Amina sings and the enlightened count familiarizes the baffled villagers with the phenomenon of somnambulism, she is considered a ghost. *Morte a Venezia* reminds the viewer that the dead have arisen, that the life that the film gives them is both immortal and transitory, as though the dead were at the same time unborn. Perhaps those images are beautiful that are traversed by this muteness, the muteness of the point of indifference of transitoriness and immortality to which no utterance comes near. The question before which the film places the hesitant viewer is whether the "That's how it is" is more than gay kitsch, the "That's how it is" of a self-indulgent and hollow aestheticism or of a complacent and no less hollow yearning that reifies beauty. The famous ball scene at the end of *Il gattopardo* opens the "cinematic circle" through its excess, even if the prince's dance with the village girl, the reflections on age and death before a painting by Greuze, and the caricature of a general who carries himself as a social lion all have a dramaturgic function. It is as though Visconti wants to lead the film to the threshold of the modern, as though by means of duration, of the turning circle of repeated entries, movements, colors, and forms become autonomous and give rise to a web that lays itself over the tracks of the plot and steadily breaks them up. There is a visible threat of a loss of overview.

Convention disintegrates, and the liberation of the compositional materials of the film directs attention to their contingency. But does not the gaze likewise dive into the peculiarity of that world of the aristocracy to which, as it is already said in the novel, specific laws apply? Indeed, this world, as Deleuze writes in his book *The Time-Image*, resembles a "synthetic crystal."[11] It has its place outside of history and nature, outside of the Divine Creation, and is perhaps nothing other than a world without acts.

In the utopia of the "cinematic circle"—to which Visconti surrenders himself perhaps above all in *La terra trema*, a film epic in which the individual passes over into the type, history into myth, the image of reality into the reality of the image—"element" and "significance," thing and thought, are immediately real. Here the abyss between reality and possibility closes, and the possible (the possibility of the "element" or "significance") no longer blocks the very way that it seems to open. But here an observation that Cavell makes in the appendix to his film book is important. He speaks of "ideas" that find "incarnation" in certain images, and he adds that a "power" corresponds to them that he compares with the "power" of a phrase of music or of poetry. This "power" is pronounced "inexplicable."[12] Is it a "power" because it is inexplicable? What does Cavell mean? Perhaps that there is no idea of the idea, no significance of the significance, no significance that could emerge from the "cinematic circle," crossing out its actuality and investing it with a definition. The significant thing, the sign, has no significance outside the "cinematic circle." In other words one never does justice to a film by explaining its significance, by assigning to each "element" and the coherence of the "elements" a significance that elevates itself above the "elements." Whenever one measures a film by whether or not one is able to explain its significance, it inevitably comes across as formalistic or melodramatic, as though it had succumbed to a surplus of thingliness or an exaggerated emotionalism. Conversely, going no further than bare descriptions of "elements," a stasis against which Cavell warns repeatedly, proves just as unsatisfactory and alien to art. The significance of the significance crosses out the actuality of the "cinematic circle," turning the immediate reality of the "elements" into something possible, into the indifferent and thus always merely possible reality of bearers of significance. Or is it the case that only by accepting a significance of the significance one can speak of a *closure* of the circle—indeed, of a circle at all? The drifting apart of word and image in *Morte a Venezia* is, for one, the lack of a context, whereas for another, it is its creation. Solely on condition that one can define art conceptually, subordinate significance and element to a specific determination—and thereby, for example, assess *every* drifting apart of significance and element as a failure, as a deficient spiritualization of the sensuous or a deficient sensualization of the spiritual—does this conflict admit of resolution: the prize for settling the dispute is however the end of art, thus the reopening of the circle whose closure is observed.

In a certain respect, then, the understanding of a film is never a purely conceptual understanding. One can never reduce a film to its concept. Art requires an indirect address. Perhaps that is true even of philosophical discourse. If there is no significance of the significance, no idea of the idea, no concept of art, no spiritual end of art, then the insight, for example, that it is always the possible but never the "immediately real" that blocks the way to Utopia, cannot be straightforwardly separated from the form of thinking, in the end not even from its own formulation. The thought has become "flesh and blood," something real, or rather it has not fashioned itself in a distinct spiritual sphere in order finally to externalize itself. The film or the philosophical text is an act, an expression of thought in "flesh and blood" to which in turn only another act can answer, another expression, another philosophical text or film that does not remain in possibility but rather itself grounds the reality or actuality of a circle of "element" and "significance." In this way the "force" to which Cavell refers communicates itself. That also befits its inexplicability.

"Utopia is blocked off by possibility, never by immediate reality." In Visconti attempts at change founder as a consequence of an orientation by the difference between reality and possibility. Almost all of his films revolve around this theme. *Lo straniero* forms an exception, *L'innocente* a limited case. In *L'innocente*, Visconti's last film, a man of the world takes it for granted that the change has already taken place. What is at issue is the experiment of a life beyond good and evil. Treating the possible as real, this life shatters against reality because the possible is not real but rather only an illusion, a deception. It is not real in the sense of the prevailing society that maintains itself through double standards. Nor is it real in the sense of a relationship that would be free of deceptions because it would no longer equate freedom with permissiveness. The "stranger," the central figure in the film of Camus' novel, passes over entirely into the anonymity of the social immanence with which he involuntarily collides, in an unexpected movement of exaggeration, of the exaggerated effect of the

sunlight whose conspicuousness Visconti ensures throughout, even strew-
ing the sand with blindingly reflective, tiny mirrors. The glinting knife
of the Arab youth stabs at his murderer's eyes. Meursault refuses to wear
the mask of subjectivity that, within the prevailing society, imposes a relationship to a transcendence—to the transcendence of a meaning whose
possibility hypocrisy realizes. Such a meaning, for which the "stranger"
is sued, can take on the shape of a son's or husband's love, reverence for
God, camaraderie, or respect for institutions. One could claim that society must first become like Meursault, that it must tear down the barrier
of the possible as the barrier of meaning grown rigid, and that it must put
an end to the confusion of reality and possibility in order to prepare the
way to utopian openness. Perhaps this thought would have emerged more
graphically from the film if Visconti had not had to bow to the wishes of
the Algerian French writer's widow. In the event, Visconti was not able
to draw the social and historical context more sharply: its exposition is
limited to vignettes sometimes bearing grotesque traits and to the use of
authentic objects and locations.[13] In a text written in 1967 Visconti refers
to the student riots and says that in the literature of the period there are no
heroes who have a stronger tie to the moment than Meursault: "The figure
that best expresses the mentality of the young belongs to their parents'
generation."[14]

Even though nearly all of Visconti's films revolve thematically around
the failure of attempts at transformation, the theme varies from film to
film. Four variations on the failure resulting from an orientation by the
difference between reality and possibility can be discerned, four groups
that occasionally overlap and in turn require differentiation.

To the first group belong those films in which the possible clings
to a love or a passion that breaks with the real, that seeks to break through
a historical, social, artistic paralysis. In *Ossessione*, Visconti's first feature
film, whose plot is drawn from an American crime novel, a drifter falls
in love with an ambitious woman, a former prostitute unable to hold out
any longer in the narrowness of a petty-bourgeois, fascistoid environment.
She seizes the opportunity for transformation but only in order to climb
the social ladder. Making his appearance as a fairground artist and portrayed as a homosexual, the figure of an entirely uninhibited veteran from
the Spanish Civil War touches, as it were, tangentially the fateful circle
drawn by reality and possibility. This figure, because it does not promise
simply a possible life, a life that has still first to be lived, opens the circle.

And because it probably denounces the lovers in their guilt, it closes the circle. In *Senso*, in which operatic melodrama and an exacting exposition of historical events keep company, a countess committed to the resistance during the Austrian occupation of Venice falls under the spell of a young officer in the occupying army and, in the name of passion, betrays her background and convictions. In *Le notti bianche*, adapted from the novella by Dostoyevsky, the forces of a love that bursts every social convention and therefore appears a delusion, a pure possibility, come up against the forces of a love for whose reality recognition according to the dominant customs stands guarantor. In *Il lavoro*, the captivating chamber play that Visconti contributes to the portmanteau film *Boccaccio 70*, a spoiled girl with a rich father in Burgenstock has to acknowledge that the Milanese count whom she has married is a conformist halfwit. Even love is not exempted from the law of exchange, proving to be labor, business, prostitution. The last shot shows a part of a woman's mouth, distorted, as though a fetishistically dismembering gaze wanted to pin itself to the body, as though such labor were the work not only of the prostitute but likewise of the camera. It thereby perhaps remains undecided whether the girl, whom her spouse calls simply "Dolly," sheds tears, with which she avows her failure, or smiles like a sphinx because she has understood that the possible blocks the path to Utopia, to a state of affairs no longer defined by socially imposed barriers. The doll becomes an adult, as a prostitute or as a wife. Valuable and beautiful objects increasingly fill the rooms traversed by the precise camera. They are either bourgeois status symbols, or in their fullness they are no longer distinguishable from vacuity, beautiful and valuable, because they no longer possess a function. In *Morte a Venezia* the sight of a desired beautiful body, like a helpless yearning pointing beyond a society in decline and an art become stale, seals the death of the artist. In *Gruppo di famiglia in un interno* the forces of an art connoisseurship vanishing completely into the past clash with the forces of an unexpected love that wavers between physical and paternal love and neglects to produce a continuity, to pass on a legacy. The son, who nonetheless is not a son, dies before his father and thereby condemns him likewise to death.

To the second group belong those films in which the possible is the occasion of a revolt against social exploitation, against the unjust distribution of property. In these films reality again and again robs the hope for a transformation of its force. *La terra trema* narrates the story of such a revolt in a Sicilian fishing village: the lack of solidarity among the fishermen, in a compact with the superior power of nature, sees to it that the possible transformation dashes against the reality of the way things are. *Rocco e i suoi fratelli* relates the tale of conformism after an attempt at change has gone wrong: transformation through conformity is a betrayal of transformation, against which some measure their success and others do not survive. *Le caduta degli dei* recounts the history of an irrevocable end to attempts at transformation, the history of their parody or travesty, of their hellish mockery by means of the alliance between capitalism and National Socialism. To this group *Il gattopardo* also surely belongs, a film concerned with the improbable maintenance of a superfluous social class, whose conventions promise freedom from the unrestrained striving for profit and gain after the revolution has extended reality, instead of realizing the possible.

The films in which not love and passion but rather art's beauty and semblance vouch for the possible belong to a third group. Here, alongside *Morte a Venezia*, a film that schematically sets in opposition two conceptions of art, and *Gruppo di famiglia in un interno*, a film that brings to the fore the beauty of works of the past and maneuvers it into a reflected antithesis to the ugliness of the present, *Bellissima* and *Ludwig* must be cited. In *Ludwig* a world of art, literally, is created: it is to remain undisturbed by the overpowering world of realpolitik, intrigues, and war, while nonetheless filmically the plain documentation continually disrupts the parade of sumptuous images. In *Bellissima* the longing to leave behind everyday misery unmasks, against its will, the appearance of cinema as mere illusion. Two short films keep company with this unmasking: *Anna Magnani*, an anecdote that deals with the real Rome of fascism and the Rome evoked by the stage song, and *La strega bruciata viva*, a sketch that tears the mask away from the face of the film diva and then restores it. She floats off in a helicopter.

There is, finally, a fourth group that, consisting of a single member, can scarcely be characterized as a group. In *Vaghe Stelle dell'Orsa* what forces itself as something possible on the modern married woman and Etruscan daughter is the enigmatic past itself. It contains the seed of a liberation from the indifference of the present, encumbering the latter at the same time with the reality of traumatic events. Into the vortex of this reality, visually brought out by meanderings and whirlings, by reflections and shadow plays, the free conduct of the women threatens to be swept.

How should one understand Adorno's proposition that the possible, not the "immediately real," blocks the way to Utopia, the insight that

Visconti's films give expression in "flesh and blood"? From the perspective of intellectual history one can discern in the proposition an allusion to the political debate over possibilism, in which, for instance, Rosa Luxemburg took part with her article on the alternative between possibilism and opportunism. Luxemburg quotes in this article a definition according to which possibilism is a politics that strives for "that which is possible in the given circumstances." She then develops the thought of a praxis that is not opportunistic: it neither renounces the analysis and consideration of the "given circumstances" nor lets itself be ruled by the axiom that "one meets with the most success on the path of concession."[15] Without referring to the debate, deconstruction takes up this thought anew. It conceives it as the tension between the possible and the impossible, between the impossible that remains dependent on the possible and the possible that remains dependent on the impossible, for example in the form of right and justice. (I say "deconstruction"—Jacques Derrida thought its insight in "flesh and blood.") From the perspective of textual history one can recognize in the proposition concerning the roadblock of the possible the impact of an anarchic impulse. It is the same impulse that leads Adorno in the mid-1960s to insist during his lectures on the theory of history and freedom that at every moment the possibility of change is present and must not be deferred into an uncertain future—as though precisely the possible as the conditional had brought about the omission of the realization diagnosed at the beginning of *Negative Dialectics*. The possible is, so to speak, in itself conservative. It prolongs the real and, as a consequence, renders impossible the change that it at the same time announces or on which it opens up a view. Would one be able to speak of change at all in a world in which everything were real? Adorno, one might conclude, denounces the transcendental illusion of possibility. The possible is not impossible enough. Or else it is all too impossible, remaining abstract and bordering on delusion. Not impossible enough and then again all too impossible, the possible becomes entangled in the conflict in which it loses out every time to the real. At the end of Visconti's *Le notti bianche*, the young woman Natalia catches sight in the snow of the hieratic figure of the feverishly awaited stranger and leaves in the lurch the kind, but dull, office worker. Thereby the concreteness of the possible that perpetuates reality is smothered by the abstractness of the possible that appears to the viewer a delusional fantasy. As a result, it is irrelevant whether or not the stranger, in fact, returns. Nearly all the flashbacks depicting Natalia's encounters with the stranger have something unreal about them, as though the object of depiction were her perception of reality. One must distinguish between two ways in which the possible is impotent, but likewise between a reality to which change addresses itself because it blocks the paths and a reality from which the barriers have been removed. Does the mysterious figure of the sister in *La terra trema* not embody this reality? Does it not embody the freedom from externally imposed barriers, from the barrier of reality and from the barrier of the twofold helpless possibility?

In his films, as in his opera and theater productions, Visconti sets considerable value on a particular sense of reality, on the significance of the "immediately real." In 1966, reviewing the experiences with the theater that he had gathered over the course of two decades, he alludes, seemingly ironically, to the image that people had made of him and put into circulation: "This lunatic Visconti, so it is believed, he wants real, authentic jewellery by Cartier, taps from which real, authentic water flows, real, authentic French perfume in the phials standing on the dressing table, Flemish linen on the beds."[16] In an essay on invention and tradition, in which six years before shooting was to start he is already thinking over the film that would come to be known as *La terra trema: Episodio del mare*, Visconti justifies the relevance that the sound of a voice or the roar of the ocean has for him, as though the authenticity of the reproduced sounds would help the work disclose an essential reality and secure it for itself.[17] The roar of the sea was for the composer Luigi Nono the true central character of the film; when he was to collaborate on producing the sound track for *Lo straniero*, he wanted to draw his compositional material from noises and thereby avoid the impression that they were being heard only "by chance."[18] Coining the phrase "visionary aestheticism," Deleuze contends that the objects and the surroundings in Visconti take on an "autonomous, material reality" that gives them an importance in themselves whereby they no longer operate as the frames, recipients, and vehicles of action. The senses, free of their orientation by the precepts of action, invest the objects and surroundings so that "dreamlike" connections arise: "It is as if the action floats in the situation, rather than bringing it to a conclusion or strengthening it."[19] Is the "dreamlike" connection not evidence of that reality that is no longer the reality of a barrier—in *La terra trema* "the grand vision of man and nature, of their perceptible and sensual unity"—which more deeply defines the "communist consciousness" than the "struggle with nature and between men"? Is that which is indissolubly possible in the event—Deleuze names it the "visionary's part"[20]—not in turn precisely this "immediately real," by no means the possible that is distinguished from the real and hence doubly helpless?

Youssef Ishaghpour claims that in some of Visconti's films there is not too much, but rather too little, sense, as though the director and viewer would take pleasure in things that extricate themselves from the "tyranny of meaning."[21] One can, however, also infer from this movement of flight that the "cinematic circle" is not made to revolve by an idea of the idea or a significance of the significance. In a review of the pioneering production of Goldoni's comedy *La locandiera*,[22] with which Visconti in 1956 visited Paris, Roland Barthes interprets the attention paid to things as a reference to the mediation that marks the historical transition from the character part to the social type.[23] The individual achieves objectivity with the object, by means of it, through the resistance that it offers. Naming Brecht, Barthes speaks of a "realistic theatre." Such an interpretation complements the remarks on the relationship between human beings and things in Visconti's early manifesto concerning "anthropomorphic cinema." Taking the place of the reified, conventional, and rhetorical, of the interest in things "for their own sake," a "reality of art" is to emerge that concerns itself with "living human beings in the midst of things."[24] What happens at the beginning of *Rocco e i suoi fratelli* is, according to the Catalonian filmmaker Marc Recha, just as inseparable from "every corner of the basement apartment" as from the "gestures" of the figures.[25]

The care that Visconti expended on the selection and display of objects in his works need not be reduced to a concern with the effectiveness of a given production design and the response of the audience. Perhaps it can be taken as a sign for that "immediate reality" that he wanted to create with every film, every theater and opera production, as a sign for an awareness of that reality that the work of art itself is. Like the text in which Adorno's proposition stands, works of art strive for a reality that comes toward them whenever between element and significance a continuity arises that for its part is not subordinate to a significance and that on no account excludes, for example, the interruption of the "cinematic circle." For philosophy this is as much as to say that one does not possess truth but rather holds oneself within it. For art this is as much as to say that art is not something possible or a proxy of a possibility, not even critically or negatively. What the successful films created by Visconti express is that transformations have always already occurred. They do so by means of their content but also by being the objects they are. They even sometimes find figures for this. Konrad, the gigolo and the opportunist whom the professor in *Gruppo di famiglia in un interno* suddenly views as a possible son, is familiar in painting with the genre of conversation pieces, in music with Mozart's aria "Vorrei spiegarvi, oh Dio," a new recording of which he comes across in the possible father's record collection. Yet the professor hesitates to acknowledge the transformation that has taken place, thus surrendering to the fatally ambiguous possibility that stands in the way of change. Death, either accident or suicide, overtakes the younger man who calls himself "son" in a note to the professor. *That* the transformation has always already taken place is clear from the irreducibility of the *expression*. Hence it is not a matter of realizing possibilities, of awaiting their realization, indeed of mourning the omitted or impossible realization. In order to sweep clean the paths, to shake off the shackles of heteronomy, it is necessary to acknowledge a reality, in other words the change that has already occurred.

A biographer describes Visconti's daily routine in a holiday resort:

During the morning, a procession of local antique dealers would come to sell him all sorts of objects. Lunch was at 1.30 and at 5 p.m. he would interrupt everybody's siesta because at 6 p.m. every day a procession of taxis took Visconti and his guests down to a café in Porto d'Ischia. From there he would take a walk with his friends, stopping at every shop to buy presents for everyone. Another ritual was that of buying the tuberoses. . . . Inside the house the scent of these white, fleshy flowers was so strong that it gave many of the guests a headache. At night television was obligatory, however bad and irritating: when the woman announcer said good night at the end of transmissions for the day, Visconti would shout at her "You swine!"[26]

Translated by James Phillips

3

Michelangelo Antonioni
The Aestheticization of Time and Experience
in *The Passenger*

ALISON ROSS

Cinema and Technique

We can schematically characterize the use to which techniques of cinema have been put by means of a three-way differentiation. First, there is the use of cinema to stage human tales. In this vein we can cite the use of cinematic techniques in the oeuvre of Jim Jarmusch, from the early *Stranger Than Paradise* to *Dead Man* and *Ghost Dog: The Way of the Samurai*.

Second, there is the use of cinema to stage a confrontation with a received pattern of meaning. Here the confrontation may have a comprehensive scope, as in Chaplin's *The Modern World*, or a restricted one, as in Greenaway's rendition of Shakespeare's *The Tempest* in *Prospero's Books* or Pasolini's treatment of the Oedipus myth in *Oedipus the King*.

Despite their different emphases, in both of these processes cinematic techniques and elements are used to screen a pattern of meaning, whether that meaning is presented as tragic or depicted in critical or rebellious terms.

Finally, there is the use of traditional characters or plots as little more than props or vehicles to stage aestheticized settings. Here the relationship between meaning and cinematic elements in the first two cases is reversed. In the most developed forms of this use of cinematic techniques, the story line has a purely evocative form, and character is treated in the abbreviated manner of a stereotype. David Lynch's films, for instance, stage an obsessive preoccupation with certain techniques and motifs that exist solely as aesthetic forms: the dwarf figure, the phallic woman, and the popular song.

Antonioni's cinema belongs, I think, in this third category. Unlike Lynch, however, whose aesthetic vocabulary includes the use of estrangement techniques and thus operates to some extent within the second category, in Antonioni's cinema a received pattern of meaning is confronted only as an aftereffect of its aesthetic treatment. In this respect the treatment of political execution and torture (*The Passenger*), institutional violence (in the photographer's planned use of scenes from a doss-house for his book in *Blow-Up*), public art, and political demonstrations or dissent (in the clowning scenes in *Blow-Up*, the strike outside the factory in *Il deserto rosso*, or the imagined destruction of the luxurious house in *Zabriskie Point*) function primarily as occasions for aesthetic exercises rather than as a content with which his cinema deals.[1] It is important to be clear about the limitations that follow from such aesthetically driven cinema: it is not the case that Antonioni uses film as a vehicle to advocate political positions or to contest calcified habits or experiences.[2] Antonioni's cinema explores the technical possibilities of film.[3] It is this aesthetic concern with the technical elements of presentation over narrative content that makes his work a potent medium for the presentation of ideas that would be otherwise obtuse to experience.

Let me be clear: in using this schematic differentiation, I do not want to suggest that Antonioni is only interested in the evocative qualities of a well-constructed scene or a beautiful face; rather, the emphasis in his films on these elements makes available themes that would not otherwise be accessible. These themes do offer a critical commentary on the contemporary world, but one should not view the treatment of these themes exclusively in the perspective of a critical intention. In other words, an adequate appreciation of Antonioni's films cannot limit itself to expounding only the critical commentary that he presumably wishes to make on the contemporary world. The critical intention neither exhausts nor motivates in their concrete forms his techniques and aesthetic renditions.

First of all, I would like to emphasize that it is in the modes of cinematic presentation that the confrontation Antonioni's cinema stages with received patterns of meaning occurs. But I would like to make this clearer by making it more specific and suggesting that the aesthetic forms forged in his cinema confront received patterns of meaning by giving sensible form to abstruse ideas.[4] Taking up this hypothesis of the primacy of aesthetic concerns in Antonioni's cinema, I will examine the different ways that the use of a number of cinematic devices in *The Passenger* makes available as experienceable form otherwise nebulous ideas and projects. For instance, in keeping with the aesthetically driven motives of his cinema, the *episodic form* Antonioni gives to the life of the central character needs to be understood less from the perspective of the narrative content of this film than in relation to the specific techniques by which the "project" of losing one's identity is staged in and, to put this point more emphatically, *as* the composition of particular scenes. This "project," it seems to me, becomes comprehensible as an effect of an aestheticizing intention. Antonioni's treatment of Locke's life, according to an episodic structure, foregrounds the aesthetic composition of scenes at the expense of narrative content; or better, the theme of the loss of identity is the narrative device that reverses the emphasis on conventional narrative in favor of formal cinematic elements. In this respect it would not be too much of an exaggeration to say that narrative is the vehicle of its own demise in *The Passenger*.[5]

Meaning and Narrative in *The Passenger*

The Passenger seems to raise two different kinds of questions: first, what kind of life would one have if one embarked on a "project" to lose one's identity and all the ties and habits that constitute a life? Second, what kind of life or experience would motivate such a "project"? As I suggested in my opening remarks, this narrative device of a "project" to lose identity is the pretext Antonioni needs for the episodic construction of *The Passenger*. Yet the film does not address these questions as such; indeed, Antonioni's final cut of the film removed scenes that would contribute a context of motivation for the protagonist's actions.[6] Rather, the film shows the temporal experience of dispersed identity in the episodically constructed life of the main protagonist and thereby opens up an aesthetic constellation in which a life is treated without any teleology of meaning.

In *The Passenger* Jack Nicholson plays the character of David Locke, a British journalist who is making a documentary film in Africa. After he returns to his hotel from an unsuccessful attempt to contact members of a guerrilla insurgency, Locke discovers the body of David Robertson, a fellow Englishman he had met earlier and a guest at the same hotel. The rough physical resemblance between the men is the premise for the film; after a brief perusal of Robertson's belongings—which include a diary of planned meetings; an airline ticket with stops in London, Munich, and

Barcelona; and a revolver—Locke drags Robertson's body into his room, switches clothes and passport photos, and engineers the deceit on the hotel staff that Locke is dead and that he "is" Robertson. The film is compartmentalized into different episodes, including scenes of the past between Locke and Robertson, as well as scenes set in both London and Africa, between Locke and his wife, Rachel; footage from Locke's interviews, as well as footage he had taken of an execution in Africa; and scenes contemporary with Locke's dissemblance, such as his meetings in Germany and Spain as "Robertson," who, Locke discovers, was a gunrunner for an African Liberation Front; the torture and harassment of agents acting for this front in Europe by African government agents; Locke's relationship with "the girl" played by Maria Schneider; Locke's pursuit as "Robertson" first by his producer, Martin Knight, and then by his wife, Rachel, in Spain; and his own death in Spain at the hands of African government agents who believe that he is Robertson, in the film's famous penultimate seven-minute take. Against the pull of a conventional treatment of this material in the genre of a political thriller in which the protagonist's time is marked by the drama of his pursuit, the film is remarkable for the languor that is the dominant mood in each of the episodic scenes, as well as the absence of a musical track that would infuse the succession of scenes and settings with pace or continuity.[7] Indeed, it is notable that the episodic structure allows Antonioni to eschew temporal continuity.

The significance of the narrative elements in this film can be seen by comparing *The Passenger* to the treatment of the topics of meaning and experience in terms of codes in Antonioni's other major films. In general, the topics of meaning and experience are treated along two axes in Antonioni's films: on one side Antonioni addresses the coding of experience as meaningful in terms of what he calls "the modern sickness of Eros" (*Un cronaca di un amor, L'avventura, La notte, L'eclisse, Il deserto rosso*); on the other side he raises the formal dimensions of coding as such as an epistemological question (*Il deserto rosso, Blow-Up*). The significance of *The Passenger* as a stage for the confrontation of patterns of meaning is that this film presents the codes of both "sick Eros" and the reflective relation to codes as having lost their orientating value.[8] In this respect *The Passenger* confronts code orientation itself as a pattern of meaning.

Antonioni describes the "sickness of Eros" as a modern malaise whose chief symptom is the overemphasis placed on Eros but whose causes are the distinctive features of modern life. These features are documented in the dissonant rhythm Antonioni's work charts between the pace of technological life with its new urban architectures, new workplaces and the itinerant populations they require, and the old beliefs that sit uneasily in these environs. It is in this sense of a "contemporaneous anthropology"[9] that the famous scenes of Antonioni's work from the 1960s—such as the long concluding takes in *L'eclisse*, in which the main characters are absent from the scenography of their urban environment, or the contrast between the bold, primary colors of the factory and the blank expanse of wall that Antonioni uses to dramatize the emotional state of Giuliana in *Il deserto rosso*—need to be seen.

For Antonioni the disequilibrium between science and morals frames forms of experience. Whereas science entertains theses and installs practices that are easily dispensed with when they become outdated, moral beliefs and values constitute a fatality for human life insofar as they orient a path of action at odds with the brute fact of our existence as historical creatures and therefore with the field of human possibilities for action. Put in Heidegger's vocabulary, the rift between science and morals installs the dissonance between what humans "are" in their historical being and the beliefs that attempt to stylize existence in relation to "values."[10] For Antonioni the drive for security, which is the motive force of moral belief, is incompatible with the historical constitution of human life. In the film *L'avventura* Antonioni tries to show the elements that characterize "sick Eros" as a binding pattern of meaning. In this context it is significant that, as Antonioni stated at his press conference for the opening of *L'avventura*, simply analyzing "sick Eros" or confronting this code in a reflective manner, as the character played by Gabriele Ferzetti does, is not sufficient to be free of it:

Why do you think eroticism is so prevalent today in our literature, our theatrical shows, and elsewhere? It is a symptom of the emotional sickness of our time. But this preoccupation with the erotic would not become obsessive if Eros were healthy, that is, if it were kept within human proportions. But Eros is sick; man is uneasy, something is bothering him. And whenever something bothers him, man reacts, but he reacts badly, only on erotic impulse, and he is unhappy.

The tragedy of *L'avventura* stems directly from an erotic impulse of this type—unhappy, miserable, futile. To be critically aware of the vulgarity and the futility of such an overwhelming erotic impulse, as is the case with the protagonist in *L'avventura*, is not enough or serves no purpose. And here we witness the crumbling of a myth, which proclaims it is enough for us to know, to be critically conscious of ourselves, to analyze ourselves in all our complexities and in every facet of our personality. The fact of the matter is that such an examination is not enough. It is only a preliminary step. Every day, every emotional encounter gives rise to a new adventure.[11]

In his films of the mid-1960s, such as *Il deserto rosso* and *Blow-Up*, Antonioni adopts a more formal perspective on the coding of experience. An epistemological question now asserts itself: if paintings and photographs present scrambled visual codes that need decoding to make sense, how do we know that our interpretations of such codes are correct? In *Il deserto rosso* the character of Giuliana is able to sense things (such as the noise that is the cry of the baby near the dock) that others deny; in *Blow-Up* it is the sources able to testify to events that are examined. Significantly, the photographer does not see the murder and the body in the bushes, and it is his decoding of a photograph that leads him to understand a scene he had earlier photographed. In both of these films, as well as his earlier works, Antonioni explores how Western industrial life imposes patterns of professionalization that dull the senses to experience in training them to the practice of repetitive codes but that also, as in the case of the "blow-up" in *Blow-Up*, provide auxiliary contexts and technological pathways for experience.[12] In the face of these features of modern life, Antonioni does not retreat to nostalgic invocations of an authentic human nature corrupted by the rapid pace of industrialization but rather provides a dispassionate documentation of the new forms of human life that these features bring into being.

The general perspective on the dissonance opened up in modern experience between a petrified and stylized world of values, on the one hand, and the historical register of human existence in changing time as well as the specific critique of the formal operation of codes as the patterning for experience, on the other, is extended in *The Passenger* into a more radical thesis by the treatment of the schematization of experience.[13] In this film the identity of the central character is described in terms of the habit-induced schematization of experience. Habit, even in the case of the profession of a journalist whose immediate context is constantly changing, intervenes in the form of the ready-made codes that stylize his context in terms of the "rules" by which he relates to events: the journalist is a detached observer, unmoved by what occurs around him, his métier is the words and ideas he uses to communicate the significance of events to others. At one point in the film, footage is screened from one of Locke's interviews in which the subject—an African opposition figure who had spent time studying in Europe—violates the code: he questions Locke's impartiality and emphasizes his point by turning the camera around to film the journalist.[14] At this moment, with Locke's discomfit registered on film, the code is placed in the foreground as a practice. This foregrounding occurs at one other place in the film, when, in another scene set in Africa, Locke's wife, Rachel, challenges the polite tone of Locke's interview on the topic of opposition forces with the president of an unnamed African country.[15] Whereas moral beliefs force experience into ill-fitting schemas that become engines for pathologies of reaction—such as neurosis (Giuliana in *Il deserto rosso*) and predatory eroticism (Sandro in *L'avventura*)—Locke recasts codified behavioral patterns (with moral pretensions) into stylized practices of a purely aesthetic type. This aestheticization then makes possible their abandonment, as Locke demonstrates when he takes on Robertson's "empty" identity. In this respect the film inverts the schema in *Blow-Up*, which is epistemological: how do we find a pattern in visual codes where no obvious pattern presents itself? This approach presupposes that there is a pattern to be found, although the film admittedly complicates this thesis by drawing attention to the contingencies involved in the imposition of a pattern; in *The Passenger* it is this idea that is put in question as the central character's project of losing his identity is presented partly as a curiosity about finding and inhabiting another life but, more fundamentally, as a curiosity about the "form" of uncoded experience.

Locke provides the definitive statement of this perspective when he challenges Robertson's view that "every place is the same": "It is us who remain the same. We translate every situation as we experience it into the same old codes, we just condition ourselves. . . . However hard you try, it stays so difficult to get away from your own habits." This statement is the hypothesis of the film, explored and given vivid aesthetic form by its episodic construction.[16] Can you leave your habits? Is it possible to have coherent experiences without a code or a framework to link them into a meaningful chain? Antonioni proposes an experiment of just this type by minimizing the presence of causal frameworks, such as motivation, to code the film's narrative, and by complicating the temporal and spatial logics between and within sequences. Like Locke, we are encouraged to struggle against easy, habit-bound interpretations.

Although the girl tries to interpret Locke's project in terms of his switching of the code of dispassionate observer to that of engaged actor, from the profession of the reporter to that of the gunrunner (an interpretation partly suggested by the European release title: *Professione: Reporter*),[17] she does so apparently because she views identity as a choice between aesthetic styles. It is hard, however, to carry this perspective to any of the other episodes than the scene in which she states it, especially in view of the structure and elements of the film, which systematically undermine any attempt at narrative integration in terms of a redemptive conversion.

LOCKE: I've run out on everything: my wife, the house, an adopted child, a successful job—everything except a few bad habits I couldn't get rid of.

GIRL: How did you get away with it?

LOCKE: It was an accident. Everyone thought I was dead, I let them think so.

GIRL (*in a flat, unquestioning tone*): There's no way to explain it, is there?

LOCKE: Now I think I'm going to be a waiter in Gibraltar.

GIRL: That's too obvious.

LOCKE: A novelist in Paris.

GIRL: Too romantic.

LOCKE: How about a gunrunner?

GIRL: Too unlikely.

LOCKE: As a matter of fact I think I am one.

GIRL: Then it depends which side you're on.

Her approval of Locke's account of the gunrunning for the guerrilla war "in an unknown part of Africa" ("I like it," she says) and later her insistence that Locke continue to make Robertson's appointments and play this role, a strategy that will end in his death, is rationalized by her because "he [Robertson] believed in something and that's what you wanted." The shift in her interpretation of Locke's situation is worth noting: whereas she saw his relation to the role of Robertson as an "accident" that she accepts to be without adequate explanation, she now attempts to suffuse this situation with the significance of an intention. Her desire is that this role be meaningful. But the film presents this as an impotent wish, particularly when she identifies his body to the police at the end of the film as "Robertson." This identification, which contrasts with Rachel Locke's ambiguous statement of refusal—"I never knew him"—cannot provide the context of his death with any meaning because even when he is dead, his death is not the death of the person the girl wishes him to be.

Two features in the film are instructive here: first, all the elements of narrative that could generate a meaningful context are stripped back, not just by the project of the main character, which is reductive in respect of narrative and necessarily privative in relation to meaning, but especially by the use of techniques of narrative discontinuity, such that at key points in the film it is a cinematic device rather than the content of a scene that is emphasized. In the scene between Robertson and Locke, cinematic elements overshadow rather than stage the conversation between the protagonists; indeed, these elements reinforce narrative ambiguities. In this scene Antonioni disjoins and then reunites the auditory and visual tracks of a previous conversation between Locke and Robertson and in doing so effects a striking temporal dislocation. At the outset of this scene Locke works on changing the photos in the passports while a voice-over of a conversation he had had with Robertson is played. As Locke speaks in this conversation, the camera pans the room to show a tape recorder playing, and as the viewer identifies this tape as the source of the voice-over, the camera pans outside to a shot of Robertson watching the desert as the visual sequence rejoins the sound. Similarly, Locke's famous offscreen death at the end of the film is a spectacular staging of a technique (this seven-minute take took eleven days to shoot and several complex technical adaptations to the equipment) rather than of narrative content. In this shot Antonioni perfects the style he had used since *Un cronaca di un amor*, in which the camera does not simply follow the movements of a character, or narrative sequences in which characters are present, but undertakes its own path of movement and its own logic of sequencing. Further, in the case of the dialogue between Robertson and Locke, not only do the devices of temporal and spatial discontinuity dramatize this dialogue, but also Antonioni deliberately leaves unanswered narrative questions such as why it was that Locke had his tape recorder running. Did he suspect that Robertson was involved with the guerrilla movement? Would he have used Robertson in his documentary? Or was the recorder running anyway, and did he simply forget to switch it off when Robertson dropped by?

The Passenger extends the theses of the other approaches to meaning and experience in Antonioni's films into a question about what the absence of a code or a binding meaning for experience would look like. What would it mean to experience life without a code? Would this be possible? These questions, which Antonioni approaches in his use of cinematic elements, undermine narrative as a sufficient way of explaining them.

Time and Mood: The Aesthetic Configuration of Ideas in Antonioni's Films

The relation between narrative and technique that uses the narrative device of Locke's "project" to undermine the significance of narrative builds up as a further theme the idea of time as the dispersion of identity. This idea is inimical to conventional character development. Instead of being the medium of character development (as in adventure films), time is deployed as a space for parading life fragments whose meanings are more or less exhausted in their immediacy. The film's reflection on the "project" of the loss of identity is executed in part by the reductive presence or authority of the main character.

Characters may be viewed as complex systems. Time is one of the ways in which character systems build up their internal complexity and ensure their own stability.[18] What I want to emphasize through the use of this terminology is the way that a normal cinematic character is built up through connections with his or her environment and how he or she stands out against that background by demonstrating stable character traits. Time is the element that allows these otherwise contradictory features to be intelligibly woven together. It is this relation to time that is radically altered in Antonioni's film. The African agents still follow Locke and believe him to be Robertson, despite the fact that he fails to approach them (as Robertson would have) at the airport. Locke reduces to sparse, arbitrary elements Robertson's character system. His decisions saturate an immediate present, and although they may be seen to be related to an intelligible overall design that unfolds in time, they do so in a blind fashion. Presumably this is one way of understanding his death: had members of the cell failed to meet the real Robertson, he would have assumed that the cell had been penetrated and ceased making his schedule of meetings. Unlike the temporal scope for the development of character in an adventure film, *The Passenger* lacks the premises, such as a genuine character and his or her time dimension, to narrate an Aristotelian end or resolution. It is in this sense that the film presents the idea of time as the element for the dispersion of identity.

This idea is heightened by the film's languor-ridden mood, as well as the major motif of waiting. Early on, Robertson describes the desert as "so beautiful, so still—a kind of waiting." It is the technical achievement of this film that "a kind of waiting" is shown that systematically undoes Locke's "identity" as a coherent system. Each decision made unfolds in only a small span of time; Locke's projects do not extend beyond the episodic structure of a scene. Even the continuity of his evasion of pursuit in the latter parts of the film does not regulate the final episodes with overall continuity, and in each of these episodes a sense of languor is the dominant mood. Many of the scenes show Locke waiting for people who do not appear (this is the motif with which the film commences, even prior to Locke's becoming Robertson) or fleeing from people who are waiting for Robertson, such as his wife and his producer, whom he does not wish to see.

What is foregrounded by the languor-ridden mood, but above all by the scenes constructed around the motif of waiting, is the question of whether the "project" of living a life reduced to the immediate is at all compatible with endowing such a life with meaning.[19] Indeed, the contrast between the equation that fuses identity with the coding of experience as habitual on one side, and the equation that fuses the evasion of codes in the project of the loss of identity with death on the other, creates a constellation in which the film confronts the idea of a meaningful life.

The Passenger shows abstract ideas, such as the dispersion of identity in time or the relinquishing of identity, as a "project." It remains to ask what insights and limitations follow from the way Antonioni presents such ideas and how this film presents these ideas in an "experienceable" way?[20] Once again *The Passenger* may be usefully compared to Antonioni's other films on these points.

Moral values, motivations, moods, and feelings cannot take a specific form but may only be "shown." Meanings of such kinds are able to be experienced in aesthetic presentations, which make accessible ideas not able to be explored discursively.[21] Similarly, temporal characteristics of experience, such as waiting, or the agency of time as a force of dispersion over identity can be shown in aesthetic presentations. Film, moreover, is the ideal medium for the presentation of ideas of time on account of its capacity to spatialize temporal forms.[22]

Antonioni's cinema attempts to give such ideas an experienceable form. Films such as *L'avventura* show the impasse between values and existence. In *Il deserto rosso* color is used to show moods and feelings but also the contrast between the time of the present and the outmoded beliefs and feelings of those who inhabit it. In *The Passenger* the abstract project of the loss of one's identity is made accessible to the audience as an experience by virtue of techniques that "present" the passing of time. This project is irreducible to any teleology of meaning or intention, as is shown by the episodic narrative of the film and the manner in which the camera follows movements that are extraneous to character and plot (such as the focus on the cars passing the café where Locke and the girl sit and discuss his life or the documentation of the events occurring outside Locke's window in the penultimate scene).

In *The Passenger* the theme of time as the dispersion of identity is presented in an experiential form. As in the case of the treatment of the theme of meaningful codes in Antonioni's earlier films, this theme has its impact on account of the way it is staged. Key cinematic elements—such as the splitting of the auditory track from visual sequences and the independence of the camera's movements from the functions of the descriptions of space and character—give a texture not otherwise to be had for this abstract theme.

In Antonioni's films the emphasis on cinematic elements reverses the conventional position of narrative. The chief consequence of this reversal is that instead of making meaning intelligible through narrative elements, Antonioni's films make available abstract themes through evocative modes of aesthetic presentation; or perhaps one should have it the other way around, that aesthetic presentation conjures such themes. Although these themes can be integrated into a critical commentary on the contemporary world, the aestheticizing intention in Antonioni's cinema does not deploy them for this purpose. Rather, his cinema makes ideas that would be inaccessible through conventional narrative—such as the "project" to lose identity or the dispersion of identity in time—available for emphatic experience precisely through his relative autonomization of aesthetic moments.

4

Robert Altman
The West as Countermemory

MICHAEL J. SHAPIRO

Altman's Politics of Aesthetics

If film is the "aesthetic matrix of a particular historical experience," it remains for us to ponder the ways in which it articulates the aesthetic with the political so that the "historical experience" is rendered politically.[1] Although there is a wide variety of relevant approaches to the political implications of artistic texts addressed to particular historical periods, Jacques Rancière's remarks about the politics-aesthetics relationship best capture the way that Robert Altman's films supply a political sensibility. Rancière notes that insofar as an artistic text can "borrow from the zones of indistinction between art and life the connections that provoke political intelligibility . . . it does this by setting specific forms of heterogeneity, by borrowing elements from different spheres of experience and forms of montage from different arts or techniques."[2] Thus, for example, in his *Kansas City* (1996), a film that features a crossroad between diasporic African American musicians and several levels of Euro-American political officials, Altman juxtaposes (in parallel montage) the macropolitics of the 1938 presidential election with the micropolitics of African American economic survival as it is functioning within a diasporic jazz culture. But rather than allowing a conventional political narrative to dominate his story, he frames the interactions and intersections of the two political cultures as a song. As Altman puts it (in response to complaints that the plot of *Kansas City* is thin), the "story" in the film as a whole "is just a little song, and it's the way it's played that's important."[3] Altman's approach was to make the movie itself into a kind of "freewheeling jazz improvisation,"[4] an approach reminiscent of the aesthetic strategy of Ralph Ellison's novel *Invisible Man*, which constructs African American history in the form of "a jazz composition or performance."[5] According to Altman:

A song is usually about three minutes long . . . but when jazz guys work on it, the song takes 17 minutes. I decided to make a song out of the story of the two women. As it developed, the whole movie is jazz. Harry Belafonte [who plays jazz club owner Seldom Seen] is like a brass instrument—when it's his turn to solo, he does long monologues like riffs—and the discussions of the two women are like reed instruments, maybe saxophones, having duets.[6]

Altman's film is therefore political not because it deals with a presidential election but because of the way it works on (in Rancière's terms) "the contraction or distention of temporalities, on their contemporaneousness or their distance, on [their] way of situating events at a . . . minute level."[7] And Altman's cinematic aesthetic accords well with other genres belonging to what Rancière refers to as the contemporary "aesthetic regime of art," which is a departure from the traditional mimetic regime by dint of its reversal of the privileging of "the primacy of the narrative over the descriptive." The aesthetic regime features instead "a fragmented or proximate mode of focalization, which imposes raw presence to the detriment of the rational sequences of the story."[8]

But with what kind of presence is Altman concerned? If we heed the ideas immanent in his cinematic form, that "presence" emerges as a *co*presence, a bringing to presence—conceptually, cinematically—of parallel streams of life. Making use of parallel montage, a technique pioneered by D. W. Griffith, a "yoking together of non contiguous spaces through parallel editing," Altman effects a "disfiguration of continuous time" to allow a glimpse of the copresence of different lifeworlds.[9] For example, in *Nashville*, in which he explores a complex racial/spatial order by creating a panorama with multiple personalities involved in different kinds of stories (in an American city that is both a place and a musical institution), Altman resists what his editor, Sid Levin, calls "the classic style . . . the conventional use of master, medium and close-up shots." Rather, there are "three or four different master angles of the same sequence, each with a slight variation in camera angle."[10]

In addition to decentering the sociopolitical order with shots taken from many angles, Altman's cuts and juxtapositions reveal the different valences and meanings that the rhythms of life have in alternative social venues. For example, in a seemingly trivial yet exemplary moment of filmic and aural montage in *Nashville*, the scene cuts from a hospital, where an elderly husband weeps over the news that his wife has just died, to a youthful, festive gathering in a music club in which someone is laughing in precisely the same rhythm as the husband's sobbing. And in *Kansas City* Altman produces a similar parallel resonance in a scene in which jazz-club owner Seldom Seen's henchmen are knifing to death the cab driver (who had conspired in the robbery of Seen's black gambling customer) in an alley. As the cab driver is being killed, there is a cut from the alley to Seen's Hey Hey club, where "at the same time the two saxophonists try to outdo each other with a rapid exchange of short phrases. [Coleman] Hawkins and [Lester] Young engage in a cutting contest of their own,"[11] and their intensity produces the same rhythm as the killing.

The politico-aesthetic sensibility that Altman enacts in *Nashville* and *Kansas City* is in evidence in his two exemplary westerns, *McCabe and Mrs. Miller* (1971) and *Buffalo Bill and the Indians: Or Sitting Bull's History Lesson* (1976). In what follows, I treat the way Altman structures his films to dislodge the imagistic and narrative clichés with which the West has been produced in classic westerns. In these two westerns Altman exercises his exemplary politics, a subversion of (in his words) "set ideas, fixed theses, platitudes, things that say this is this."[12] In the process he offers a cinematic politics of history that rethinks and restages America's western experience.

Resisting the Cliché: *McCabe and Mrs. Miller*

What has been the dominant figuration and story of the American West? From the three aesthetic genres of legendary history, painting, and fiction—of Theodore Roosevelt, Frederic Remington, and Owen Wister respectively—to the classic western films of John Ford, the West, as it was narrated and figured throughout much of the twentieth century, has been primarily a heroic story about Euro-American cultural and political expansion on a large panoramic frontier, under a big sky. The movie screen to which Altman brought his work was thus not blank; it was already filled symbolically with figures, spaces, and narratives. The conceptual implications of the already-saturated historical West with which Altman was faced when he decided to do a western is addressed in Gilles

Deleuze's treatment of the painter Francis Bacon, who faced a similar historical plenitude. As Deleuze insists, it is wrong to assume that the artist "works on a white surface." Rather, "everything he has in his head, or around him is already on the canvass, more or less virtually, before he begins his work."[13] To resist what Deleuze calls "psychic clichés" and "figurative givens," the artist must "transform" or "deform" what is "always-already on the canvass."[14]

The same is largely the case with the silver screen. John Ford's West, for example, is the vast open prairie located in Monument Valley, where he filmed eight of his westerns. Altman needed to find a different kind of landscape, filled with characters other than Ford's heroic types, in order to achieve a different, more complicated and politically perspicuous West in his *McCabe and Mrs. Miller*. He called his film an "'anti-Western' because the film turns a number of Western conventions on their sides, including male dominance and the heroic standoff; gunplay is a solution only after reputation, wit, and nonviolent coercion fail; and law and order do not always prevail."[15]

Altman's resistance to the clichés of the classic western is pervasive in *McCabe*, beginning with the opening scene, whose deformation of the earlier westerns becomes apparent if we can contrast it with the opening scene in Ford's *The Searchers* (1956), which depicts the slow arrival from the large open prairie of Ethan Edwards (John Wayne), viewed by his sister-in-law from the interior of her cabin. This shot, repeated at the end of the film, with a different figure in the doorway, as Ethan's departure is again viewed from within a domestic venue, is a moment of referential montage that reflects the nation-building theme that lends coherence to most of Ford's westerns. The "Anglo couple" or "family on the land" thematic is part of a "nationalist ideology" in Ford (as in D. W. Griffith's earlier silent westerns). Although Ford eventually evinced ambivalence about the advance of Euro-American civilization westward (in his *The Man Who Shot Liberty Valance* and *Cheyenne Autumn*), most of his films have participated—but not without ironic qualifying moments—in the figuring of the Euro-family as a bastion against the threat of interracial marriage and against a competing model of familial attachment, the Indians' clan- or lineage-based system of intimacy and attachment.[16]

In *The Searchers* the theme of domesticity and belonging versus migrancy and separation is reinforced by the sound track. As the credits run against a playbill-style font face on an adobe brick wall, we hear the

Sons of the Pioneers singing the Stan Jones ballad "What Makes a Man to Wander?"

What makes a man to roam?
What makes a man leave bed and board
And turn his back on home?
Ride away, ride away.

As becomes apparent in the opening scene as the credits are run in *McCabe and Mrs. Miller*, Altman's film is not a story about the importance of establishing a stable, Euro-American domesticity in the West. The contrast between McCabe's opening ride and Ethan Edwards's overturns the Ford clichés in various modalities. First, as John McCabe (Warren Beatty) rides toward the town of Presbyterian Church in the opening scene, the sound track begins with a ballad, in this case Leonard Cohen's "The Stranger Song." While the ballads by the Sons of the Pioneers in *The Searchers* and Leonard Cohen's in *McCabe* manifest the typical ballad style—they are both narrative poems with repeated refrains—Cohen's presents a very different kind of character. Rather than a heroic wanderer, Cohen's "stranger" is an antihero, a hustler looking for shelter rather than a tough loner, the typical western hero who is unfit for domesticity, even though he helps those who are weaker achieve it:[17]

It's true that all the men you knew were dealers
Who said they were through with dealing
Every time you gave them shelter
I know that kind of man
It's hard to hold the hand of anyone
who is reaching for the sky just to surrender
who is reaching for the sky just to surrender . . .
He was just some Joseph looking for a manger,
He was just some Joseph looking for a manger . . .

It should be noted, however, that Ford's Ethan Edwards is not entirely the stereotypical western hero either. Although Edwards is the rugged loner who saves those who are not as tough or wily from destruction, his departure is not simply that of one too individualistic to accommodate a social or domestic existence. Because of his racism he cannot accommodate himself to a multiracial society. Ford's ambiguous hero is therefore exiled from America's future because his racism has no appropriate place, not because he is merely an individualist like some of the classic western's heroes, for example George Stevens's Shane (Alan Ladd) in *Shane* (1953). In deforming Ford's approach to the hero, Altman is thus deforming something already deformed.

Ford's landscapes, however, remain unaltered clichés. As the Joseph line is sung in Leonard Cohen's first ballad on the *McCabe* sound track, the outskirts of the town of Presbyterian Church come into view with a church in the center background. It is evident that Presbyterian Church contrasts dramatically with John Ford's frontier. As the story unfolds, what is presented is not the displacement of a wilderness with a garden, as the wild West becomes civilized (imagery both shown and verbalized in Ford's *My Darling Clementine* and *The Man Who Shot Liberty Valance*) but rather a chaotic and violent mélange of unenviable characters. Rather than a vast frontier, Presbyterian Church is a muddy town in a rainy mountain venue that is far from the exemplar of an outpost for building national community in the wide-open West. Filled as the story progresses with hustlers, derelicts, profiteers, and predatory corporate advance men, Presbyterian Church's antiwestern tenor is coded not only by the difference in landscape and character but also by cinematically evinced moods—Vilmos Zsigmond's dark tones and washed-out, almost colorless landscapes and Leonard Cohen's melancholy ballads.

Cohen's "The Stranger Song" complements the moody, unsure, and blustering McCabe; his "Winter Song" resonates with an emotionless, opium-distracted, managerial Mrs. Miller (Julie Christie); and his "Sisters of Mercy" song accompanies (while playing into the pervasive religious idiom) the arrival of the homely, disheveled "chippies" (in McCabe's unbusinesslike, sexist idiom), prostitutes whom McCabe plans to employ in his under-construction saloon-bathhouse-bordello. The somber cinematic mode evoked by sound, light, and color is of a piece with the "somber mood of the new western history,"[18] which in recent decades has lent complexity to a West that had been represented as a beckoning destiny rather than a site of imperial expansion, involving, alternatively, negotiation and violence, trading and exploitation among European, Native, and Spanish Americans.

The color tones play an especially important role in Altman's attempt to code the West. As Altman implies, the washed-out tones are intended to give the audience a historical sense of the West: "I was trying to give a sense of antiquity, of vagueness, and to make this not a life that you're living but a life that you're looking through."[19] And he had to invert his characters as well in his cinematic coding because of the way the West already existed in the audience's received stock of signs. Given what is always already on the screen as one attempts to write and direct a western—the platitudes and clichés of the advance of civilization, of the heroic gunfighter taming a lawless wilderness, and of women who are vehicles for expanding a stable domesticity westward—Altman's *McCabe* is thoroughly subversive. McCabe is a dressed-up dandy and low-level card shark who achieves charisma after his arrival because of the character vacuum that precedes him and because of the false rumor that he has "a big rep," spread by a saloon owner, Mr. Sheehan, who claims that McCabe shot the dangerous Bill Roundtree. And in contrast with the canniness of Ethan Edwards in *The Searchers*, a man who anticipates dangers and survives while rescuing others with his daring and deep knowledge of the land- and ethnoscape of the West, McCabe is a bumbler. He cannot control his "chippies" (one of whom is shown attacking a client with a knife); he proves unable to do the math when he and Mrs. Miller go into business together; and, fatally, he fails to discern the consequences of rejecting an offer from the large and predatory mining company to buy out his business. Unable to convince him to take their generous offer, they send a hired killer to get him out of the way.

It is not simply a lack of intelligence that ultimately dooms McCabe, however, who dies in a snowdrift after being wounded by the company's hired gun, Butler (Hugh Millais), whom McCabe dispatches as well with his derringer before he dies. McCabe is done in by his stubborn adherence to the myth of the small independent entrepreneur; he puts off Sheehan's early offer of a partnership, aimed at excluding outsiders, with the words, "Partners is what I came here to get away from." And he is prey to a naive, moral economy code mouthed by the lawyer he consults, Clement Samuels, who, full of pomposities and clichés, says, "When a man goes into the wilderness and builds something with his own hands, no one is going to take it away from him." Referring to "the very values that make this country what it is today," Samuels adds that "'til people start dying for freedom, they ain't goin' to be free." Ultimately, Samuels encourages McCabe to "strike a blow for the little man." Clearly the reversed name of Samuel Clemens (Mark Twain), a writer whose tongue was always planted firmly in his check, helps to convey Altman's disdain for self-destructive and unrealistic platitudes. By the time McCabe realizes that pious platitudes will not save him, it's too late. Unable to make a deal with the hired gun-man who says he doesn't make deals, McCabe flees to an assortment of buildings that represent other (architecturally materialized) pieties—the church, from which he is flushed out by a gun-wielding parson, and a "house of fortune" run by a local entrepreneur.

The overturning of verbal and visual clichés does not, however, ex-haust Altman's cinematic strategy in presenting a critical version of west-ern history. The perspective on the facticity or the nature of what is taking place that the film invites the viewer to adopt is assisted by characters who bear only a tenuous relationship with the film's dramatic narrative—the catastrophe that befalls the McCabe-Miller enterprise. A young African American, Sumner Washington, shows up in a wagon with some of Mrs. Miller's sex workers, whose wagon had broken down. He introduces his wife to Mrs. Miller and says that he's a barber by profession. Thereafter, he and his wife are present to the action at various moments, offering by dint of shot–reverse shot sequences a perspective from their points of view.

To understand their role in the film's aesthetic strategy, we can re-turn to Deleuze's treatment of Francis Bacon, where Deleuze points to the presence in some of Bacon's canvases of a figure or figures that have no narrative relationship to the central figure. Deleuze refers to these figures as "attendants" whose role is to serve as "a constant or point of reference." The attendant is a "spectator" but not in the ordinary sense. He or she is a "kind of spectator" who "seems to subsist, distinct from the figure."[20] This spectator plays an epistemic role, according to Deleuze, providing the basis for determining the facticity of the scene, or, in his words, "the relation of the Figure to its isolating place" or "what takes place."[21]

Invariably, the look the viewer gets from the Washingtons' point of view, each time the camera cuts from a group of men to the observing couple, reveals childish, self-centered behavior associated with interaction among crude, uncivil men. Whereas the Washingtons always appear well dressed and dignified, the disheveled men they watch, at times cavorting and at times brutalizing each other, are the opposite. The point of view and contrast offered by these cuts to the Washingtons-as-attendants establishes a mode of facticity in the West that was largely fugitive in the classic west-erns. What the Washingtons' gaze tends to emphasize is the unreliability of the culture "among men" to establish a mode of communal intimacy. And what we see (as we see with them) is reinforced in numerous scenes, as well as in Altman's characteristic multilayered sound track. From the early scene in Sheehan's saloon, through the other male gatherings, the peripheral conversations taking place outside of the main camera shots are audible. They often involve the exchange of unreliable and / or mythic information. In contrast, the scenes among women reveal a playful, caring, and supportive communal harmony.

A telling moment of parallel editing emphasizes the difference: while a group of Mrs. Miller's sex workers, which includes a Chinese woman, is sharing a bath and engaging in playful exchanges, the scene cuts to the men playing cards in another room. As the scene cuts back to the nude women, one of the men's voices can be heard as he passes on a rumor about the distinctive physical attributes of Asian women, a rumor that is belied by what the viewer can see. Throughout the film, once the contrast between the bumbling McCabe and the canny Mrs. Miller is established, inept, violent, and uncivil men are contrasted with what appears to be an orderly and civil women's society within the brothel. In scene after scene the viability of the "among women" trumps that of the "among men" as a basis for community. Certainly John Ford, in his early film *Stagecoach*, displays a generosity toward the former prostitute, Dallas, who turns out to be a promising prototype character for the West-to-come. But the value of her character for such a role is inextricably connected to her coming marriage (an identity shift from prostitute to wife) to the hero, the Ringo Kid (John Wayne), who also emerges from a damaged identity, a change from "outlaw" to inchoate rancher / settler.

Doubtless even the classic westerns sought to note the importance of strong women in the emerging Euro-dominated West, for example "extraordinary heroines from Mae West's Klondike Annie and Doris Day's Calamity Jane, to Joan Crawford's Vienna and Barbara Stanwyck's Jessica Drummond."[22] But Mrs. Miller is a different type. Her toughness is entrepreneurial. Having the knowledge and experience needed to develop and manage a sex-work enterprise, she has to convince the town's only innovator, McCabe, to develop a larger vision because he has the only building that would make a viable space for her business. And although McCabe becomes her occasional sex partner, it is through canny economic talk and a no-nonsense approach to all areas of the business that breaks down McCabe's initial resistance and makes him her business partner.

When they first meet, and Mrs. Miller asks to be taken to a place for breakfast, McCabe's face registers amazement as he watches her attack her meal without the least hint of a stereotypical feminine delicacy. Here again, Altman's camera work carries the burden of mapping the encounter of the characters. In particular, the face shots of McCabe—subsequently repeated in other scenes, in which Mrs. Miller displays an unladylike manner—convey what McCabe's agency is about in the film: a puzzlement stemming from an inability to evade stereotypical thinking. Face shots, or what Deleuze calls the "affection images," locate the intentionality of the self. The face is where the meaning of all the bodily movements, as an ensemble of the agency of the self, is registered. It is responsive to the questions "What are you thinking about?" and "How do you feel?"[23] In contrast, except for the dreamy moments when Mrs. Miller is high on opium, the face shots of her demeanor register the determination of someone in control of her surroundings.

Ultimately, however, a structural dynamic overpowers whatever effects issue from the force of their personalities that constitute the McCabe–Mrs. Miller enterprise. Here it is apropos to refer to what Noël Burch has famously called two kinds of filmic space, that within the frame and that outside of it.[24] Two visits, one by the mining company's advance men and one by their hit men, take place within the frame. In confrontation with the advance men, who try to buy him out, we witness a cocksure McCabe who rejects their offer. When the hit men arrive, riding in like all strangers in westerns, we witness a different McCabe, a fearful ingratiating version whose attempts at mollifying these new representatives go for naught. But the two sets of visitors, whose interactions with McCabe reveal McCabe-the-antihero's instability, are connected to a powerful force outside the frame, the force of capital.

Altman's attention to the way that corporate capital displaces the efforts of the small entrepreneur impugns the clichés that attend settlement in the classic westerns and, most significant, challenges various narratives of "the winning of the West," especially those based on notions of civilizational superiority. At a minimum the heroic cowboys are displaced by bumbling maladroits, who appear as mere children compared to the women, whose civic skills create the only communal stability. But even the more perspicuous narratives that emerge from Ford's films—that the law book has displaced the gun (*The Man Who Shot Liberty Valance*) and that "words won the West" (*Cheyenne Autumn*)—are overturned by the lesson in political economy offered by *McCabe*. All that was missing from *McCabe* by way of an important political pedagogy was the fate of the "Indian." But Altman turned to this pedagogy explicitly five years later in his *Buffalo Bill and the Indians: Or Sitting Bull's History Lesson*. In this film Altman turns his attention not simply to the unjust immiseration of Native America but also to an issue that preoccupied John Ford: the distinction between history and legend.

History as Countermemory:
Buffalo Bill and the Indians

Altman's *Buffalo Bill and the Indians* draws on elements from both *Nashville* and *McCabe*—*Nashville* because the film is "about show business" and *McCabe* because it is aimed at sweeping away mythic or legendary forms of history. He wanted, he said, "to take a more honest look . . . at some of our myths . . . to see what they are. It's no accident that the picture is subtitled *Sitting Bull's History Lesson*."[25] Yet, as Altman puts it, "It's going the opposite way from *McCabe*—it's saying that this idea of the West is all show business."[26] Whereas Altman's *McCabe* becomes intelligible as a critical intervention in the symbolic production of the American West when viewed *against* some of John Ford's cinematic clichés, his *Buffalo Bill* articulates the Ford inspiration constitutive of the narrative in Ford's *The Man Who Shot Liberty Valance*; Altman's *Buffalo Bill*, like *Liberty Valance*, renders the heroic story of the West as mythic. Although competence with the gun (a feature of the heroic cowboy) remains very much in the moral center of *The Man Who Shot Liberty Valance*, Ford's most complicated western, the gunplay is mythical rather than heroic, and the typical narrative of the classic western—the taming of the West by the spread of eastern culture and the territorial extension of the white American imaginary—is undercut by the paradoxes the film explores.[27] And most significantly for purposes of comparison with Altman's *Buffalo Bill*, publicists are some of the film's major characters.

Ford's *Liberty Valance* begins with Senator Ransom Stoddard's (James Stewart) account—told to the editorial staff of the local paper and shown as an extended flashback—of his experiences from the time he first arrived in the town of Shinbone. Toward the end of his account, while he is covering the moment of his nomination as territorial representative, the then newsman, Dutton Peabody, stands up at the nominating convention and provides a soliloquy about the accomplishments of the candidate, Ransom Stoddard, a young lawyer who arrives as a victim of violence at the hands of Liberty Valance (Lee Marvin) and ultimately builds a reputation—which leads ultimately to his election to the United States Senate—on the mistaken assumption that he bested Valance in a gunfight. Thus, what seemed like a simple, heroic nation-building narrative, a man from the East bringing law and order to a violent West and subsequently incorporating his region into the nation as a state, turns out to be a commentary on the role of myth in the nation-building process.

When the narrative returns to the present, the film's most famous line is uttered by the newsman, who having learned that Stoddard is not the man who shot Liberty Valance, and having been asked if he will print this revelation, says, "This is the West, Sir. When the legend becomes fact, print the legend." At a minimum, Ford displays an ambivalence toward myth inasmuch as his main character, Ransom Stoddard, displays a "chronic inability to give authority to his assertions until be becomes the man who shot Liberty Valance . . . until he becomes the person he's not."[28] Ultimately, the reverence for words and books, for which Stoddard is supposedly an avatar, is undermined by the moral ambiguities afflicting his identity.

In *Buffalo Bill* Altman takes up Ford's concern with the mythic West, not to debunk myths but, in his words, to have "another look at them," to move "to a place where I can look at them from a different angle."[29] The "look" that Altman provides is distinctive, for his *Buffalo Bill* is shot almost entirely with a telephoto lens. While the historical trope in Ford's *Liberty Valance* is largely a function of the black-and-white tone, Altman's is a function of the historical tableaux produced through telephoto zooming effects. Although there are some panoramas in the film, Altman uses the telephoto lens "even [in] those big wide shots, in order to compress images [because] . . . long lenses change the image and evoke antiquity."[30] Thus while he uses color tones to connote antiquity in *McCabe*, it is the telephoto lens that achieves the time image in *Buffalo Bill*. But the "time" at the center of *Buffalo Bill* is not ethnohistorical time—not the events involved in the whites-vs.-Indians encounters in the West—but media historical time. This temporality is signaled early in the film; as the credits are run, the sound track plays a tinny version of the music associated with cavalry charges in classic westerns, and when later, Sitting Bull enters the combat ring during the show, the sound track replays a Hollywood version of Indian drum music.

Who is looking and listening, and what are they/we hearing and seeing in *Buffalo Bill*? The time image achieved by Altman's telephoto lens and sound track articulates the film's primary trope of history as enter-tainment. With the telephoto effect, which situates the viewers as outside spectators, Altman's *Buffalo Bill* is constructed as a show, a metacommen-tary on the kind of West that Buffalo Bill's Wild West Show produced— the West as entertainment. As one treatment of *Buffalo Bill* puts it, "In this film, the subjects are merged in the word 'show,' which represents both The Wild West *Show* of Buffalo Bill and the movie *show* about Buf-falo Bill."[31] The sequence of events in the film is more or less homologous with the performance sequence in a Wild West show, especially in the way the key characters appear in sequence: Buffalo Bill, Sitting Bull, and President Grover Cleveland.

How then does the subtitle *Or Sitting Bull's History Lesson* play into the show-framing of the film? Once again, the answer is supplied by the form of the film. Despite acknowledging that his "Wild West" is a show, Buffalo Bill, his publicist, John Burk, and his emcee, Nate Salisbury, rep-resent their reproductions as accurate portrayals of history. As a voice-over announcement at the outset of the show states, "What you are about to experience is not a show for entertainment; it is a review of the down-to-earth events that made the American frontier." And to enhance that history—conveyed as the heroic victory of settlers over blood-thirsty sav-ages—they decide to enlist a historical "Indian" character and fit him into the most violent scenario that white America had been willing to acknowledge, the defeat of General Custer at Little Big Horn. Accord-ingly, Sitting Bull is represented (fraudulently) as the killer by the emcee, Nate Salisbury, who, at the beginning of the show, introduces Sitting Bull as "the wicked warrior of the western plains, the cold-blooded killer of Custer . . . the untamed scavenger whose chilling and cowardly deeds cre-ated nightmares throughout the West and made him the most feared, the most murderous, the most colorful redskin alive . . . the battling chief of the Hunkpapa Sioux . . . Sitting Bull."

Yet a silent Sitting Bull's body undermines Salisbury's introduction, just as he had undermined earlier expectations when he first appeared. If we heed the "cinematographic body,"[32] realized in *Buffalo Bill* with the shots of Sitting Bull's bodily comportment, we see a different relationship between narrative and body from its familiar portrayal in classic cinema. Vincent Amiel notes that the tendency in classical cinema was "d'utiliser le corps comme simple vecteur du récit, abandonnait son épaisseur au profit exclusif de sa fonctionnalité" (to utilize the body as a simple vector of the narrative, abandoning its density for the exclusive benefit of its functionality).[33]

In contrast, certain directors (Amiel singles out Keaton, Bresson, and Cassavetes) use the body differently. Its comportment is not an "instrument . . . au service d'articulations narratives" (instrument in the service of narrative articulations)[34] but rather the primary vehicle for producing what is to be known. In some contemporary films (and here *Buffalo Bill* is an exemplar), "the cinematographic body is no longer an object of film or knowledge; rather it is a model of knowledge via editing. . . . [It is] simultaneously that which is filmed and that which (re)organizes the film in the mind / body of the spectator . . . [becoming the] source rather than the object of cinema."[35]

The "knowledge" to which Amiel refers requires a distinctive frame. In the case of *Buffalo Bill*, Sitting Bull's body supplies a history lesson by effectively subverting the image that the show is trying to construct (exemplified in Salisbury's opening soliloquy). The Wild West show's attempt to turn history into both entertainment and a Euro-American vindication, through the construction of a blood-thirsty savage to be bested by Buffalo Bill in the ring, is belied by the dignified body of Sitting Bull. First, Sitting Bull's inflated reputation as a savage killer is supposed to be reflected in his size. As he and his entourage ride in when he first joins the show company, his very large associate, William Halsey, is mistaken for him. Sitting Bull turns out to be quite diminutive. Then as he rides into the ring for his appearance in the drama of Little Big Horn, Sitting Bull, as a silent and simply adorned old man, with a dignity and wisdom in his carriage that radically transcends the "show" in which he is displayed, has a dramatic effect on the audience. Their initial jeers turn to applause, for he has managed to move out of the antagonistic role to which the show has assigned him.

On another level silence is the historical role to which Native Americans have been consigned in Euro-America's dominant Indian imaginary. The stoic and inarticulate Indian, an image perpetuated in novels, paintings, and films, was part of a construction of the civilizational superiority that helped justify encroachment into Indian territories. In Altman's *Buffalo Bill* the "silence of the Indians" is portrayed as a function of white inattention to their words. While Sitting Bull's silent dignity during the staged invention of an alternative Little Big Horn engagement in the show subverts one narrative, that of the violent blood-thirsty savage, his silence in another scene is imposed. As the film progresses, it becomes clear that Sitting Bull was willing to subject himself to the indignity of false representations because he had hoped to meet President Cleveland in order to air his people's grievances. When, however, President Cleveland visits Buffalo Bill's Wild West Show and appears at an evening gathering, he refuses to speak with Sitting Bull.

While the "Sitting Bull" expected by the Wild West production company is a product of the fraudulent media publicity that emerged from Custer's defeat at Little Big Horn, Buffalo Bill himself is also a constructed identity, shown in part through the many scenes in which his look is a function of the wig, makeup, and buckskin he puts on to appear in the show. But well before his Wild West show, the historical Buffalo Bill was an invention of Ned Buntline's stories in dime novels, which turned a minor scout into a frontier hero. And the mythologizing that constructed "the West" is emphasized by the nature of the main personae involved in making Buffalo Bill a media creation, first in the dime novels and then in his role in the narratives dramatized in his traveling show. There is a producer, a publicist, a journalist, an interpreter, and an old soldier who verbalizes false legends. And as is the case with Altman's *McCabe*, much of the mythology is simply overheard in peripheral conversations. For example, there is one early in the film when someone off-camera can be heard saying that "Sitting Bull is famous for scalping folks in their beds."

As was the case with his *McCabe*, in *Buffalo Bill* Altman makes use of attendants, in this case of characters who have no relationship with the main narrative about the show—its exploitation of Sitting Bull, its fraudulent version of the Battle of Little Big Horn, and its failed attempt to separate image from fact (there is a last encounter between Buffalo Bill and a postmortem appearance of Sitting Bull as an apparition who, says Buffalo Bill, "isn't even the right image"). In *Buffalo Bill* one of the attendants is an old soldier who delivers nothing but clichés about Buffalo Bill's heroism and a bartender who articulates the myths surrounding both Sitting Bull and Buffalo Bill, thereby serving as a vehicle for the primary facticity that the film delivers: the Western hero as invention.

In an early scene, as Sitting Bull's party appears, the bartender states that Sitting Bull is seven feet tall. And subsequently, when Buffalo Bill forms a posse that fails to track and apprehend Sitting Bull's party, under the mistaken assumption that they were fleeing (but had in fact left temporarily to perform a ritual celebration of the first moon in the mountains), the bartender expresses amazement as he looks at the forlorn hunting party that has returned empty-handed: "that's the greatest Indian Hunter of them all!" The bartender/attendant, a peripheral character, thus has some of the most important lines. But then, in film after film, bringing the periphery—both visual and aural—into the mix that constitutes a story's intelligibility is what Altman does.

"What Kind of a Man?" None of the Above

The question that Ransom Stoddard poses to the outlaw Liberty Valance in Ford's *The Man Who Shot Liberty Valance*—"What kind of a man are you?"—is central to the issue of the making of the West for Ford. Will he be the hero of the gun, the hero of the law, an ambiguous mixture of the two, or what? If Ford seemed to remain ambivalent about the answer to that question, he showed little ambivalence about the role of gender. If community rather than anomie was to win in the West, it would be a result of some kind of masculine agency, whoever those male agents might turn out to be. His films, both through their story lines and their forms, are centered by male heroes, however flawed those heroes might be (as is the case with Ethan Edwards in *The Searchers* and Ransom Stoddard and Tom Doniphon [John Wayne] in *The Man Who Shot Liberty Valance*).

In Altman's West the men are antiheroes. In *McCabe*, as it is put in Leonard Cohen's lyrics, we encounter a different kind of man from what is characteristic in the classic westerns; it's "that kind of man . . . who is reaching for the sky just to surrender . . . just a Joseph looking for a manger." And in *Buffalo Bill* we encounter a thin media invention with a poor grasp of history and reality. In contrast, Mrs. Miller and her sex workers/employees in *McCabe* display the strength and social sensitivity that is almost totally absent in the men of Presbyterian Church. If community is at all possible, it will rest with their initiatives. And in *Buffalo Bill*, Annie Oakley, who threatens to quit if Sitting Bull is fired and forced to return to custody, is the only character who displays a respect for history and for Native American alterity. If a negotiated, nonexploitative sharing of the West would have been at all possible, it would have had to rest with a woman like Annie. Altman, as was his intention, gave us another look, and that look has to be assessed in terms of the challenge it offers to the heroic Euro-American nation-building narratives it deforms.

5

Carlos Saura
Cinematic Poiesis

KRZYSZTOF ZIAREK

Disjunctions and Doublings

The most striking feature of Carlos Saura's films from the 1970s, in particular of *Cousin Angelica*, *Cría cuervos*, and *Elisa, vida mía*, as well as of his later "dance" films such as *Carmen*, *Tango*, and *Salomé*, is the compositional rhythm through which the complex narrative and temporal structures of these films unfold. This labyrinthine and forking organization of the films—Saura himself mentions Borges as one of the sources for his approach to constructing film images—is often described and analyzed, whether by Saura himself or by film critics, in terms of the subjective experiences of the main characters, for instance, Ana in *Cría cuervos* or the doublet Luis / Elisa in *Elisa, vida mía*. In such analyses the films are taken to reflect the characters' complex mental experiences, in which the boundaries between memories, actual events, fiction, and fantasy become not only blurred but often undecidable. Departing from this emphasis on subjective experience, I focus my analysis of *Cría cuervos* and *Elisa, vida mía* on their "poetic" rhythm, as Saura himself describes it, understood here in terms of the progressively unfolding interaction between image, movement, and sound, on the one hand, and temporal planes, both actual and possible, on the other. This intricate interplay gives Saura's films their characteristic compositional rhythm, both within shots and between them, linking their various temporal moments, whether real, imagined, or remembered, into an elaborate filmic architectonic. Seen this way, this cinematic-poetic rhythm exceeds any "subjective" perspective operating in Saura's works, and reflects instead their properly cinematic, "poietic," force, that is, the force that propels the sequence of images and underlies the overall design of the films. This cinematic poiesis enacts and makes us "see" the temporal unfolding of experience, where the planes of presence, recollection, and possibility (e)merge both within and into one another.

The intricacy of this cinematic rhythm finds perhaps its most telling manifestation in the opening three-shot sequence of *Elisa, vida mía*, which begins with a complex simultaneous overlaying and disjunction between the image and the text read in voice-over. The first shot shows a hilly Castilian landscape near Segovia, with two visible stretches of a dirt road: one starting from the twop of a hill far away from the camera, the second running from the top of a closer hill, and continuing toward the camera, which rests immobile on the right side of the road. A white car emerges at the top of the further hill, and then disappears behind the hill closer to the camera. As the noise of the approaching car becomes audible, the car reemerges at the top of the closer hill, moves toward the camera, and drives past it. The engine noise dies down, and we hear a voice-over (later we learn that it is the voice of Luis, Elisa's father, played by Fernando Rey), which starts reading from what, during the course of the film, turns out to be a kind of an autobiographical memoir / narrative, which Luis writes about "his" life. However, the "imagined" perspective from which he writes this text is that of Elisa (Geraldine Chaplin), his daughter, whom he has not seen in a long time:

I hadn't seen my father for years, nor had I really missed him. I almost never wrote him . . . [the first shot ends; the second shot shows the car coming down a dirt road, turning by the camera, which follows its movement toward an old farm house, as the voice-over continues] just a few postcards to say I was fine, and that Antonio and I sent our love. I didn't want to see him sick, struggling to recover from a recent operation. At the time, my marriage was in crisis . . . well, one of a series of crises. When I got my sister Maria's telegram, telling me of our father's sickness and then an anxious call from my family that revealed how serious it was, I decided to go to Madrid. Selfishly speaking, finally I had an excuse to get away from home [the third shot begins, showing the car drive into the yard, follows its turn, and shows it park in front of the house. People get out of the car; all through the shot the voice-over continues] and calmly reflect upon my own situation. As I got further away from Antonio, I realized I couldn't go back to the man with whom I'd spent seven years. I left, I now realize, knowing I'd never return.

Even though the spectators remain unclear about many important elements of the story inaugurated in the initial shots—details that are explained later and often become more complex as the film continues to unfold—by the time of the synchronized endings of the third shot and of the first voice-over, they have registered, albeit confusedly, the critical disjunction between the overlaid text and images: the text about Elisa visiting her sick father in Madrid and the image of Elisa arriving with her sister's family to celebrate their father's birthday in his secluded house in the countryside near Segovia. At the same time, the film has introduced another disjunction / doubling, namely the one between the father, Luis, and the daughter, Elisa, as the voice(s) supposedly commenting on the images unfolding on the screen. The relation between image and text and the doubling / identification of Luis / Elisa, playfully underscored by the sound echoes between their names, become the mobile frames of the film, shifting, changing, and modifying one another as they become enriched and developed through the subsequent scenes.

This hermeneutic confusion created by the initial sequence, and the interpretive task assigned to the spectators, which, as Marvin D'Lugo suggests, "demands that its audience actively choose a position of 'reading' that story, which is to say, that we elect a way of looking at the world defined within and in relation to the on-screen fiction,"[1] constitutes one of the crucial aspects of the film. Interpretive choices arise immediately from the opening of the film: what is the relation of the image to the text? Is the image what "really" happens in the film and the text simply an autobiographical narrative being written by Luis, though from the point of view of Elisa? Or is Elisa in fact the author of the memoir and just imagines her father writing it from her perspective? This possibility seems also in play, though it is not on a par with the alternative suggested by the film's overall development, namely, that Luis passes on his "authorship" to Elisa, enticing her to take on "her own" voice. Though initially created by Luis, "Elisa's" voice indeed becomes, in the last scene of the film, appropriated and made her own by Elisa, as the subtle changes introduced into the repeated initial voice-over, now read by Elisa herself, suggest. Saura clearly wants to involve his audience in a hermeneutic exercise, in which it becomes obvious that, as Luis remarks in the film, "everything is but representation." This observation simply verbalizes what the filmic texture continuously instantiates in *Elisa, vida mía*, namely the constructed nature of the (represented) reality, which is repeatedly challenged, revised, and opened up to future possibilities and modifications. This deliberate way of filming constitutes an unmistakable challenge to the purportedly stable and "essential" nature of reality, on which a regime like Franco's based its self-representation and which Saura continues to tacitly call into question, even though the film does not include any explicit political allusions. As Saura leads his audience to unlearn its ways of seeing and hearing reality by becoming actively engaged with the questions and ambiguities that the film proceeds to open up all the way through its ending, however, one comes to realize that the interpretive task entailed by the film, though integral to it, does not constitute its focus. Rather, the film centers on the very interplay between possibility and actuality, reality and fiction, as different or alternative possibilities of events and points of view emerge in its course.

The film's focus on emergent possibilities is made clear by its structure, which not only does not resolve the ambiguities introduced in the beginning but instead opens them up to new possibilities, raising them anew as (still unanswered) questions. Where the film's emphasis lies is illustrated pointedly by its ending, in which the initial scene is doubled and, at the same time, both slightly modified and presented from a new perspective: while the final scene repeats the opening image with a nearly identical text, this time the text is read by Elisa. The differences in the text between the beginning and the end, though few, are also significant. The sister's name is now Isabel (and this is indeed how Elisa refers to her sister throughout the film), and Elisa's marriage to Antonio is said to have lasted nine, rather than seven, years as suggested in the opening voice-over. These differences, or discrepancies, illustrate the change of the voice from Luis to Elisa, though it remains unclear whether Elisa "corrects" Luis in order for the memoir to reflect her life more "accurately" or reinvents her father's story. Most important, the final scene reveals Elisa as the author of the memoir/narrative, indicating a new possibility for the status of the reality depicted by the film: it suddenly becomes possible that the entire film is just a series of images showing different possibilities that Elisa is working out as variants for the text of the "memoir" she is writing. The ending makes it evident that the film is never simply about interpreting the ambiguities and finding answers for the visual puzzles it presents but, rather, about undergoing a complex temporal experience of newly arising possibilities, whose rhythm of emergence makes up the film's structure. Through the pronounced undecidability and open-ended character of the questions raised by the film—for instance, the spectators never learn where the boundaries between reality, fantasy, and fiction lie, nor can they decide with certainty who authors the text read in voice-over—Saura makes a statement about the nature of film: film for him functions as a temporal space that comes to be experienced as a cinematically unfolding play of new possibilities emerging from one image into another and often folding back into or overlaying preceding images.

What gives Saura's films their unique tenor is the manner in which the cultural and political interplay and contestation of representations not only come to constitute part of the temporal experience of emergent possibilities but also become themselves revised by various modifications and displacements introduced through these possibilities. This is the case because the possibilities brought cinematically into play by Saura are characteristically projected toward the future and thus remain themselves intrinsically open to further transformation. Their emergence within the film's composition can be either explicit, that is, these possibilities become actually presented on the screen, as happens with the imagined scenes of Elisa's murder, or it remains only implied *as a possibility* through a telling juxtaposition of scenes or frequent use of the same actors to play different, though related, characters; for instance, Angelica's mother and adult Angelica played by Lina Canalejas in *Cousin Angelica*, Ana's mother and adult Ana played by Geraldine Chaplin in *Cría cuervos*, or Elisa and Elisa's mother played again by Chaplin in *Elisa, vida mía*. Because of this intrinsic capacity for transformation and invention, the folding back on itself of *Elisa, vida mía* in its last scene does not simply end the film but also opens up a different perspective on what we have just seen. This remarkable ending reinforces the way in which Saura succeeds in keeping the temporally closed cinematic space of his film intrinsically open both to different ways of seeing the material and to newly appearing possibilities of its further transformation. In a way the further *Elisa, vida mía* unfolds, the more it keeps being traversed and animated by new possibilities associated either with potential or latent scenes or with implied shifts in perspective, possibilities that, even though they never materialize into specific images, continue to trouble any interpretation of the film. As a result the film ends up being not simply about producing multiple readings or interpreting proliferating ambiguities but, primarily, about experiencing cinematically the temporal unfolding of possibilities and the revisions / transformations of reality they make possible. Crisscrossing Saura's films, these imaged, implied, or virtual possibilities fashion their distinctive cinematic rhythm, which invisibly overlays and modulates the sequence of images that actually make up the films. This rhythm, at work already in *Cousin Angelica*, but fully in evidence in *Cría cuervos* and *Elisa, vida mía*, and later in *Carmen* and *Tango*, enacts a particular experience of temporality, one in which past, present, and future—whether real, remembered, or imagined—keep interacting in ways that hold them intrinsically open to new, often unexpected, possibilities that (might) emerge within the cinematic images and transmute them.

The Rhythm of Emergent Possibilities

This temporal rhythm of emergent possibilities is signaled brilliantly in the beginning of *Elisa, vida mía*. The opening shot of the road and the moving car literally images movement and traversal, suggesting the start of a cinematic journey, of an experience taken in its etymological sense of traversing a danger and heading toward an unknown future. In this case the experience involves a temporal disclosure of disjunctive possibilities that reenergize and reframe the cinematic material we are seeing. The film presents the everyday, and therefore often disregarded, experience of how one finds oneself always already moving in time, which continuously reopens the present onto the future. This sensation of being already underway is underscored by the fact that the road in the opening shot appears on the screen as though without an origin, emerging seemingly "out of nowhere" at the top of a hill that "screens" the direction from which the road is coming. This absence of origin becomes reinforced through another visual rupture in the road introduced by the second hill, positioned closer to the camera. This second rupture also produces the repetition of the car's emergence after a brief visual lacuna, this time much closer to the camera and moving almost directly toward it. The imaged absence of origin and the gaps and lacunae in the road, literally exposed and brought onto the screen for us by the car's movement, become the constitutive elements of the specific temporality of experience in Saura's film. The initial shot is composed as two segments of the car's movement: the first, without origin, has "always already" begun, but it is possible to see it only when the car appears at the top of the more remote hill; the second segment is introduced, after a gap of several seconds, by the growing sound of the car's engine, which we hear before the car actually reemerges onto the top of the closer hill. Though it seems that the shot will end when the car has moved past the camera, as if disappearing into the frame of its lens, the shot continues for a few more seconds, without any movement on the screen, but with the surprising irruption of Luis's voice-over. Thus, the shot becomes a sequence composed of ruptured stillness, movement, and voice: a moment of stillness (the "always already" nonpresent origin), the rupture of the car's first emergence, the lacuna when the car disappears behind the closer hill, the sound of the approaching car, the car's reemergence, the second brief moment of stillness, and the surprise at the sound of Luis's voice.

This juxtaposition of simplicity and complexity in the composition of the opening shot, evocative of Saura's style in general, announces the way in which the film will unfold by characteristically giving the spectators a second, or even a third, look at the "primary" scenes of the film. Just as the opening shot has the car reemerge from behind the hill so that we can see it closer and notice several persons inside it (a key disjunction from the subsequent voice-over, which speaks of Elisa traveling to Madrid, implicitly by herself), the film is punctuated by the repeated emergence of alternative possibilities for the initial scene and for the fragment read from Luis's / Elisa's memoir. The text from the opening scene is heard again during the film, and its slightly altered version is read once more at the end of the film by Elisa, in a scene that suggestively restarts the film, as though it were to begin anew, only this time from Elisa's perspective. The rhythm established through these cinematic loops is one in which scenes (can) recur or (re)emerge as their own transformed possibilities. Whether a specific scene actually recurs or not, Saura composes the film in a manner that keeps every scene open to possible recurrence and alteration. An exemplary instance of such implied alteration occurs in Elisa's account of her dream memory about a family meal, in which as a child she remembers a shaking chandelier and a silver family tea set. Though the scene does not recur in the film, its alteration is suggested in another scene, in which Isabel, Elisa's sister, shows her a photograph that proves Isabel's earlier point that the tea set was china and not silver. Isabel's comments are enough, though, to keep the alternative version of events in play as a possibility, that is, as a possible, and different, actuality from what we see happen on the screen. And it is precisely this idea of keeping scenes open to a future reemergence, whether as an alternative rendition, a corrected version, or simply as a reimagined occurrence, that gives the film its characteristically open rhythm, a rhythm whose force is that of "making possible."

In the opening shot, the second appearance of the car, closer to the camera, is the first and framing instantiation of this intensifying transformative rhythm, which in this specific case literally makes possible another "look" at the car. Accordingly, the possibilities enacted in the film keep increasing the complexity of the narrative, as their expanding or shifting horizons accumulate and interact, complicating, rather than facilitating, the choice between presented and / or implied versions of events. For instance, by the end of the film, the authorship of the memoir is no longer decidable: while the initial scene points to Luis as the author, it also casts the narrative in Elisa's voice, scripted by her father. The ending shows Elisa taking over the authorship, as she not only becomes liberated from her inscription within patriarchal representations of women (and, literally, within her father's writing) and acquires her own voice, but also reauthor(ize)s and modifies "her" (father's?) narrative. Thus, the authorship in question could be in fact a joint one, Luis's and Elisa's; or, in an alternative possibility, the film could be a reflection on the fluidity of authorship, on multiple borrowings and cannibalizations, as Saura refers to them, that circulate between Luis and Elisa and that characterize artistic creation as such.

Whatever these expanding possibilities of the authorship implied by the film, they end up pointing beyond the screen narrative to Saura's own authoring of the film as one more, and all encompassing, possibility, brought into play more and more suggestively as the film continues to unfold. Thus, one more indication at issue in *Elisa, vida mía* is not just finding out or deciding who finally "authors" the text, and, by extension, the film; rather, what organizes and animates the film is the reciprocal traversal of scenes and perspectives, as well as their being simultaneously traversed by new possibilities that keep materializing as alternatives to the already presented scenes. To keep these possibilities active *as* possibilities, Saura incorporates in the middle of the film scenes in which Elisa is seen with her bedridden father, apparently in their old family home in Madrid, the only scenes that correspond to the version of events recounted in the fragments of Luis's / Elisa's narrative read in voice-over. Most likely, these scenes belong among the imagined scenes in the film, as their fictional status is further emphasized by their correspondence to the text of the "created" memoir and differentiated from the events unfolding on the screen. Yet the status of these enigmatic scenes remains ultimately undecidable, for it is possible that they could be the only "real" scenes in the film, which would make all the other scenes "merely" different possibilities imagined by the memoir's author(s). In terms of the film's rhythm of poietically expanding possibilities, the scenes from the family home in Madrid can be interpreted as the imaginary / real pivot of the work, which would lead to a critical displacement of the entire surrounding narrative into the realm of fiction and creative imagination.

It is important to remember here that these repeated appearances of new narrative and interpretive possibilities do not form any recognizable sequences but are, instead, spread out and spaced by gaps. These pauses rhythmically reenact the initial time lapse between the appearance and the reemergence of the car in the opening scene. For instance, Elisa secretly reads in her father's journal an account of her final breakup with her husband, Antonio, only to have that breakup dramatized in a later scene, in which Antonio comes to Luis's house to try to reconcile with Elisa, and in which Elisa, as though playacting, recites the words she read earlier in her father's text. In a structurally similar instance of the reciprocal echoing of scenes, Luis writes down in his journal a version of Elisa's earlier remarks from his conversation with her about her disintegrating relationship with Antonio, in which Elisa wonders how a person with whom one has lived for years can suddenly strike one as a total stranger. To complicate matters further, Elisa's remarks constitute an echo of Luis's own unstated reflections that had led him to leave his family nearly twenty years earlier. These episodes illustrate the intricate connections and borrowings that characterize the relationship between Luis and Elisa, the two authors whose personas seem to merge at one point (into that of an androgynous author?) in a scene that could be an (imagined or real?) recollection of Luis caressing his wife or, alternatively, a scene of incest. Either way, it remains undecidable whether what is seen actually takes place or is just imagined, and by whom: Luis, Elisa, Luis / Elisa? As Saura himself puts it, "Is this Luis' story (Elisa's father) or Elisa's? Does the story belong to a character who is double, half Luis, half Elisa, which in the final analysis would be me, the filmmaker?"[2]

These gaps and ambiguities in the narrative are both doubled and displaced in the closing scene, which, in the last brilliant stroke, restages the film's rhythm of emergent possibilities. In the scene the spectator gets cinematically projected into a new "future" for the film's entire narrative: not simply into a possible reenactment of the film's material from the point of view of its new, or newly dis-covered, authoring persona, Elisa, but into an as yet unmarked, barely opening up, "feminine" variation of the rhythm of possibilities that, as the spectator can sense, open again into the future, signaled by the car's repeated advance toward the camera lens. Beyond the details of the stories of Elisa's family, her marriage, and her rapprochement with Luis, what has the most impact on the spectator is this visually and textually generative rhythm, which structures the ways in which the image and the text appear to cross-engender each other throughout the film, as though thematizing not only the relationship between film and literature but also between the script and its cinematic realization. In short, the specificity of the cinematic rhythm in *Elisa, vida mía* lies in its capacity to envelop the spectator in the future-directed energy of arising possibilities. This temporal force comes to be instantiated cinematically by Saura through a characteristic interactivation of movement (both of the camera and within the shots), sound, color, and voice-over.

This idiomatic experience of time in Saura can be understood and recapitulated through the prism of the opening scene in *Elisa, vida mía*, especially through its generative interplay of movement, spatial and temporal gaps, and sound. Like the car in this crucial scene, time is shown by Saura to be "always already" underway, and without a specifiable beginning, so that spectators find themselves projected into a cinematic experience marked not only by a literally visible absence of origin but also by recurrent gaps and characteristic temporal loops, in which events that had already transpired can be traversed again, either explicitly, as in the closing shot of the film, or, more often, implicitly, as in *Cría cuervos*, when the appearance of the adult Ana speaking about the past from the imaginary future moment in 1995 (the film's action takes place in 1975, the year in which it was made), instantly reframes and opens to speculation both the scenes that we have already seen and those that follow in the remainder of the film. Shots that appear to have unfolded as present events in front of the spectators all of a sudden become destabilized in their ontological status: they all now seem to be Ana's recollections of the experiences she had as a nine-year-old girl, experiences that further blur the already fragile boundaries between memories, actual occurrences, and imagination. Scenes already seen thus seem to come alive again and, without having to appear for the second time on the screen, as happens in *Elisa, vida mía*, become filled with new possibilities, ambiguities, and gaps, which make judgment about their status as real, remembered, or imagined even more difficult.

One has to remember that in *Cría cuervos* the point of view embodied in the figure of the adult Ana, played by Geraldine Chaplin, who also plays Ana's mother in the scenes Ana remembers and / or imagines as a nine-year-old in 1975, instead of stabilizing the film's narrative, makes it hinge precariously on the perspective that is not simply imagined but essentially futural. Literally projected into the future, which will arrive only twenty years later, this perspective is imaged in the film as intrinsically possible rather than actual. Moreover, within the temporal frame in which the film is set up, that future moment will never arrive; that is, it will always remain within the film as its opening onto the future, as the imaged / imagined, always yet to come, year 1995. The very composition of the scene, which reframes the child Ana's already "unreliable" point of view through the not-yet-existent perspective of the adult Ana, underscores this open-ended projection toward the future, a projection that becomes the temporal mark of the emergence of possibility qua possibility. As the adult Ana, Chaplin appears in a close-up against a nondescript, uniform background, address-ing the camera directly yet, at the same time, positioned "always" at a dis-tance, as though removed from the present moment and from presence as such. With the exception of the projected date of 1995, the scene remains deliberately unmarked, and its setup clearly announces the "artifice" of the shot. Giving no hints about Ana's life in 1995, the scene places the emphasis primarily on Ana's transformed future understanding of the events of 1975, which in turn allows the spectator to take distance to what transpires on the screen in the "present," that is, in 1975. The scene thus functions as a mark-er of the present's intrinsic dislocation by the coming future, since what matters is not what the future will look like but instead the awareness that the perception of the "present," presented on the screen, will have changed. And this imagined future, as Saura shows, remains always "unimaginable," for its function is that of a moving horizon, which continuously ruptures and reframes the present, and with it, the past. In this way the shot of the adult Ana becomes the image of possibility itself and of temporality as the force of rendering possible. This disjointing future, which inscribes different possibilities into the film's "present," that is, into its 1975 scenes, comes to frame the whole narrative. It indicates that reality in Saura's work is the "present" that is never fully present but that unfolds instead as both intrinsically open to and already traversed by the transformative arrival of the future. Through this dislodging of the present—which intensifies the ambiguity concerning the imagined / real / remembered / projected status of all the scenes in *Cría cuervos*—Saura pushes the film toward a dramatized state of playful undecidability.

Far from being negative, however, this futural dislocation comes to signify both the force with which the new possibilities emerge and the potential they have to alter what is being seen as the "present" on the screen. The scene with the adult Ana speaking to the camera clearly functions as a marker of future qua possibility. The scene illustrates that in 1995 Ana *will have come* to question her own childhood judgment about her parents' marriage and thus also to cast doubt on her own perceptions in 1975, which may have colored all the scenes, especially the ones in which Ana remembers (or imagines) her parents, since her mother is already dead when the film begins and her father dies in the opening scene. This is why this scene, coming as it were from the nonexisting future, does not help clarify the status of any of the scenes that make up the film, as the spectator becomes even more unsure as to what extent the events on the screen actually happen(ed), were imagined, or simply distorted by Ana's idealized perception of her mother. While the spectator's understanding is being purposely questioned, put to the test, and repeatedly reframed during the film, the reminders of Ana's possibly different future perspective on the events of her childhood never allow the viewer to forget the transformative force of the coming future. One could even say that it is indeed this sense of the coming change and of the transformative character of existence that suffuses the entire film, whose atmosphere would otherwise be almost claustrophobic, heavily determined by closed spaces of the house and its garden, and compounded by the dark interiors in the many scenes that take place at night.

"¿Por qué te vas?": Finitude and Futurity

The projection of the adult Ana into 1995 makes *Cría cuervos* appear as though it were projected from the future back into 1975. The effect of this temporal distancing, however, is not so much to suggest that the film can be read as basically a series of recollections of real or imagined events, often complexly embedded within other recollections, as to underscore the passing, insubstantial, essentially temporal character of existence. It seems no accident that the main musical motif associated with Ana is Jeanette's song "¿Por qué te vas?" because not only is the song about passing and going away, but it is also as simple, banal, and catchy as the everyday passing of time, in which we are always already caught. There is an inescapable sense of sadness associated with the song, as its lyrics talk about departure and, throughout the film, remind Ana and spectators about her mother's passing away. Yet at the same time this refrain about the inevitable passage of time brings hope: even if nothing concrete, it suggests that time continuously opens out of the present into the future. That is why "¿Por qué te vas?" plays also, and one could say, most importantly, not only when Ana and her two sisters dance together in one of the most touching and serene scenes in the film, but especially in the closing shots, when, after their school vacations, Ana and her sisters emerge from the enclosure of the house, and thus also out of their past, onto the sunlit, noisy, and very-much-alive streets of Madrid, and walk to school. As they near and enter the school, the girls merge into the crowd of other students, with the last, surprising shot giving us a lingering panoramic view of the city. This closing shot not only generalizes away from the family scenes we have been watching but also projects, within this suddenly opened up and generalized perspective, the time that has passed within the film onto the future as a new possibility, already suggested by the shot of the adult Ana in the year 1995. The conclusion of *Cría cuervos* does not exude any easy optimism,[3] but it does bring into focus the complex temporal experience presented in the film. Within her specific, and often very painful, familial, cultural, and historical circumstances, associated with the end of the Franco era and of the family life emblematic for it, Ana undergoes intense experiences in which she becomes acquainted with the passing of time, with loss, and with mortality. Yet Ana's painful "existential" education, which, significantly, takes place at home and away from school, is framed by an overall experience of the complexity, one might even say, of the density, of time, an experience of the present that is not only flooded with recollections of the past but also marked by a recurrent opening onto the future and its possibilities. It is with this intricate, both painful and playful, experience of time as the force of possibility that the film leaves the spectator, the experience that is reflected in Ana's eyes as she listens to the Jeanette song she clearly loves.

This coexistence of transience and futurity, of sadness and anxiety, on the one hand, and hope, on the other, frames the development of Ana's character through the film. Even though the song suggests sadness and invokes the passing away of her mother, Ana listens to it often, which indicates that she not only does not want to flee from the sadness in her life but that, as she becomes increasingly aware of mortality, she delves deeper into the emotions associated with transience and loss. Although it is true that Ana tries to control and even manipulate death (for instance, in the scene when she plays with her sisters and commands them to die, only to quickly resurrect them), as she not only has poisoned her father but also attempts to poison her aunt, who becomes the girls' guardian after their father's death, the film can be taken to illustrate Ana's becoming familiar with death and then growing to accept not only the death of her parents but mortality as such. Her entranced listening to "¿Por qué te vas?" implies a gradual opening up to the experience of time's passage and, by implication, to finitude. During the course of the film, and especially when she is listening to the song, Ana learns to remain in time and thus to become more accepting of the transience of existence. Through Ana's growing familiarity with the sadness accompanying the passing of time, the film leads the spectators, as it becomes evident in the scene with the adult Ana, to the recognition of the impermanence and fragility of life. Yet what is most important in Saura is that, together with this acceptance comes also the recognition of the possibilities that open up from the present into the future.

Saura's films do not simply recognize these possibilities as intrinsic to time, that is, as futural, surprising, or transformative. The cinematic rhythms of Saura's works, as well as their narratives and composition, are in fact premised on the force of such possibilities. Approached in these terms, *Elisa, vida mía* appears to be constructed as one long temporal loop, as, quite literally, another film take, made possible by the direction of the film's development. What the film dramatizes in this way is nothing other than the very rhythm of filmmaking: a take, then another one, which brings with it a new possibility of seeing/filming the material. But rather than exhausting or completing the first take through the second, or the third, and so forth, the temporal loops in Saura's films keep revealing the possibility of yet another loop, thus inscribing incompleteness and openness into the very nature of the film material. In a similar vein *Cría cuervos* ends with Ana's recognition and acceptance of the death of her parents, which also becomes emblematic of her recognition of finitude. But this acknowledgment of finitude, without diminishing any of its painful sadness, brings also the awareness of an opening future and thus of new possibilities, which the ending of the film begins to disclose cinematically for the spectator when the camera gets literally released from the enclosed spaces of the house: first onto the street and subsequently onto the panorama of Madrid, as the previously intense focus of the camera and of the narrative on Ana suddenly opens up onto "life" in mid-1970s Spain. In this way the ending also recalls the projected / future scene with the adult Ana and becomes another cinematic marker of temporality experienced as the force of emerging possibilities. The power of Saura's *Cría cuervos* comes from this complex cinematic blend of the painful experience of the transience of existence with the presentiment of new possibilities that owe their transformative force to the banal and everyday passage of time.

The two entwined markers of temporality in Saura's films—finitude and possibility—which *Cría cuervos* presents through the prism of Ana's remembrance of her childhood initiation into the finite character of life, constitute the explicit parameters of *Elisa, vida mía*. They become literally visible in Luis's death, which, leaving an indelible mark of finitude on the film, also makes possible the transformation of Elisa into the "true" voice behind the memoir. This link between finitude and transformation is underscored by two other scenes, in which Elisa becomes substituted for a murdered woman whose body Luis claims to have found one day on the road near his house. In both scenes "Elisa" gets murdered by a man played by the same actor as Elisa's husband, and although one of the scenes seems to be invented by Luis, the other appears to be imagined by Elisa herself, who apparently envisages a murderous conclusion to the disintegrating relationship with her husband. In either case the spectator is violently reminded of Elisa's mortality, as the film visually encloses within the horizon of finitude the newly emerging possibilities in Elisa's life that are brought about by the ending of her marriage and her subsequent replacement of her father as the author of the memoir and the teacher at a local religious school. Within the experience of temporality presented by Saura's films, death becomes ubiquitous, from *Cousin Angelica*, through *Cría cuervos* in particular, to *Elisa, vida mía*, and functions as the recurrent marker of finitude, a reminder that whatever one sees on the screen, whether it be a memory, a fantasy, or a real occurrence, becomes subject to displacement and revision, made possible at least in part by the force of the future, whose finite horizon has its limit in death.

Cinematic Poiesis

The temporal rhythm in Saura's most important films can be defined as the rhythm of finitude, of conjoined passing away and opening onto the future, where an ending signals also a new possibility. Describing Saura's cinematic style, especially the intricate mesh of temporal threads that weave together reality, memory, and dreams, film critics, as well as Saura himself in his interviews, refer to its "poetic" character. In these remarks the term *poetic*, though most often taken for granted and left undefined, appears to refer to the density and dreamlike logic of the temporal relations, which render memory, reality, and imagination fluid and permeable in many of Saura's signature films. This ostensible link between the notion of the poetic and the complex temporal design of the films points, indeed, to their structuring rhythm, which can be characterized as a type of "cinematic poiesis," found at work most explicitly in *Cría cuervos* and *Elisa, vida mía*. What makes possible calling Saura's filmmaking "cinematic poiesis" is precisely its reliance on the generative and transformative rhythm of possibilities, which come to be disclosed by means of complexly embedded perspectives and temporal planes. To explicate in more detail this cinematic poiesis in terms of its force of the possible, I turn in the remainder of this chapter to Heidegger's rethinking of poiesis as a temporal play of concealment and unconcealment, in which relations unfold in terms of the force of emergent new possibilities.

To begin with, it is easy to note the connections between the temporal rhythm of Saura's films and Heidegger's discussion of *Dasein* in *Being and Time* in terms of being-toward-death, in which finitude, possibility, and transformation are woven into a complex temporal manner of being-in-the-world. Heidegger characterizes death as "that utmost possibility [*Möglichkeit*] which lies ahead of every factical potentiality-for-Being of Dasein [*Seinkönnen des Daseins*], and, as such, enters more or less undisguisedly into every potentiality-for-Being of which Dasein factically takes hold."[4] As the utmost possibility, death renders existence into being-toward-death, where all possibilities that unfold within the projected opening toward the utmost possibility (death) become marked by finitude. Thus, human existence is projected always ahead of itself and becomes a traversal of and a deciding between emerging possibilities, all of which come to be permeated with the sense of finitude: "In Dasein there is always something *still outstanding*, which, as a potentiality-for-Being for Dasein itself, has not yet become 'actual.' It is essential to the basic constitution of Dasein that there is *constantly something still to be settled*. Such a lack of totality signifies that there is something still outstanding in one's potentiality-for-Being."[5] In this projection Dasein is raised away into the possible, "into the possible in its possibly being made possible, namely into something possibly actual."[6] This means that Dasein relates itself not simply to what becomes possible, and thus possibly actual, that is, to what is capable of becoming actual, but, first and foremost, to making-possible, or to possibilization (*Ermöglichung*). Dasein thus relates first not to possibilities but to the force of the possible, that is, to the force of rendering possible, which Dasein maintains by binding itself to possibilities qua possibilities. "Every projection raises us away into the possible, and in so doing brings us back into the expanded breath of whatever has been made possible by it."[7] In this way the projecting opens a world and holds this whole before us in terms of possibilities. But what is possible prevails, as Heidegger remarks, only if we bind ourselves to it in its being made possible, that is, if we participate in its becoming possible by holding it open as a possibility.

At the basis of Heidegger's explanation of temporality lies this tension between possibility and finitude, the tension that not only enables Dasein's understanding of itself as temporal but also makes possible its relation to temporality, and thus to being, in terms of potentiality-to-be (*Seinkönnen*). In short, understanding itself to be finite, Dasein also becomes capable of relating to itself and to the world around it through the prism of its various possibilities for being, that is, in terms of the different modes of being that become possible for it within its historically and culturally situated existence. This is why Heidegger places the emphasis in his description of temporality and historicity of being on the quiet force of the possible.[8] It is being-toward-death and finitude that allow for the recognition of this quiet force, which, through its silent openings, makes and keeps all that is possible. This force is "simple," everyday, even "banal," yet it is also extraordinarily enabling. On the one hand, it is the force of "nihilation" (*Nichtung*), disappearance, and death. On the other hand, however, this force "makes possible," that is, it enables an openness onto possibilities that arise with the coming future: "the 'force' of the possible gets struck home into one's factical existence—in other words, that it comes toward that existence in its futural character."[9] As Heidegger explains in "Letter on 'Humanism,'" "As the element, Being is the 'quiet force' of the favoring—enabling, that is, of the possible. . . . When I speak of the 'quiet force of the possible' I do not mean the possible of a merely represented *possibilitas*, nor *potentia* as the *essentia* of an *actus* of *existentia*; rather, I mean Being itself. . . . To enable something here means to preserve it in its essence, to maintain it in its element."[10] To maintain something in its element means here to hold it open to its possibilities for being, that is, to enable something to be, in its being, open to and futurally projected into its unfolding possibilities.

This force of enabling, envisioned always with regard to one's futurally unfolding possibilities for being, comes to be associated by Heidegger in his later writings with a rethought notion of poiesis. In this reformulation poiesis does not refer simply to its etymological sense of making, or to artistic creation, but designates a mode of revealing, that is, the temporal play of concealment and unconcealment, in which beings come to be both disclosed into and maintained within their array of possibilities for being. "Such favoring is the proper essence of enabling, which not only can achieve this or that but can also let something essentially unfold in its provenance, that is, let it be. It is on the 'strength' of such enabling by favoring that something is properly able to be."[11] Poiesis refers, then, to letting beings be, which means letting them unfold in the temporality of being proper to them, that is, always in relation to the opening sheaf of possibilities whose emergence punctuates being and gives it an open, futural direction. This "open region" disclosed through poiesis, though pertaining to ordinary and familiar beings, recasts truth into an intricate weave of concealment and unconcealment:

At bottom, the ordinary is not ordinary; it is extraordinary. The essence of truth, that is, of unconcealment, is dominated throughout by a denial. Yet this denial is not a defect or a fault, as though truth were an unalloyed unconcealment that has rid itself of everything concealed. If truth could accomplish this, it would no longer be itself. *This denial, in the form of a double concealment, belongs to the essence of truth as unconcealment.* Truth, in its essence, is un-truth.[12]

What makes the ordinary extraordinary is precisely the admixture of concealment, or un-truth, into the way in which everyday being discloses itself. Truth never comes unalloyed, as Heidegger remarks; that is, it is never neatly or precisely separable from what remains hidden or denied to our seeing. Rather, truth thought as unconcealment is always mixed with concealment, uncertainty, even undecidability.

Considered in this context, Saura's films, from *Cousin Angelica* and *Cría cuervos*, through *Carmen*, *Tango*, or *Goya in Bordeaux*, can be taken indeed as paradigmatic of the kind of unconcealment at work in Heidegger's notion of poiesis. For if there is "truth" in Saura's films, it is not associated with certainty or precision but instead with the complex play of disclosure and concealment, which blurs and leaves as undecidable the boundaries between reality and fiction, the disclosed and the hidden, the explicit and the implied. For example, the "truth" of *Elisa, vida mía* does not lie in the impossibility of resolving the ambiguities running through the film, for instance, deciding the authorship of the memoir or the status of the "incest scene" and so forth. In other words, it does not lie in a defect or a fault of understanding but rather in Saura's ability to keep emerging possibilities open, that is, to maintain them in play as possibilities. In short, "truth" in Saura becomes an "open region" of cinematic possibilities, which his films repeatedly traverse by interlacing temporal threads or by juxtaposing characters (Ana's mother / Ana as an adult, Elisa / Elisa's mother, Angelica's mother / adult Angelica, etc.). The same can certainly be said about *Cría cuervos*. The film's entire cinematic texture comprises layers of concealment and unconcealment, memory and imagination, reality and the intimation of nonexistent, though possible, future frames.

This characteristic embedding and exfoliation of the past, the present, and the future, combined with the incessant interplay of reality, memory, and dream, constitutes the filmic rhythm in Saura. This rhythm reflects the cinematic poiesis happening in the films and organizes their temporal development. As Agamben suggests in *The Man Without Content*, such rhythm is to be understood as the principle of presence, which opens and maintains the work of art in its original space, that is, in the realm of unconcealment. Approached this way, the poietic rhythm is neither calculable nor rational, without ever becoming irrational. Rather, this rhythm is the measure and the *logos*, conceived as that which gives everything its proper station in presence. However, such rhythm, as Agamben observes following Heidegger's reconceptualization of temporality as ekstasis, is not a sequential flow of instants but an ekstasis in a more original dimension of temporality:

There is a stop, an interruption in the incessant flow of instants that, coming from the future, sinks into the past, and this interruption, this stop, is precisely what gives and reveals the particular status, the mode of presence proper to the work of art or the landscape we have before our eyes. We are as though held, arrested before something, but this being arrested is also a being-outside, an *ek-stasis* in a more original dimension.[13]

Rhythm designates thus a reserve that gives and at the same time hides its gift, namely, being as temporality. This reserve is, in Greek, *epoche*: a way of offering and bringing into presence, which at the same time holds back and suspends.

This double meaning of bringing into presence and holding back describes aptly the workings of Saura's films, in which many scenes function as such double gestures of a disclosure that simultaneously holds something back, in effect introducing more ambiguity into an already complex text. What is crucial in Saura is that this holding back is not limited to denial or obscurity but involves also a futural perspective: an opening on the not-yet-existent future, which "holds back" the present from closing on itself and stabilizing its perspective. The poietic rhythm in Saura does not produce "simple" disclosures, which would allow something to be fully or unquestionably present, but evolves a more complex play of possibilities, which keeps the future inscribed in the present as a force opening the present to new possibilities. This force is manifested remarkably in the ending of *Elisa, vida mía*, which, folding the film back on its opening scene, ends up intensifying its play of possibilities, since the image of Elisa rereading / recreating the memoir reopens the film and projects it into the future beyond the film's ending.

In Saura's oeuvre from the 1970s, *Elisa, vida mía* holds a special place, since it presents this kind of cinematic poiesis as an explicit thematization of the problem of artistic creation and of filmmaking. This autotelic gesture becomes evident already in the initial overlaying of the image with Luis's voice in the opening shot. Indeed, *Elisa, vida mía* can be taken as Saura's signature portrayal of the workings of the artwork, and specifically of the film-work. In "The Origin of the Work of Art" Heidegger remarks that art in its poiesis is eminently historical, in the specific sense of making history, that is, of opening up the temporal dimension of possibility as the proper realm of human dwelling. That is why Agamben declares that humans have a poetic status on the earth, which means that it is poiesis that opens, makes possible, for humans the originary space of their world. Writing in a clearly Heideggerian idiom, Agamben suggests that rhythm should be thought precisely as what grants human beings this poetic dwelling: "In this authentic temporal dimension, the poetic status of man on earth finds its proper meaning. Man has on earth a poetic status, because it is *poiesis* that founds for him the original space of his world. Only because in the poetic ἐποχή he experiences his being-in-the-world as his essential condition does a world open up for his action and his existence."[14] Thus rhythm here does not concern structure or style, *aisthesis* or artistic creativity, but instead describes the originary poietic dimension of the work of art, in which human being-in-the-world and its relationship to truth and history are in play. The adjective *originary* refers here to art's force of rendering possible, that is, to its ability to disclose reality as originative of possibilities, whose futural direction keeps the present intrinsically open to transformation. Saura's most successful films from the 1970s work in terms of such a poietic rhythm. In their continuous play with displacing and reformulating cultural and personal representations, *Cría cuervos* and *Elisa, vida mía* allow the spectator to experience poiesis as a play of possibilities continuously emerging within the cinematic space. In *Cría cuervos* Ana's initiation into mortality and finitude allows the spectator to see the world become, as though for the first time for a discovering child, a space of finite existence. Saura's brilliant filmmaking achieves a reciprocal intensification between the particulars of Ana's story and the experience of finitude evoked by the film. In fact, it is this reciprocal enhancement that makes the film convincing as a traversal of the continuously ruptured space of finite possibilities.

Elisa, vida mía locates this space of emerging possibilities expressly within the artwork's poiesis. The key scene, in which Elisa visits her ailing, possibly dying, father in Madrid, encapsulates the way in which such artistic poiesis traverses the undecidable boundary between seeming and appearance. Since the scene appears fictitious in the context of the rest of the film, seemingly made up only for the sake of the semiautobiographical memoir, it raises the question of whether what appears on the screen "appears" in the sense of "seeming" or in the sense of "coming to be." Is the scene we are witnessing imagined or real? But this question also makes the spectator remember that the entire film is a "fiction," a cinematic appearance. Since among various arts, film is literally a matter of appearance and seeing, this scene raises the question that becomes decisive for *Elisa, vida mía*, and perhaps also for all of Saura's works: what are the parameters both of filmmaking and of the kind of disclosure that film is capable of? Because of the nature of the medium, film is perhaps best positioned to show through cinematic image what at once "is" and "seems to be." By interweaving memory, dream, and reality, Saura's films make evident this twofold character of appearing, as their spectator is constantly made aware of seeing what appears on the screen as both what *comes to be* and what *only seems to be*. Yet in Saura's case this way of filmmaking is less about epistemological uncertainty, or perceptual and cognitive ambiguities, than about making explicit the force of the possible and of the transformation enabled within such space of undecidability. The interval between appearing and seeming, the proper "space" of filmmaking, becomes for Saura the space of cinematic poiesis, that is, the space of being as the "quiet force of the possible," which, exfoliating continuously revised representations of the past, and thus of the future as it arrives into its becoming past, keeps evolving new possibilities, a future open for another, albeit finite, retake.

6

Glauber Rocha
Hunger and Garbage

JAMES PHILLIPS

The trouble with most films of the left is that they are not truly revolutionary. The revolutionary cinema should stimulate not the conformity of the public but the revolt of the public. A film like *Z*, for instance, is very Hollywoodian. I think a truly revolutionary film is Godard's *Weekend* because it is a film that provokes the public.

—*Glauber Rocha*[1]

A LATE SLOGAN from the Brazilian filmmaker and critic Glauber Rocha reads: "The subject is KYNEMA." To interpret this, encouraged by the eccentric orthography, as simply the declaration of an aesthete would be an error. Rocha's entire work constitutes an exposition of the political essence of cinema. Formalism is the mark of the revolutionary filmmaker, since, for Rocha, cinema is properly cinema when it is political and properly political when it takes itself as theme.

Of course, all cinema can be said to be political inasmuch as it inevitably encodes a political position. In most instances, however, cinema is political merely by extension: it is no more than a means of communication of an independently existing politics. Cinema only comes into its own when it contests this subordination and participates in the suspension of instrumental rationality that, following Hannah Arendt, is a trait of the political realm. This suspension of instrumental rationality is improperly understood as the affair of aestheticism, since in its refusal to engage in political struggles aestheticism colludes with reaction and subserves its ends (as Rocha reveals in his condemnations of Hollywood, a transcendent theme can always be found for the purportedly immanent world of illusionist cinema). Hence film takes itself as theme precisely when it forbids itself the specious liberties of make-believe. The theme of cinema is the freedom of cinema itself.

Yet cinema cannot enter on this freedom so long as the masses are exploited and the earth laid waste, because by jumping ahead of the revolution, cinema anticipates a freedom that is simply the corollary of illusion, thereby forfeiting all claim to freedom and becoming an instrument of colonialist oppression. For Rocha the theme of cinema is its impossibility, and his films are made out of the agony that is their condition of existence. The autonomy of the work of art, which in bourgeois aesthetics functions as an axiom, here becomes the problem itself of politics. The theoretical fascination of Rocha's work lies partly in its political reinvention of the autonomy attributed to the modern work of art.

Cinema can only feel asphyxiated in the liberties of aestheticism. As soon as the question "What is to be done?" concerns itself with the achievement of particular aesthetic effects, cinema turns away from its own possibility in the political. Given that aestheticism is intrinsically illusionist, extrication from illusionist cinema cannot be secured by adherence to an aesthetic manifesto. In this regard Rocha does not share the naïveté of the DOGMA 95 filmmakers. If Rocha denounces the technical sophistication of Western commercial cinema, it is not because he believes the problem of film, which is immediately the political problem of the third world, can be solved by renouncing sets, lighting, makeup, and so forth. For one thing, Rocha does not have the luxury of possession that precedes renunciation. No aesthetic choice informs the austere production values of his films. To be sure, Rocha appropriates the austerity imposed by economic underdevelopment—most famously in the text presented in Genoa in January 1965, "Aesthetics of Hunger"—and sets it to work. But what is at issue is a mobilization of the political force inherent in the simple fact of the backwardness of the Brazilian film industry, rather than an artistic fetishization of the frugal and the deficient. The title "Aesthetics of Hunger" refers to what Rocha analyzes as the European delectation in the misery of Latin America: "For the European observer, the processes of artistic creation in the underdeveloped world only interest him to the extent that they satisfy his nostalgia for primitivism."[2] Such an aestheticization of hunger is the very last thing that Rocha desires, since the extraction of an aesthetic value from indigence contributes to its political apology.

The problem confronting the filmmaker of what is to be done does not lend itself to aesthetic solutions. Rocha is merciless to the point of humor on this score. In 1963, on grounds of its reputed aestheticism, he dismissed unseen Mário Peixoto's *Limite* (1930), a film withdrawn from circulation early by its director and long held in such high esteem that it could be accounted the "La chasse spirituelle" of Brazilian avant-garde cinema: "In their bourgeois, sentimental subjectivity, films that are *beautiful for the sake of beauty* are without interest for Brazilian cinema, just as they always were for any cinema."[3] Cinema cannot come into its own through aestheticism, and it is perhaps in protest against the aesthetic detachment he suspects behind the international reception of his first two features, *Barravento* (1962) and *Black God, White Devil* (*Deus e o diabo na terra do sol*) (1964), that Rocha articulates the critical position of the "Aesthetics of Hunger" and thereafter breaks with stylistic austerity. The agony of hunger passes over into the cinematic image itself, convulsing it in *Land in Anguish* (*Terra em transe*) (1967) before overseeing its disintegration in the final provocations of the garbage cinema of *The Age of the Earth* (*A idade da terra*) (1980).

Rocha, of course, did not see himself as cinema's destroyer. Cinema, for him, does not yet exist. Notwithstanding his admiration and affection for Godard, Rocha rejects his definition of the revolutionary filmmaker as destroyer. This rejection is consistent with his advocacy of the new Brazilian cinema. Rocha was tireless in promoting the works of fellow filmmakers, attending screenings at international festivals, giving interviews, and writing articles in their defense. He was intensely aware of the fragility of the constellation of economic and political factors that allowed Cinema Novo to come about. The system of production and distribution that, for Godard (and other filmmakers of what has come to be known as Second Cinema), possesses the domineering dead weight of a fact was as yet, for Rocha in Brazil (and Third Cinema in general), barely more than a possibility. Rocha's rejection of Godard's definition is consistent, however, not only with his cultivation of a national film industry but also with his aversion to aestheticism. To recognize the political collusion of the cinema of spectacle and then to define one's task as the destruction of this cinema is to remain within aestheticism, because it is to remain within the dishonest aestheticism of aestheticism's bare negation. As cinema still awaits to be born in its essential politicality, it is not a matter of destroying it.

What, then, is taking its course in the violence that Rocha inflicts on the academicism of cinematographic discourse? It follows from the political essence of Rocha's work that it cannot be analyzed in terms of problem and solution: anything that is not the emancipation of the third world cannot be regarded as a solution. Rocha's work does not realize itself in violence. The violence is neither a means nor an end. On the basis of a sober insight into the relations between politics and cinema, Rocha, whom Carlos Heitor Cony is right to call an "envoy of delirium,"[4] is an artist of a frenzy without return. Cinema must not shy away from its own incapacity, its constitutive condition of impossibility. As there is no aesthetic solution with regard to what is to be done, Rocha's abandonment of the critical realism of his early films in favor of an underground cinema in *The Age of the Earth* is a gesture of political desperation rather than of artistic acumen. Without a stylistic degree zero or terra firma, Rocha's cinema contents itself with neither the Rossellinian asperities of *Barravento* nor the "garbage aesthetic" that came to the fore in the late 1960s as a reaction to the perceived gravity of Cinema Novo. *The Age of the Earth*, which was years in the making and which drained the resources of the government funding body, Embrafilme, only to premiere in Venice to general execration, is a stupendous film by virtue of its defiance. Passages of dialogue are repeated without coherence or affectivity; a nude black Christ (Antônio Pitanga) solicits from a tree outside Brasília; an apocalyptic pantomime in sequins plays itself out involving ventriloquism with a skull; and John Brahms—in an enrapturing performance by Maurício do Valle that is half Falstaff and half Ubu—declares it his mission to destroy the earth, "this poor, small planet." Rocha's last film practices that defiance of the spectator's taste and narrative expectations that is more characteristic of underground filmmakers such as Júlio Bressane and Rogério Sganzerla than of Cinema Novo proper, and he subjects this defiance to a defiance of its own from the quarter of the political problem of cinema. *The Age of the Earth* cancels out Rocha's other films, but they in turn cancel it out: one-sided approaches do not complement one another to form a solution. There is no way to make cinema, and it is the greatness of Rocha's work to realize itself in this impossibility.

If the impossibility of cinema is (without any mediation or reflexivity) a political impossibility, if the birth of cinema is postponed so long as the masses remain exploited, it is nonetheless not a question of the people's seizure of power. For Rocha power is not the object of politics. Subscribing to a conventional terminology, René Gardies misconceives the prerevolutionary character of Rocha's work: "The Nothingness of today (the absence of the people) appears as the utter negative of the Everything of tomorrow, of the People-King."[5] In the "Aesthetics of Dream," a text delivered in 1971, Rocha denounces "the People" as the myth of the bourgeoisie.[6] The people that knows how to rule is a people that has surrendered its last vestige of resistance to colonialism, since the very notion of control is colonialist. The extremism of Rocha's position, which appears to forbid itself any comprehension of expropriation in pre-Columbian societies, is directed properly against the spurious autonomy of Brazil. As the country's independence from Portugal was declared by the Portuguese prince regent himself in 1822, the struggle against colonialism, such as it was carried out in Algeria and Vietnam, was preempted rather than won. Brazil was independent but a Bragança still sat on its throne. A self-assertion of national identity is not in and of itself the answer. Rocha says in a statement first published in *Positif* in 1970: "The seizure of political power by the colonized is fundamental. But the seizure of power is not enough."[7]

In *Cinema 2: The Time-Image* Gilles Deleuze writes of the changed political perspective of Rocha, Youssef Chahine, and black American cinema: "The death-knell for becoming conscious was precisely the consciousness that there were no people, but always several peoples, an infinity of peoples, who remained to be united, or should not be united, in order for the problem to change. It is in this way that third world cinema is a cinema of minorities, because the people exist only in the condition of minority, which is why they are missing."[8] If the task of third-world cinema is not to mobilize the masses for the bourgeois myth of the sovereign people, it is just as little to hypostasize the powerlessness of the masses as their essential condition (such a hypostasis would be simply the cynical complement of the bourgeois notion of popular sovereignty). The problem to be changed will be changed at its roots by a dismantling of the concept of power.

The essence of cinema is tied to a future revolution. Cinema cannot assert itself because it lies in the very nature of this revolution to withhold itself. In its contestational potentiality, the revolution stands over the actual as its caveat and comes between power and the proof with which power provides itself in realization. The desperation of Rocha's cinema is both an acknowledgment of the impossibility of revolution and the modus operandi of this revolution with respect to the ontological foundations of power. The impossibility of the revolution is not to be converted into a fact, an aspect of the prevailing state of affairs and a negative actuality. Just as cinema cannot assert itself, it also cannot resign itself without betraying the revolution's radical objection to the status quo. The impossibility of the revolution is its pure possibility: it is impossible not because it lacks the specific conditions in which it could be actualized but because actuality itself, in which beings are decidable and lend themselves to identification and control, is incompatible with it. Possibility presses its philosophical priority. If, for Rocha, cinema remains to be created, if it is not a fact to be destroyed, it is because it is a becoming in Deleuze's sense: it is a nonexistence that is again and again to be realized, as the expression of a people to come, never to come.

In his monograph devoted to Rocha's cinema (his "text"), Gardies offers a historical explanation for the absence of the people: "During the decade (1961–1971) in which this text comes about, the Brazilian working class [la classe populaire] suffers from an almost total alienation."[9] Given the harshness of the military dictatorship of Artur Costa e Silva and, later, Garrastazu Médici, Gardies should not be accused of sociological reductionism. With the imposition of curfews and the revocation of habeas corpus under the infamous Institutional Act No. V of 1968, the people, quite literally, were missing from public places. Nonetheless, Gardies's account needs to be supplemented by a far more mundane explanation. Even if Rocha had desired to stage crowd scenes in the manner of Eisenstein, the budgets for his films would not have permitted it. Whenever there is a crowd in Rocha's cinema, it is not a drilled corps of extras assigned the role of "the people" but rather a chance assemblage of onlookers.[10] The women of the village of Milagres, for example, show themselves interested but not altogether convinced by developments among the cast of *Antônio das Mortes* (*O dragão da maldade contra o santo guerreiro*) (1969). The gulf in Rocha's films between the professional actors and the people is perhaps at its deepest in *The Age of the Earth*. Seated at a sidewalk café in the center of Rio, Ana Maria Magalhães and Tarcísio Meira impassively deliver their flowery lines in what comes across as a tribute to *Last Year at Marienbad*, while a few bemused and bored passersby with time on their hands loiter in front of the camera.

Public places have almost never been invested by the People in its bourgeois conception. In the classical polis the public place is the domain and demonstration of free men, and its loss in the generalized house arrest of tyranny is dreaded as a leveler of social and sexual differences. In the urban cinema of Brazil, for its part, the public places are left to *meninos da rua* (street children), the homeless, the unemployed and underemployed, and "office boys" (more a social group with its own dialect and sexuality than a profession) whose ingenuity expends itself in prolonging the out-of-office trajectories of their errands. The isonomy of the classical *agora* is remembered in the garbage anarchically proliferating in the streets: the authority and responsibility of the house, which sees to it that everything is in its proper place and of which tyranny and the society of control are the essentially antipolitical magnifications, does not extend beyond the threshold out into the open. Rocha does not suppress these figures of the square and the pavement for the sake of constructing an illusion of the People. Instead, they remain as the guilty conscience of the operatic dramaturgy and oratorical exchanges of the professional cast. Given that there is no way to avoid a guilty conscience—Hollywood and the local *pornochanchada* (sex comedy) certainly do not bridge the gulf between the cinematic image and the misery of the third world—the work of art, with its pretensions to aesthetic immanence, must shatter itself against the masses.

Rocha's cinema begins with this shattering. The guilt of the work of art is that it is not yet truly autonomous, that the theatrical excesses of a Baroque sensibility never go so far as to transgress the aesthetic sphere, challenging the reactionary political investments of the quarantine of the work of art. The ethical or political moment, which is transcendent with regard to the aesthetic sphere, leads Rocha to the creation of a work of art rather than to the repudiation of art, since a work of art rooted in the irrational reality of the Brazilian people will be traversed by forces disconcerting the equilibrium in which it might otherwise give itself up as an object for a reductively aesthetic appreciation. The seamless and the lapidary are the criteria of another culture. For Cinema Novo and the later underground directors, the circumstance of an underdeveloped film industry, with its minuscule budgets and poorly trained technicians, becomes the occasion for a heated debate concerning whether achieving the polished production values of first-world cinema is even desirable. This is, in one respect, a simple question of box-office returns. The lesson from the early 1950s, when the glossy productions of the Vera Cruz studios of São Paulo failed to win a public in Brazil, was that a sustainable Brazilian film industry could not model itself on Hollywood. Critics from the right and left will take issue with the new cinema for essentializing the nation's backwardness, for making not exactly a virtue of necessity but a national characteristic of poverty and clumsiness. These critics, however, address the question of the Brazilian people within the discourse of the nation-state. Something besides a petulant chauvinism apologetic of underdevelopment and its attendant misery is involved.

In the Guevarist manifesto "The Tricontinental Filmmaker: That Is Called the Dawn," published in *Cahiers du Cinéma* in 1967, Rocha declares that the tools belong to Hollywood and then, in an analysis of the components of Brazilian civilization, characterizes the Tupi by intelligence and artistic incompetence.[11] To make incompetence an object of militancy is not enough to single out Brazil among the nations. Convinced of the inimitability of Greek art and hence suspicious of the imperatives of Winckelmann's neoclassicism, Hölderlin had already asked if a specifically Western poetry could come into its own by means of the—definitively Greek—mastery of the presentation of material. Gombrowicz, in turn, will reject the rallying cry of many Polish artists, "Catch up to Europe!" in order to make a program out of immaturity: "Bad art may be more representative of a people."[12] Arguably, neither a people at home in its unique characteristics nor the People of bourgeois cosmopolitanism is represented in art that falls short of itself, since it is with the masses, with the people to come as unidentifiable multiplicity, that the unmanageability of the gap between expectation and accomplishment is populated.

It would be easy to attribute to Rocha, on the basis of his mistrust of aestheticism and the bourgeois myth of "the" People, a stance at odds with the Enlightenment, or at least with its bastardized form in liberal ideology. In place of the disinterested appreciation of the beauty of the work in which humanity sees itself reflected in its universality, there is pursued a violation of the apathy of taste for the sake of an image of an unrepresented, unrepresentable populace. But even if the Enlightenment sought to isolate beauty as a phenomenon for analysis, it would be an unduly prim account of the movement that labeled its efforts to see beauty for what it is as mere aestheticism. Is it out of opposition to Enlightenment aesthetics when a cinema does not wish to hear the judgment passed on it, "This is *merely* beautiful"? The merely beautiful (the beauty that is innocuous because it keeps within the political and social limits set for beauty in general) is not necessarily identical with the beauty that the Enlightenment endeavored to grasp in its distinctness, since the distinctness of beauty is not necessarily identical with the place beauty occupies in existing conditions. One of the distinguishing features of the beautiful, as discerned by Kant in his third *Critique*, is its relationship to subjective judgment. The judgment "This is beautiful" claims to speak in a universal voice ("we are agreed that this is beautiful"), and hence—so it might seem—to speak for "the" People, whereas "This pleases me" claims to speak only for the speaker. When the judgment "This is beautiful" is made in response to Rocha's cinema, it amounts to a covert expression of discomfiture and hostility, but only if it claims to extract from that which endeavors to be resolutely minor an *empirical* proof of universal community (the *claim* to speak in a universal voice does not of itself demonstrate the empirical existence of a universal community). Similarly, the beauty discovered in an image is not straightforwardly its point of weakness with respect to reactionary politics, as though what should expose the intolerability of a minority's situation here and now occasions instead a flight from the here and now to the pleasure of participation in the universal community of taste. What has been held against aestheticism from the nineteenth century on is that the engagement with the here and now that is coextensive with the work of art's sensuous immediacy is vitiated in the existential neutrality of the universalizing judgment "This is (merely) beautiful." The sensuous immediacy of the work of art, once it is no longer allowed to communicate with the sensuous immediacy of political action, is reinvented as the beautiful complement of the bourgeoisie's disingenuous resignation of political action to the universal laws of history and economics.

If in the history of art since the Enlightenment, in nineteenth-century French poetry as much as in Brazilian underground cinema, the ugly is embraced, this is not because the release of the work of art from its state of suspended animation—in the abstract white space of the museum, in the abstract dark space of the cinema—can be brought about through recourse to the ugly. In the judgment "This is ugly" the same claim to be speaking in a universal voice is put forward that differentiates "This is beautiful" from "This is agreeable *to me.*" The incorporation of the ugly signals not so much a break with Enlightenment aesthetics as with the templates of the beautiful with which in the eighteenth century Kant, following Johann Georg Hamann and followed by the romantics, already broke.

The battle against the recognizability of the beautiful by objective criteria is a battle for the political essence of the beautiful. This is what makes the *Critique of the Power of Judgment* a preeminently political work.[13] Kant suggests that the community announcing itself in the judgment "This is beautiful" is unable to close ranks: it occupies the space of plurality by which Arendt understands the political.[14] The beautiful is the problem rather than the proof of universal community: in aesthetic judgment there is a *claim* to universal validity rather than universal validity as such. It is only when the beautiful takes on the stability of a fact that antiart appears the opposite of art. In the *Critique of the Power of Judgment* the Enlightenment philosophy of art declares itself in advance impervious to the shocks resulting from the later general substitutions of the pleasing and the unpleasing. For Kant, disagreements between individuals over whether a particular phenomenon is to be judged beautiful or ugly do not have an impact on the universality with which aesthetic judgment is invested. The disagreements are irresolvable because beauty cannot be read off from the object as one of its properties, but that they arise at all is because aesthetic judgment invokes a subjectively universal validity. The beauty of the beautiful work of art is, following Kant's argument, more akin to a promise of universal community than the emblem of its realization. Beauty is the unredeemable bond that prevents community from closing in on itself and rediscovering a more numerous egotism. In *Peregrinations: Law, Form, Event* Lyotard writes: "The unanimity concerning what is beautiful has no chance of being actualised. . . . This kind of consensus is definitely nothing but a cloud of community."[15] It is also the solidarity without solidity by which Heidegger understands Being-with-one-another and Arendt understands human plurality. As soon as it sees itself solidifying, as reflected in a received opinion, this community breaks up, some denouncing the received opinion as a cliché, others maintaining its acuity and expressiveness. Only if there is the possibility of disagreement does beauty maintain the tenuous manner of existence peculiar to it, and only if there is the sociability of a universal feeling of participation does humanity distinguish itself from what Kant assumes to be the inviolable egotism of animals.[16] Having retired the objective criteria of neoclassical art manuals, Kant foreshadows a philosophical and political task for the ambiguous transitions between the ugly, the beautiful, and the kitsch. The uncertainty with which any given object is to be judged beautiful (or ugly or kitsch) is the mirror proper to Kantian humanity, since in beauty's resistance to reification community dispenses with empirical identity and attains the higher universality that is otherwise reserved for the transcendental. Bearing witness to the unpresentability of community, the aesthetic is the volatility of the here and now, as the site of indeterminacy, of decision and political action. Whereas the disingenuous aestheticism of bourgeois art worship betrays the unpresentability of Kant's community through the very recognizability of the domain that it marks out for the autonomy (i.e., the existential neutrality and quarantine) of art,[17] an artist such as Rocha, who combats the mere aestheticization of art and, by extension, the confinement of aesthetic judgment, opens the work up to the revolutionary promise of the beautiful.

When the beautiful no longer brushes up against the ugly, when it no longer divides its audience, it ceases to be beautiful. If the undisputed masterpiece nonetheless does not cease to be beautiful, it is because its institutionalization brings it to teeter on the edge of kitsch, thereby restoring it to the disputability of the beautiful. The "aura" of the work of art, which Walter Benjamin denounces as a vestige of the cultic, can be explained also in terms of the shimmer of objective uncertainty with which aesthetic judgment recognizes a specific work of art as beautiful. The beautiful cannot be pinned down as an objective trait. In its nomadic itinerary, abandoning what was considered beautiful for something new, it resembles a swarm of locusts in search of fresh sustenance. In its appetite for the new, beauty is comparable to imperialism; nevertheless, where imperialism aspires to a universal of control, beauty appeals to a universal of dissent. It calls forth to community by means of its invocation of universal validity, yet it disavows the community able to read off its unity from the unequivocality of an object. The subjectively universal validity of aesthetic judgments is strictly unpresentable, since the appeal is being made not to a property of the object whose stability is the condition of universally binding judgments with respect to it but to the universality that inhabits the judging subject in its irreducibility to its empirically conditioned desires.

The universalism of aesthetic judgment is its possibility rather than its actuality. The community of aesthetic judgment can never realize itself as the truth and decidability of what is—in short, it can never mistake itself for the majority—because it is in possibility, in thought's overreaching of the actual, that Kantian humanity comes into the insubstantial community proper to it as a community of thinking beings. Thought is not an activity of an actual subject but rather the possibilities within which the actual is a point of realization. That which unites humanity is the possibility of a contestation of what is. This contestation results from the existence of thought rather than from the existential neutrality of the general concept. Actuality is even the moment in which existence comes closest to the existential neutrality of the concept, insofar as what is offers the decidability of its actuality to the concept as a point of entry: actuality is existence's hour of metaphysical temptation.

If we think at all, it is community that thinks in us, breaching the hermetism of the particular. Kant, who is often passed off as the philosopher of liberal democracies, elaborates a conception of sociability that has nothing to do with the extrinsic harmony of selfish interests. Should it be objected that the transcendental dignity of a sociability of thought is likewise far removed from the humiliations of the daily political struggles of minorities, this says more about the anemia of Kant's reception than about Kant's philosophy itself. The movement of thought is bilateral: thought abstracts from the here and now, but it also returns to the here and now as its dislocation and utopian promise.

Rocha's humanism is explicit, and for the public that takes away from Heidegger's "Letter on 'Humanism'" and its French legatees no more than a handful of catchwords this humanism is an object of Enlightenment nostalgia, and, as an element in the aesthetic spectacle of primitivism, its stridency is "moving." If Rocha, and left-wing discourse in Latin America generally, adheres to the ideals of the eighteenth century (and of Marx), this is for the "European observer" of the "Aesthetics of Hunger" just a further manifestation of underdevelopment. The assiduity and reflectiveness with which Cinema Novo takes underdevelopment as its theme cautions, however, against such a patronizing account. Heidegger's dismissal in his postwar text of the task of restoring a sense to the term *humanism* does not take in its compass a humanism that grounds itself in underdevelopment. The humanism of which Heidegger is wary is the humanism from which he traces a genealogical line from the Renaissance's exalted conception of the human being as the master manipulator of material (a trope with which Jacob Burckhardt accosted Heidegger's generation) to the racial breeding programs and spoliation of the earth in modern technicism. To revive the dignity of the human subject after Hitler's dictatorship is to pay the excessive price of a debasement of the world to stock. In contrast to the masterpieces of the Renaissance, where, according to bourgeois histories of art, the autonomy of the human spirit asserts itself in overcoming the refractoriness of brute matter, Rocha offers a cinema with "inferior cameras and laboratories, and therefore crude images and muffled dialogue, unwanted noise on the soundtrack, editing accidents, and unclear credits and titles."[18] Rocha's humanism is not a humanism of the empowerment of the subject, just as his cinema does not provide the grislier consequences of such a humanism with their artistic gloss. To protest against the perfectionism of Hollywood is to protest against the esteem given to the preeminent manipulator of material, once embodied in the Renaissance by the artist of genius but now a role reserved for American studios with their vast technological resources. Outside Hollywood all art, by comparison, inevitably assumes the appearance of a cottage industry. By politicizing the backwardness of the Brazilian film industry, by mobilizing the relation to the benchmarks against which it is seen to fall short, Rocha intimates that the artist has another task than proving the superiority of Man over Nature. Even if Nature remains defined by the actuality of material, it is no longer subordinate to Man as infinite possibilities, and humanity even comes most into its difference from the actuality by which material things have been understood—the difference that humanism has always endeavored to illuminate—precisely when our possibilities fail to be realized, when our pretensions to control are rebuffed, and when expectation and execution part company.

Rocha finds ever new ways to make cinema falter and stammer. For the sake seemingly of the open space of experimentation by which Arendt understands the political, his films turn their back on perfection. Something is always missing from the perfect work of art, because in the exact correspondence of its means and ends, of its conception and implementation, it does not reach beyond the categories of labor to the freedom and spontaneity of political action. In *The Human Condition* Arendt writes: "There is in fact no thing that does not in some way transcend its functional use, and its transcendence, its beauty or ugliness, is identical with appearing publicly and being seen."[19] This transcendence, however, cannot be conceived in terms of perfection. In a sense the work of art that is held to be perfect does not appear publicly, because, by virtue of the immanence of means and ends, it occupies a sphere of realization inviolably secured against the possibilities of the political and the erraticism of the public's judgments of taste.

Where liberal-minded art critics adopt the meretricious language of a celebration of differences and posit the immanence of individual works, the fickle community of aesthetic judgment is also foreclosed. Every work, once it is considered perfect in its own way, folds in on itself in replication of the atomization of community in liberal political philosophy: the work now consummates its relationship with its own concept. The anarchic moment in the exercise of the Kantian faculty of judgment—that moment in which the process of judgment still plays havoc with the discrepancy between intuition and concept—is elided in favor of a sedimentation of differences in which each work is perfectly itself and merely different from all others. Given that it is the community of aesthetic judgment that discovers the work's ontological undecidability, perfection and immanence stand between the work and the indeterminacy in which humanism sees itself reflected. For a number of Brazilian filmmakers, to be judged different appeared not to be enough. The community of aesthetic judgment is

to be weaned away from the automatic responses of instrumental rationality (the work is a "success" because the artist has realized his or her intentions) by a militant artistic incompetence.[20] Art is to be judged bad, but as
it should not simply escape the immanent perfection by which it serves a
reactionary political agenda, it must likewise bring to its shortcomings an
aggression that sets them in conflict with the technicism reasserting itself,
in the transcendent model of perfection, over every deviation.

The volatility with which Kant's aesthetic judgment alternates between condemnation and approval is more auspicious for a "minoritarian"
cinema than the complacent postulate according to which everything is
different. For Rogério Sganzerla, Brazilian cinema is both the greatest and
the worst cinema in the world: the swings in assessment can be ascribed
to the ontological undecidability in which the community of aesthetic
judgment exercises its freedom from objective criteria. If many Brazilian
directors of the 1960s and 1970s admit to an inferiority complex in relation to their counterparts in North America and Europe, this need not
invite the consolations of the language of the celebration of differences.
A revitalization of aesthetic judgment is at issue behind the psychological
condition. Similarly, if Rocha persists in employing the derogatory phrase
"the third world," it is arguably not only because there is a quantitative
difference in living standards that should not be trivialized under the cover
of the qualitative difference of the exotic but also because the revolutionary task of Brazilian cinema with regard to the apparent self-evidence of
technicism is informed by the very gap between the means of production
in Brazilian cinema and the prevailing standard imposed by international
technicism. The judgment that this cinema is beautiful, if it seals the gap
and glosses over underdevelopment, continues to tie beauty to notions of
perfection and immanence. It delivers the critical realism of Cinema Novo
up to exoticism and opposes the ontological undecidability by which the
community of aesthetic judgment can here break with the hegemony of
technicism and neocolonialism.

Rocha's work frustrates the taste for the exotic without opting for
an insipid internationalism. The myths of Brazil are called up and ranged
against Hollywood, but they articulate an oppressive national identity
from which the masses likewise have to flee. There seems little sense in discussing Rocha's treatment of myth, as some have done, in terms of Jung's
archetypes of a collective unconscious.[21] In Rocha myth arises with the
failure of history: it constitutes an aspect of the problem facing the masses

rather than a phylogenetic resource in the struggle against colonialism. *Black God, White Devil*, with its *beatos* (holy men), *jagunços* (hired killers), and *cangaceiros* (brigands), ransacks the imaginary of northeast Brazil, but as these figures, familiar from the chronicle of Euclides da Cunha, the ceramics of Mestre Vitalino of Caruaru, and innumerable *músicas sertanejas* (regional folksongs), are far from inhabiting anything remotely suggesting a prelapsarian Brazil, they are of little use to chauvinistic ideology: they do not denote a self-sufficient national identity that could serve as a pretext for denouncing foreign influence. Here myth is not a relic of the primordial but a symptom of underdevelopment and exploitation—nothing ever seems to change. With progress having been withheld, events and personages enter into a single time. Although he acknowledges a fascination for the *literatura de cordel* (the illustrated pamphlets of the backlands in which news of events, such as the murder of the brigand Lampião in 1938 or the suicide of President Getúlio Vargas in 1954, in the dilatoriness of their dissemination pass out of the historical continuum to be reworked in the mythic contemporaneity of the popular imagination), Rocha does not indulge the nostalgia for primitivism by transcribing their tales and drawings cinematically. The violence in *Black God, White Devil* conspires against the mythic dimension of the film, in which acts are denied their consequences and characters are reduced to types. Ismail Xavier, among others, has argued that the violence in Rocha differs from the violence that the Hollywood western extracts from a Manichean conflict between the good of the solitary hero and the evil of his decadent surroundings.[22] Whereas the western signs a pact with myth, repeating late antiquity's disavowal of the openness of the political in favor of the adventure of absolute subjectivity, *Black God, White Devil* depicts the revolutionary extermination of myth at the hands of the amoral Antônio das Mortes. The film ends with a traveling shot that accompanies Manuel and Rosa in their nonetheless still desperate, headlong rush from the grips of the mythical.

Apathetic and frantic by turns, the denizens of Rocha's northeast Brazil belong to a cinema of the colonized. The nationalistic elements in the Brazilian bourgeoisie and military government, which were receptive to calls from filmmakers to foster a local industry through investment and legislation, were to be denied a cinema that would leap from the nonexistence of a local industry in a colonized market to an industry that would fabricate an image of Brazil washed clean of the stain of colonization. Neither the foreign audience with a taste for the exotic nor the local audience with a stake in keeping things as they are is interested in an image of Brazil in which the stain of colonialism is laid bare. There is an overt asymmetry between the nationalism of Cinema Novo and the nationalism of the political and economic bodies without which Cinema Novo could never have gotten off the ground (Rocha's needlessly blunt declaration of support in 1974 for Ernesto Geisel's presidency during the military dictatorship remains an open sore in his biography, in part because it made light of this asymmetry). *Black God, White Devil* reflects a lacerated Brazil. The catatonic rhythms of the characters are an index of a political state of affairs rather than of the physiological constitution of a "race." According to Fanon, the French colonial psychiatrists for whom the lethargy and sudden violent outbursts of Africans evoked "lobotomised Europeans" were, wittingly or unwittingly, transforming a consequence of colonialism into a justification of colonial rule over a people without application or self-control.[23] The immutability of Rocha's mythic Brazil corresponds not so much to a national essence as to the entrenchment of contingent national and international structures of power.

Inventing a cinema of the colonized masses, of the "lobotomised European," Rocha deploys speeds and slownesses irreconcilable with that which Deleuze, in his book on roughly the first half-century of cinema, calls the "action-image." In postwar European cinema Fassbinder's zombies, who do not always possess a motive for running suddenly amok, betray the strongest family resemblance, even if there is also something of the rhythms of Rocha's figures in Visconti's superannuated, neurasthenic aristocracy. In two of the films Rocha made while in exile—*Der leone have sept cabeças* (1970) and *Claro* (1975)—the catatonia of Cinema Novo comes into direct contact with the catatonia of the *nouvelle vague* through the performances respectively of Jean-Pierre Léaud and Juliet Berto (the latter best known from Godard's *La Chinoise* and Rivette's wondrous *Celine and Julie Go Boating*). Rocha, who for his part appears in Godard's *Vent d'Est* (1969) giving "lessons" on the path of political cinema, discerns behind the stylistic similarities between Cinema Novo and the New European Cinema a political solidarity. In question here is not the symbiosis that the Russian avant-garde of the 1920s was briefly allowed to posit between political and artistic revolution (as in Mayakovsky's dictum, "Without a revolutionary form revolutionary art does not exist"). The artistic revolution of cinema is immediately political because the object of revolution is no longer the seizure of power by *the* people or *the* proletariat but rather the institution of the "minoritarian" rhythms by which processes of subjectification are waylaid and the aesthetic community more plainly enters political action's domain of experimentation. Cinema Novo, regardless of the intentions of its conservative backers, was not to conceive the establishment of a Brazilian film industry in terms of a process of subjectification. In place of either a self-assertion of the masses raising their voice against colonization as a people-subject or the admission to the bourgeois canon of a Brazilian filmmaker on the strength of his or her perfectionism, personal vision, and mastery of material, there is catatonia, spontaneity, and improvisation. What becomes clear in Rocha, perhaps even more explicitly than in Godard, is that a new road for art—a deepening and elaborating of its essential possibility—thereby opens up.

Land in Anguish is a delirious collective utterance. To be sure, Rocha himself advocates an auteur cinema as the polar opposite of commercial cinema, and the meticulousness, resourcefulness, and originality that he brings, for example, to the editing of his films are evidence of an extraordinary will to art, but it makes little real sense to subsume Rocha under the bourgeois conception according to which the artist is the legitimating myth of subjectivity. The beauty, indispensability, and artistic ambition of Rocha's work lie in its overtaxing and dismantling of this myth. With the concept of the "auteur," Cahiers du Cinéma sought to raise the prestige of film by insisting on the director's participation in the figure of the artist prevalent since the Renaissance. This theoretical move, however, encourages a misunderstanding of the new works that Cahiers du Cinéma sought to champion, as though what the New Cinema, as a whole, rejected in the studio system was the obstacle it posed to the auteur's articulation of a bourgeois interiority. For Rocha what is objectionable in commercial cinema is ultimately not its anonymity but the political ideology of which it is an instrument.

Commercial cinema even seems to define itself by the refusal to extract from the polyvocality of its conflicting interests the stutter of a collective utterance. Regardless of how many people collaborate on a so-called commercial film, the proliferation of perspectives is generally checked; a neutrality is presupposed that has little in common with the anonymity in which the delirious collective utterance of Land in Anguish frustrates processes of subjectification and objectification. As the audio was not recorded directly at the time the scenes were shot, the dialogue in Land in Anguish occupies the same acoustic space as the many interior monologues, thereby problematizing the distinction between the public and the private. An expedient of subindustrial cinema is here turned to account. Rocha's film acquires tremendous drive from the absence of local sound. The imposition of a new shot does not distract the spectator with the task of orienting himself or herself within the space of the shot by means of the acoustic clues delivered by the cast and any items in shot: such orientation would diminish the unsettling effect of the feverish flight of images—verbal, visual, and sonic—of which *Land in Anguish* is composed. Given the impossibility under the military dictatorship of making a film about political conditions in Brazil, Rocha resorts to an allegorical setting, but rather than play down the artificiality of the cipher country of Eldorado, he substitutes the homogeneous spatiality of the dubbing studio for the existential thickness of the actual soundscapes in view. Just as the question "Where?" is unanswerable, the question "When?" is meaningless in face of the difficulty of knowing how much of what is shown is to be attributed to the dying delusions of Paulo Martins (Jardel Filho) and how much can pretend to an "objective" history. In the film's remarkable finale there is even a difficulty in knowing who is talking. Dom Porfírio Diaz (Paulo Autran) is seen in full harangue at his coronation, but it is Paulo Martins that we assume we hear in the voice-over. The aggressive and pervasive sound track, with its machine guns, diverse drumming styles, and operatic music, then breaks off: declaiming against hysteria Paulo Autran, in one of the great close-ups in the history of cinema, induces from the latent insanity of the human face a grin of scarcely conceivable ferocity and malevolence. Raquel Gerber contends that *Land in Anguish* was quickly seen as the filmic key to modern Brazilian culture because, situating the problem of Brazil in the broader terms of the development of international capitalism, it inaugurated *Tropicalismo* as an experimental (anti)method, across the arts, of addressing Brazilian reality.[24] It is a realistic document of an exaggerated reality; the deviations and distortions of allegory are themselves the truth of Brazil.

With a film such as *Land in Anguish* commentary cannot content itself with joining the dots, pointing out the links between a supposed project and its execution, and inferring the totality that would establish the coherence of each element in the work. The labor of criticism, where it exhausts itself in spelling out the agreement of means and ends in its object of analysis, presses the case for the bourgeois respectability of the work in question. More is to be lost than gained by a defense of this kind, since the sense that is made of art in such criticism is the sense of instrumental rationality. In the case of *Land in Anguish*, under the cover of praise an explicitly political work is smuggled out of the domain of the experimentation and spontaneity of human plurality. If the thesis from the bourgeois history of art concerning the autonomy of the work of art is taken seriously, the work has to overcome its instrumentalization, even as it shows up in the fulfillment of its own ends, and push through to the political itself: the highest praise, following Rocha, is due the work of art on account not of its perfection but of the politicization of both its form and content.

In the hunger and garbage of his cinema Rocha is suspicious of the principle of adequateness by which technicism is motivated in pursuing means to its ends. According to Arendt's retrieval of the *vita activa*, this suspicion animated the Greek polis. Rocha's work is classical not because it recalls the "perfection" of classical art but because it recreates the anarchic conditions in which the Greek cities differentiated themselves from the despotism of their Persian and Egyptian neighbors. In this anarchy, the Greek is a citizen and not a subject, a means to the ruler's ends. Rocha's novel *Riverão Sussuarana* (1977) is too anarchic to be recognizable as a novel. It begins as literary criticism, with a text that could serve as a preface to a festschrift for the Brazilian writer João Guimarães Rosa. Its pseudography yields to nonsense words. Episodes from Brazilian history rub up against paranoiac conspiracies relating to the Cheese Manhattan Bank, slaves nourish themselves on anteater soup, and a detailed account is offered of the death of Rocha's sister in a lift shaft in Rio. Rocha's delirium is classical to the extent that it appears, by the standards of the society of control, barbaric. His is a pure cinema to the extent that it is a political cinema. In the cinematic image there is a becoming-discourse of light, a murmuring, a babbling, a screaming; there is a barbarism of discourse, an irreducibility to the conceptual and the actual, in which the undecidability of the *vita activa* and aesthetic judgment takes hold.

7

Margarethe von Trotta
Leviathan in Germany

CECILIA SJÖHOLM

Leviathan

When in prison in the 1970s, the members of the German "urban guerrilla" the RAF, the *Rote Armee Fraktion*, or the so-called Baader Meinhof group, communicated with one another through coded names taken from Herman Melville's novel *Moby Dick*. Chasing the big white whale, the members figured themselves as enemies of the *Leviathan*, another name for the whale, or the beast.[1] *Leviathan* is also the sovereign power of the state as named by Thomas Hobbes. The first line of Hobbes's *Leviathan* is quoted in Melville's work: "For by Art is created that great LEVIATHAN called a COMMON-WEALTH, or STATE, (in latine CIVITAS) which is but an Artificiall Man; though of greater stature and strength than the Naturall, for whose protection and defence it was intended."[2] In this creature, adds Hobbes, sovereignty is the artificial soul, and the contracts tying the body together are the words of creation or *fiat*. Of course the allusion to *Leviathan* was intended to reveal the beastlike nature of modern, German democracy. The terrorist attacks of the RAF—firebombs in warehouses, bank robberies, kidnappings of businessmen, and then hostage-taking for the sake of securing the release of other RAF-members—aimed to sever the bond between modern democracy, imperialism, and capitalism (as seen in the war of the United States against Vietnam, for instance) and to reveal the monstrosity of the capitalist state. The RAF were in many ways more successful in demonstrating the message of their politics from within prison than outside of it. The imprisonment was supposed to show the violence of the state as great or greater than the violence of the RAF's own making. As if swallowed by the monstrous whale, the Leviathan, they revealed the inherent violence of the state's submitting its citizens to the term of a contract it had itself dictated. When in 1968 Baader and Ensslin were tried and convicted, after having set fire to a warehouse in protest against the U.S. war in Vietnam, Ulrike Meinhof spoke at a public debate on "the duty not to obey," in order to dismantle the fascist interior of the German republic. In other words, the actions of the RAF were not a political project in the sense that the activists were demonstrating resistance to capitalism and imperialism; the RAF was an urban guerrilla collective in the sense that it wanted to dismantle a state whose legitimacy it refused to recognize.

Terrorism today is associated with religious and / or separatist fanaticism and with the blind violence of suicide bombers. It is considered as a serious attack against Western democracy and treated as such. In Europe in the 1960s and 1970s, however, terrorism was associated with forms of political extremism that were intent on revealing the failure of European democracy to create justice and global solidarity. Although it was violent, it was not altogether blind. Until it became too bloody, too murderous, and too fanatical, political terrorism was not universally condemned. In fact, the RAF itself had stunningly high figures of silent support in the German population before its actions became too violent. It was not an unmentionable option among radical intellectuals to promote "ethical terrorism," associated with bloodless attack without casualties on an oppressive state. "Ethical terrorism" became a concept in the 1960s and 1970s, supported across a vast range of intellectuals not only in Germany but also in France. For instance, Sartre and Beauvoir were selling a radical journal on the streets that was in fact promoting "ethical terrorism."[3] Across Europe in the 1970s the agenda of the RAF was published and made known to the public. For instance, the RAF manifesto was printed in its entirety in German and covered up as a Swedish popular novel.[4] It was printed by a left-wing publisher in Sweden in 1977 and then smuggled back into Germany. Figures like Andreas Baader, Gudrun Ensslin, and Ulrike Meinhof sparked if not adoration then at least fascination across the left. However, the murders by the RAF and the Brigato Rosso that took place in Italy in the 1970s shifted public opinion against the urban guerrillas, the demarcation line between terrorism and activism having become clear to those who had earlier sympathized with both. The attacks that were intent on revealing the shortcomings of modern democracy turned out to be a real threat against democracy. Toward the end of the 1970s European terrorism was no longer showing an acceptable face. Nevertheless, the interest in the main characters of the RAF continued to grow, their personality and fate becoming a favored theme in German art, literature, and film from the late 1970s onward, in novels by Heinrich Böll, films by Margarethe von Trotta, and paintings by Gerhard Richter.

For most intellectuals and artists the specificity of the German heritage was immediately intertwined with the surfacing of terrorism in the postwar generation. For intellectuals both the phenomenon of the urban guerrilla and the history of the recent past imposed an obligation to scrutiny pertaining to the question of German identity. In German cinema of the 1960s and 1970s one of the most prominent themes (as was perhaps to be expected) was that of a continuous questioning of the Nazi phenomenon, its history and persistence in the postwar fabric of society. For German filmmakers of this period the persistent background imposing itself is that of *Deutschland bleiche Mutter* (1980, a film by Helma Sanders-Brahms), a pale, violated mother that has gone under and then resurfaced, remodeled as the fragile shell of a modern, democratic state that has yet to work through the burdens of its past. Quite a few films have examined the link between Germany's Nazi past and its terrorist present, indicating the unease of the postwar generation not only in carrying the burden of guilt but also in identifying with contemporary German society. The violence of the RAF is not merely depicted as the rage of the confused sons and daughters of Nazism. Instead, it is more or less explicitly exposed as a reaction to a certain persistence of violence underneath the surface of contemporary society, a violence in which the state, the media, and the repressive morality of the petite bourgeoisie are complicit. Films linking Nazism to the urban guerrillas of the 1970s include *Germany in Autumn*. Made in 1978 with the collaboration of many writers and directors, Fassbinder, Kluge, and Schlöndorff among them, the film refers to the autumn of 1977, when the Baader Meinhof members took their lives in prison (afterward stories surfaced claiming they were murdered). The suicides were depicted as symbolic but unknowing manifestations of guilt—terrorism as the ultimate expression of guilt, terrorist violence as the symptom of another violence, deeply embedded in the fabric of a German society that has not managed to redeem itself. In *The Lost Honor of Katarina Blum* (1975), an adaptation of a novel by Heinrich Böll, Volker Schlöndorff and Margarethe von Trotta show a young woman's life being torn apart by media and police alike, after a brief love affair with a man who has turned out to be a bank-robber, a menace to society similar to the RAF. The extraordinary interest shown in this man by the police and the media makes us regard him as much more than a criminal—his crime is not treated as a particular instance of transgression but appears to suspend the laws of society.

Katarina Blum, originally published in the respected magazine *Der Spiegel*, is an open attack on the intrusive journalism practiced by *Bild-Zeitung*: in the 1970s this newspaper engaged not only in vulgar "boulevard journalism" but also in tainting the reputations of left-wing intellectuals it suggestively called "sympathizers." This is also why the film is less interested in the possible guilt or motivations of Katarina, or even in her fate, focusing instead on the method through which her personal integrity is taken apart and crushed by the media. The film ends with her taking the life of one of her tormentors, a journalist, thereby contending that the violence of the state and the media in fact provokes counter-attacks. The media, however, was not depicted in isolation from its consumers. In the analysis of the critics of the Frankfurt school—Adorno, Horkheimer, Kracauer—Nazism was a phenomenon that grew out of an intolerant, small-minded, confused, and disappointed petite bourgeoisie. The link made between Nazism and terrorism in these films includes the (im)morality of the petite bourgeoisie, as well as the violence of the media and the state. Since the moral and social conditioning of the petite bourgeoisie had not radically changed after World War II and the downfall of the Nazis, the question of guilt had not been properly worked through. This meant also that the soil that had prepared the ground for Nazism had not been turned over or burned but rather left in its original condition. This fact is what was behind the desperation of younger generations who found themselves incapable of identifying with Germany not only because of its history but also because the social norms of the existing society seemed to prohibit real progress. This was, at least in principle, the artistic analysis to which filmmakers, writers, and intellectuals returned— the terrorist as a disgruntled and Shakespearean figure, struggling with the rot in his or her home country.

This was an image that was motivated by the actions as well as manifestoes of the RAF. According to its own manifestoes, the violence of the RAF was directed toward capitalism and imperialism, implicating the United States for instance. The group protested against the Vietnam War and the placing of American military bases in Germany. It may appear odd, therefore, that all of the RAF's actions either took place in Germany or were directed toward German citizens. Such a paradox must be considered a symptom, revelatory of the kind of rejection that was at stake. The RAF, in its manifestoes, explicitly rejected citizenship and identity as Germans. Such failure to identify as citizens of Germany, in turn, indicates the source of the violence of the RAF. Not only did the organization disagree with the politics and ideology governing the modern German state. The terrorism of the RAF was a rejection of the state of Germany in its entirety—its history, its laws, and its modern constitution.

The German Sisters

After her collaboration with Schlöndorff, however, the filmmaker Margarethe von Trotta approaches the question of terrorism from a more subjective point of view. Clearly showing that it cannot be analyzed at merely a political or social level, or simply as a symptom of the national past, von Trotta makes it a question of subjectivity, while adding a strong, allegorical-historical background to the emergence of such a subjectivity. In the tradition of German political philosophy, through Kant, Arendt, and Habermas, for instance, the emancipatory potential of political negotiation is dependent on its location in public space. Terrorism would therefore have to define itself as apolitical and secretive, associated with the dark forces attempting to overthrow the ideals of peace and tolerance that are the heritage of the Enlightenment. Von Trotta's films, however, make such a standoff between public space and terrorist action, between enlightenment and fanaticism, between emancipation and extremism inherently problematic. She shows the tradition of the Enlightenment, which has marked not only German philosophy but also its political and cultural history, as producing contradictions that exist side by side rather than in exclusion of each other. Von Trotta's films depict a Germany marked by violent geographical, social, and political divisions. Serving as allegories of those divisions and their particular history, her characters indicate the extremes that marked political life in the 1970s: a traumatic separation between East and West, between politics and terrorism, between media and morality, between the consciousness of the individual and collective guilt. The issues depicted cut across the boundaries defined in the philosophical tradition and problematize them; the promise of emancipation that has been the guideline of German political philosophy ever since Kant is shown to be not only stifled but in fact made impossible through the development of German history.

One particular thread that runs through von Trotta's films is connected to what has been said above; it depicts a privileged link between femininity and violent revolt, portraying the question of terrorism as not only a problem of German history, or a political problem, but also as a problem that crosses into a domain where the question of femininity would have to be analyzed in relation to the function of the state. The films of von Trotta open up questions in relation to politics that have been engaging contemporary feminist philosophy. What deficiencies define the female subject in relation to the state? In what sense can we relate current definitions of femininity to a contractual tradition where women, historically, have been oppressed? To what extent can terrorist acts be interpreted as symptomatic not only for the feminine subject but for the subject as such in relation to the state? Von Trotta's films suggest that there is a link between female terrorist acts and the kind of suppression that modern democracy has been proven not only to tolerate but even to help produce. In other words, the question of terrorism is not only answered through historical references but, more important, through the way subjectivity—and female subjectivity here is particularly symptomatic—is produced by the modern state. Von Trotta's women are terroristic by nature or by proxy: Katarina Blum is in love with a bank-robber who can only be allegorically a terrorist; the insubordinate sister in *Marianne and Juliane* is placed in jail as a result of her uncompromising resistance; and the main figure of von Trotta's best-known film, Rosa Luxemburg, leads a movement whose agenda included attacks on the establishment. Such fascination for the female terrorist is built not merely on psychological interest, or solidarity, or catharsis; the films show female subjectivity to be the product of an impossible double bind; the violence directed against the state is produced by the violence exerted by the state on the female subject. In this way the female subject becomes an exemplary subject of violence, not only oppressed by the state but violated by those same laws that are said to carry the promise of emancipation. Von Trotta does not merely depict the destiny of female terrorists; she places herself on the side of the modern subject of disavowal in her analysis of society. Rather than lamenting the heritage of the German nation, she is attacking the fabric of its current constitution.

Released toward the end of the flourishing years of New German Cinema in the 1970s, *Die bleierne Zeit* (*The Leaden Years*)—or, in English, *Marianne and Juliane* or *The German Sisters* (1981)—is a film about two sisters, one of whom chooses the terrorist path, the other that of a politically motivated journalist. The film is inspired by the life and fate of Gudrun Ensslin, one of the founders of the RAF and, together with Ulrike Meinhof and Andreas Baader, one of its leaders. As Thomas Elsaesser has shown, *Marianne and Juliane* is really about Germany.[5] The most poignant level of the film operates on an allegorical plane. The sisters are figures of Germany divided, between East and West. In the context of this essay, however, the split between the two nations is less important for our interpretation than the split that the two sisters represent in terms of identificatory processes, a split that has to do with their status as women, as well as Germans. It is necessary to consider their actions in view of their refusal to identify, as implied by von Trotta, with the postwar German democratic state. Von Trotta shows two women who function like mirrors of each other. As was typical for the New German Cinema, the film shows the historic and social conditioning of individuals, revealing and criticizing what was dysfunctional in their national environment. The film displays the multilayered complexity at work in the relation between the sisters both at a symbolic and at a relational, inner level.

The collapse of a national imaginary is incarnated in the sister of Marianne, who comes to represent the impossibility of nationalism. Key scenes include visits of the sisters to the cinema, where they (and we) witness footage from Alain Resnais' *Nuit et brouillard* (*Night and Fog*, 1956), a searing documentation of Germany's concentration camps of World War II. "I am not guilty. Who is guilty?" asks the voice of the documentary, leaving its viewers to answer. The sisters leave the salon, throwing up as a result not only of the scenes of dead bodies but also as if accused by that very question. Later the question will return, when Juliane accuses her imprisoned sister Marianne of being as extreme and fanatical as the Nazis. "Ich bin nicht schuldig, wer ist schuldig?" (I am not guilty, who is guilty?) shouts Marianne. These scenes demonstrate the collapse of a national imaginary that bears immediately on the possibilities of identification for the two sisters. Marianne is the sister who is bound to the past in her vehement rejection of it. She is shown in the film to be identifying with the father, which in the film also immediately translates into the need for a strong, symbolic order. In this impossible position, identifying with the law as an absolute while rejecting it at the same time, she incarnates the reversible positions between terrorism and National Socialism. The most important aspect of the sociopolitical level of the film is thereby, according to E. Ann Kaplan, to be considered at an Oedipal axis, where the terrorist-sister, Marianne, is shown to be identifying with the father and is thus susceptible to a fanaticism also associated with Nazism, originating in an excessive identification with patriarchal law.[6] This is also pointed out by Juliane herself, when she says accusingly to her sister that she might as well be a Nazi. The strong identification with the patriarchal translates, also, into a relation to the nation, to its history and its current status. The terrorist Marianne incarnates a position of an exaggerated *hatred* of the nation: this hatred is reversible in relation to an exaggerated *love*, as exercised by the Nazis and represented by the father. Nazi Germany was made possible through propagating the erroneous belief that a direct identification with a strong leader would strengthen the sense of German identity. The promise, however, ended in disappointment and subsequent rejection, with terrorist internationalism, as embodied by Marianne, being the exaggerated version of this rejection. The other side of terrorism performed in the name of international solidarity is, naturally, hatred of one's country. Hatred and love of the nation are reversible in the subject: both affects create the delusion that national identity is at the core of one's being.

Kaplan also points to the fact that the other sister, Juliane, is identifying with the mother and is thereby more able to protest in a constructive way. In the beginning of the film this seems to be true. The film shows Juliane to have been the rebellious sister, reading Sartre in her youth and perpetually challenging conservative gender roles. As an adult she works as a journalist for a feminist magazine. Juliane is engaging in traditional work for emancipation in compliance with the rules set up by society, using public space for political work, writing in the press, demonstrating for the rights of abortion, for instance. Juliane's belief in the system comes to a standstill, however, at the moment of her sister's death. From that point on, Juliane will dedicate her life to prove that her sister did not take her own life but was murdered, the victim of a state more violent than the criminal it imprisoned. Juliane inherits Marianne's stance of disavowal. Not only the fate of Marianne, but also that of Juliane, is symptomatic of a lost generation.

The sisters are thereby pitting two kinds of identificatory processes against each other, making the Oedipal mechanisms normally associated with gender identification allegorical of the impossibilities relating to the German state and its history. Here Margarethe von Trotta will succeed most convincingly in showing the incapacity of the postwar generation to identify not only with the German nation, and to negotiate the guilt of its past, but also with the current conditions of the contract binding its citizens to its laws. The film ultimately shows the collapse of both of these women; both of their positions prove impossible. Neither terrorism nor the public space traditionally considered the space of emancipation allows for the freedom of the subject to come into being. Beyond the contract of protection and freedom lies an imaginary space of projective identification, nationalism being built into the construction of the nation-state. When the promise of the nation is made too strong or may seem too weak, the nation-state begins to appear transparent and faulty, producing rejection and hatred as a consequence, thus disjoining the possibilities of emancipation and the national imaginary as construed through history and culture.

Disavowing the Contract

Toward the end of von Trotta's film, however, as Marianne dies in prison, and as Juliane swears to reveal her killers, we are faced with a more complicated issue than the one relating the destiny of the sisters to a German imaginary. When Marianne dies in prison, we are faced with the issue of the intrinsic violence of the law. As the RAF would have it, the violence of the state appears to be even more destructive than the violence of particular acts; the death of Marianne is symptomatic of a situation in which the legitimacy of the state, representing the law, has been undermined to the point of representing an even greater terror than the urban guerrilla.

Von Trotta's film is thereby symptomatic of a deeper split, symptomatic not only for the German but also for the European subject. Although von Trotta's films are preeminently concerned with the history of Germany, they also point to a broader issue: the formation of the subject under the European tradition of the Enlightenment. Rather than choosing to identify with democratic ideals offered by the Western republic, the film shows that the only remaining option for the sisters is disavowal of the terms left for identification altogether—thereby disavowing, as suggested, not only national culture and history but all contractual relations to the state. The film shows a double collapse of the terms of identity: both a collapse of a national imaginary and a collapse of the contract of the modern democracy through which the citizen has been promised the terms of his or her emancipation. This double collapse is embodied by the two sisters. The contractual situation through which the citizen is recognized and given his or her freedom is not merely a construction of reason but also a product of a law whose nature is, in itself, steeped in a history of violence.

This is an interpretation that was, in fact, suggested by the RAF itself. There are, however, more issues brought to our attention by the RAF; the group confronts us with a political violence that is to be interpreted not only as a struggle with the German historical burden, or with the intolerance and small-mindedness of contemporary society, but also as a disavowal of all those Enlightenment ideals that have molded German political philosophy. The violent rejection of the German state as expressed by the RAF is different in kind from the critique and guilt in relation to the historical nation of Germany as expressed by many intellectuals, writers, and filmmakers. The RAF never engaged in a historical or cultural analysis of German identity. Its acts called for disidentification with modern, Western capitalist democracies. Naming themselves as figures swallowed by the great *Leviathan* in prison, members of the RAF suggested that the problem was not a historical one but a current one, involving the terms of the contract of modern democracy under which the subject of the state was submitted and the intrinsic violence through which this contract was constructed.

Hobbes describes the social contract as the submission of the citizen under an unconditional law, thereby endowing the head of the state with a "monstrous" claim to power. The monstrosity of such power corresponds to that of the sovereignty of the state and is unconditional in that the citizen will lose not only his or her guarantee of safety in attacking the state but also his or her freedom. The citizen's only claim to freedom lies in the sovereign power of the state. Therefore, Hobbes argues, any attack on the laws of the sovereign state will threaten its stability and allow for total war to erupt. The state can only guarantee the safety and freedom of its citizens if the latter give up their individual desires: "I Authorise and give up my Right of Governing my selfe, to this Man, or to this Assembly of men, on this condition, that thou give up thy Right to him, and Authorise all his Actions in like manner."[7] Here power is absolute, and Hobbes is not interested in whether it is a good or bad form of rule. The sovereignty of the state relies on the sovereign power of its authority, creating a body politic through which the citizens of the state are obliged to identify with the laws and rules that have been laid down by a sovereign authority. In Hobbes's politics a citizen is part of a body, thus identifying not only with his peers, the people, but also with the sovereign. If the sovereign fails, however, this leads to a war of "every man against every man,"[8] indicating that the body of the state has fallen apart and that, obviously, the mechanisms of identification are no longer at work.

It was precisely in promoting total war in the Hobbesian sense—as attack on the state itself—that the RAF members encoded themselves after Melville's novel. Of course, RAF politics cannot be easily translated into the terms of early modern philosophy. But the reference to *Leviathan* offers a poignant figure of what was at stake. It indicates not a critique of the state, or the system, or the ideologies and politics of a certain government. It makes explicit a rejection of a contractual relation to the state and thereby a rejection of any adherence to the body of the state. The rejection of such a contract is, in fact, a rejection not only of German politics but of any kind of body politic as formed in the European traditions of modernity and Enlightenment.

In a similar vein the films of von Trotta point to a problem that cannot be isolated to the German context. The mutual collapse of the sisters, and the double collapse of a German imaginary, as well as the deep mistrust in the laws of the state that is depicted, indicates that the problem of the subject in relation to the law goes beyond the history of National Socialism. It is not only for reasons of historical guilt that von Trotta is interested in the fate of the German Jew. In her films the fate of the Jew is linked to that of women, a fact that gives us a further clue to her depiction of terrorist subjectivity in *Marianne and Juliane*. In von Trotta's films women and Jews are alike in failing to identify not only with the ideology of German nationalism but with the construction of the contractual relation between citizen and state. In *The Women of Rosenstrasse* (2003) she examines a historical episode in which German women, married to Jews, managed to reclaim their men from Nazi persecution. This historical incident evokes not only the intrinsic relation between German femininity and Jewishness, both disidentifying with certain aspects of German history, but also the intrinsic threat posed to those who are excluded by the contractual conditions offered by the state—Jews and women alike—thereby showing the implicit mechanisms of violence in its contractual construction. After the film *Marianne and Juliane*, von Trotta's biggest success was the film *Rosa Luxemburg* (1986), depicting the fate of the eponymous anarchist leader.

In her essay on Rosa Luxemburg, Hannah Arendt considers it more important that she is a Jew than that she is a woman. In her film von Trotta makes it more important that she is a woman. Both, however, come to the same conclusion concerning her anarchic activism: the violence directed toward the state is the result of a necessary disidentification, not to be seen as mere destructiveness but rather as the attempt to liberate another way of defining citizenship and the relation between subject and state, allowing for European politics to leave the Enlightenment tradition of a contractual body politic behind.[9] Von Trotta, like Arendt, wants to show that Luxemburg incorporated the true possibilities of a proletarian cosmopolitanism at a certain historical moment. Her murder by the *Freikorps*, a right-wing extremist paramilitary group later to form the core of Hitler's supporters in the history of his rise to power, incarnated a true watershed in European history. It put back the revolt of the left and the worker's movement, or the anarchist movement, and was, above all, a setback for all internationalist attempts to think and form Europe otherwise, to place international solidarity above nationalism in the wake of World War I and to form an alternative to the nation-state in European politics.

Thematizing female activism / terrorism and the relation to the state, von Trotta's films may be considered in the light of a problem placed on the philosophical agenda by Julia Kristeva in her article "Women's Time," published in 1977: is female terrorism a response to the double bind created by the so-called sociosymbolic contract, as Kristeva puts it, or to the situation in which the possibilities of the subject become both suppressed and limited in the modern state? The fascination with the female figures of Ensslin and Meinhof has always been much greater than with the male members of the RAF. Ensslin was raised in a God-fearing, middle-class Protestant home—von Trotta's film depicting her as the "good girl" and paternal favorite. Meinhof inspired even more questions. Her turn toward the RAF, after having been a successful journalist, a wife, and a mother, was considered an enigma, and she was seen as less a menace to society than a tragic figure, confused and self-destructive. The capacity of Ulrike Meinhof and Gudrun Ensslin to resort to violence and political fanaticism was not expected from women. Therefore, many considered whether there was a specific link to be made between the politics of terrorism and the state of femininity.

In "Women's Time" Kristeva mentions Ulrike Meinhof as an example of a woman whose actions must be considered symptomatic not of a specific national or political situation but of the status of femininity in modern society. There is, Kristeva suggested, a link between terrorism and the feminist revolt, although terrorism is rarely about women. This means, then, that the status of femininity (rather than the political agenda of "women") is what is at stake in any terrorist action undertaken by a woman, although the ideological motivations may not make that explicit. Written in the 1970s, Kristeva's essay, with its reference to terrorism, includes the many left-wing factions that were active in Europe at the time, Brigato Rosso (the Red Brigade, an Italian organization), and the Baader Meinhof; she is fascinated by the presence of women in these organizations and by Ulrike Meinhof in particular. Kristeva argues that social structures keep women repressed under an impossible double bind, forcing them to commit completely to existing structures of power or to reject them altogether. Either way, women are forced to respond to the conditions under which power is claimed and exerted. This is the reason why so many women engage in terrorism; they reject not only the oppressive forces of power but the existing structures and conditions under which society has been erected. These structures are not the remnants of patriarchy, or the age-old "ethical order" beyond the structure of the state, as discussed by Hegel. On the contrary, these structures are the backbone of the contracts erected between citizens and states in modern society, contracts through which the recognition of the citizen passes exclusively through the parameters of a discriminatory and exclusionary logic. Submitted to such a contract, women are forced to submit to a certain form of identity, which will exclude or deny other aspects of their subjectivity. This means that the options of women are very limited, if one subscribes to the ideals of emancipation that dominate the modern state: the ideals of justice and equality are constructed on the premise that the citizen is male, heterosexual, and so forth. If one, on the other hand, attempts to define a feminist politics according to the specificity of women, one ends up accepting the definition of sexual difference that has been set up by patriarchal society. Therefore, the only true feminist revolt must consist in the absolute rejection of the social rules and symbolic conditions of identity that have served to define women in modern political life and thereby in the total rejection of the social contract in its modern form. Kristeva indicates that terrorism is thus a form of violence that may be destructive and defeatist but in the end is an unavoidable outcome of certain structures of Enlightenment politics.[10]

One may pursue Kristeva's thought further: perhaps terrorism is a revolt on the part not merely of the female subject but of the subject disavowing the terms of identification offered in postwar Europe. What does terrorism say about the involvement of reason in politics and thereby about reason's claim to be the source of emancipation? According to Kristeva, postwar European terrorism involving women is not only a misguided form of feminist revolt but a direct consequence of reason's claim to construe justice and equality under universalistic banners. It is a symptom of the fact that the social contract is premised on a certain symbolic understanding of sexual difference through which feminine identity is based on a sacrificial logic through which a woman must cease to claim her specificity. If one is to follow Kristeva's logic, then perhaps we do not necessarily need to limit the argument to concerning the question of femininity. Her text could also be considered a critique of the conditions under which the subject is formed through its relation to the state. Her argument about women terrorists could be extended and taken to address terrorists. If so, we are to consider European terrorism as a violent rejection of the conditions under which identity is formed, a rejection of the conditions offered by the nation in the cultural and emotional sense, as well as a rejection of the abstract imposition of the social contract of reason. Terrorism would then not be considered the outcome of discrimination or repression but an attack against a certain sacrificial logic of identity that strikes at the core of the subject. This might explain why reason, enlightenment, and associated concepts such as tolerance, communication, and education in fact do very little to prevent terrorism (which would be confirmed by the fact that the RAF terrorists were well educated and middle class yet at war with the democratic state of Germany). The ultimate claim by Kristeva, therefore, merges with that of the terrorists; they are only responding to the terror of the state and the violence imposing itself through it. It is as if the force of reason has subtracted itself and created a force of law so horrifying that freedom has annihilated itself. As argued by Hegel, such terror is the consequence of a logic that has been set in motion by the social contract itself.[11]

The End of Violence?

When the wall fell between East and West Germany in 1989, one of the questions casting a shadow over the celebrations was that of a fear of a possible resurfacing of German nationalism. Jürgen Habermas suggested that the threat of nationalism must be readily undone. Therefore the citizen of Germany ought not to identify with the flag or other German symbols. The identification with Germany or German patriotism should be replaced by "constitutional patriotism." Proposing that the citizens of the new Germany should be voting in a referendum on the constitution, Habermas saw the possibility of a "republican self-understanding" for future generations take shape: "if we do not free ourselves from the diffuse notions about the nation-state, if we do not rid ourselves of the prepolitical crutches of nationality and community of fate, we will be unable to continue unburdened on the very path that we have long since chosen" toward a multicultural society and federal state.[12] The new republic ought to be based on a new constitution, replacing what was called the "Basic Law." Only a common referendum would make it possible for the population of East and West Germany to agree on a new kind of self-understanding, thereby escaping the threat of a new kind of nationalism. If one follows Habermas's argument in terms of identification for the subject, then Germans would be able to escape the historic burden of nationalism that would follow with an identity based on language, culture, and history. A new constitution, however, would form a German subject identifying with a "constitutional patriotism" that would wholly break with the past and create an identity open to multiple and changing forms of "Germanity." In his dialogue with Derrida in *Philosophy in a Time of Terror* Habermas argues that only the constitution can serve as a protection against terrorism, provided that the constitution does not set boundaries on tolerance of minorities; a democratic constitution must, in the end, tolerate also civil disobedience and other forms of protest that, for some, may appear to threaten the constitution.[13] It is difficult to get over the impression, however, that Habermas's idea for a new constitution that would be normative rather than restrictive is a new form of social contract. In the light of terrorist nihilism when it comes to comparing "just" and "unjust" violence, the complication added to Habermas's idea of constitutional patriotism is that Habermas does not discuss the possible violence implied in the founding of a new law. Certainly the unification of Germany must have enacted a certain kind of violence in that two political and economic systems were united. No contract or founding law can avoid the violence implied in relation to the subject, as has been argued by Kristeva and by, as will be shown, Walter Benjamin. As has been argued, von Trotta's obsession with Germany and her staging of Germany in the symbolic figure of two women must be seen as complicating the Habermasian belief in "constitutional" patriotism—there is no "neutral" ground on which to stand from which we are to consider the terms of citizenship or the conditions through which we place ourselves as citizens under a certain nation. One may even argue that the violence exerted by the RAF is motivated by an incapacity to identify with either a national heritage or a contractual law that is as binding and violent in character as it is weak in promises for future emancipation. The RAF undid the social contract through baring the violent character of the law itself and the presumption that the state would symbolize an end to violence.

Von Trotta's film depicts the state of Germany and the violence inherent in its construction in the aftermath of World War II. She shows a culture where the work for international solidarity has become perverted in the form of terrorism and where the work for emancipation in the form of rights for women finds difficulty in being realized. *Marianne and Juliane* is in many ways preoccupied with the same themes as the film *Rosa Luxemburg*, the two sisters attempting to pursue the work of Rosa Luxemburg. Whereas Rosa has a constructive vocation for international solidarity and peace, the political engagement of the two sisters is marked by death and confusion. It is interesting to return to the political climate in which Rosa Luxemburg was active, thereby to lay bare the road toward the final collapse in the incarnation of the two sisters. Walter Benjamin's essay "Critique of Violence" (1921) was written just after the death of Luxemburg in 1919. Historically, the essay brings us back to a time of an internationalist, visionary socialist struggle, when the worker's movement was to be founded on international solidarity and, most important, pacifism. Benjamin, in a complex inquiry into the nature of violence, brings up all the issues propagated by Luxemburg, although he adds a messianic moment to it. His essay is a radical critique of violence, showing that the sovereignty of the state can be based only on violence. Although Benjamin's own essay ends in a meditation on the violence inherent in the mythical and divine foundations of the law, one must also consider his text in conjunction with the internationalist and pacifist movement of which Rosa Luxemburg was part. The premise of the essay is that any cause becomes violent when it bears on moral issues. But can violence, he asks, be a moral means to a just end? The concept of natural law assumes man to be violent as in a state of raw nature, before the conclusion of the contract through which he agrees to give up violence. This thesis, Benjamin says, appears to assume that man has a natural right to violence given that it is used for rightful ends, as in the case of the French Revolution, for instance. Such an idea of violence as natural to man is applied also to the thesis of social Darwinism. But this is the main problem of the modern European philosophy of right: the assumption, in any theory discussing natural right, that violence may or may not be justified, whereas the moral implications surrounding the force of violence are never discussed in themselves. Thus the philosophy of right discusses only the principles on which the law is to be based, never the violence inherent in any enforcement of the law. Benjamin distinguishes between a founding law that is enforced through a "law-making force" and a law that is perpetuated in the organization of a political community through a "law-conserving force." The state would appear to make use only of the "law-conserving force" through the police, for instance. But in reality it is not that simple. In fact, the state is using both, not least through the sometimes erratic and threatening acts of the police, thus exposing the fact that any law must be based on an original violence that is then perpetuated in the sovereignty of the state, upheld through what Saint-Just called "the double-edged weapon of Terror." The power of the police is "formless, like its nowhere tangible, all-pervasive, ghostly presence in the life of civilized states."[14] This state of facts is incorporated into the European tradition of human rights, where the social contract is supposed to guarantee the safety and the promise of freedom for every subject. But, as Benjamin points out, the fascination exerted on people by "the figure of the great criminal" shows that this is simply not the case.[15] The great criminal in Benjamin's text does what the latter-day terrorist in Germany has aimed to do: he exposes the violence at the heart of a legal system that is based on the presumption that justice is to put an end to violence. Thus both the foundation of the law and its maintenance are excessive to the principles on which they are based. Benjamin's text, as Derrida has pointed out, shows the foundation of the law as an undecidable at the heart of the sovereign state: "the founding violence is always represented in a conservative violence that always repeats the tradition of its origin and then ultimately keeps nothing but a foundation destined from the start to be repeated, conserved, reinstituted."[16] While illuminating the singularity of each instance of the law, the discourse on mythic and mystic (divine) lawmaking violence, toward the end of Benjamin's text, illuminates the iterability of the violence itself.

Von Trotta's film, like Benjamin's text, takes recourse to the divine when, toward the end of the film, the terrorist sister inexplicably dies in prison. Here her status of being a defender of divine laws in opposition to the state becomes clear. The surviving sister, who has chosen to identify with the law of the state, is left with the impossible task of claiming justice for her sister. The Antigonean theme of von Trotta's film, however, is not simply to be interpreted as a dialectics between two kinds of right. And even if the film is focused on the fate of two women, thus indicating, as had been argued, the sacrificial demands and violence exerted on the feminine subject in relation to the European tradition of the social contract, it does not end there. What is at stake, ultimately, is, as in Benjamin's text, the baring of an inescapable violence at the heart of any law. Shown as mirrors of each other, the sisters, although adhering to two kinds of laws, will both be subject to the ultimate demands of sacrifice as pressed by the law. When Juliane demonstrates for the right to abortion, she is already transgressing the alleged status of the absolute dictum of natural law (against violence and death) on which the social contract is supposedly based. The film shows Marianne's identification with the law to be as complicated as Juliane's attacks against it: to what extent does the state have the right to force women into unwanted pregnancies, and to what extent does a woman have the right to claim the death of her fetus? Since the sisters are parallels of each other, the violence of the law finds a corresponding image in each one of them. Whereas Marianne's violence is explicitly directed against the state, Juliane's work is complicit with it, although she is merely aiming to realize the promise of emancipation that is supposedly inherent in it. What is shown, therefore, is the undecidable nature of "justice" and of violence, particularly in relation to feminine subjects that are situated on either end of the contract in relation to the state. The law, who is the law? For the female terrorist Marianne, the question of the legality, or justification, of the violence is irrelevant. But toward the end that stance will appear not as nihilistic but rather as the expression of a need for another, new kind of divinity. The riddle behind Marianne's death can only be solved if one reads the narrative of the film, following the sisters toward adulthood through their visits to the cinema and their throwing up at Resnais' images: "Who is guilty? I am not guilty!" Whereas for Walter Benjamin in 1921, the foundation of the law was a question of violence, it has now become death. Marianne's like rejection of Germany and the law is shown, toward the end of the film, to produce the need for divine justification in the same way that Benjamin did. Therefore, in the end her actions do not seem to be that far apart from the terrorism of latter-day religious extremists, although I stated at the beginning of this chapter that these terrorisms appear different in kind. Baring the final truth of her being not as German, or feminine, or as tied to any kind of cause, but as death, Marianne will in the end appear as the radical revolutionary referred to by Benjamin. This is a revolutionary who has seen through the possibilities of terrorist action as being motivated by a belief in justice. Benjamin quotes the activist and writer Kurt Hiller: "If I do not kill, I shall never establish the world dominion of justice. . . . That is the argument of the intelligent terrorist. . . . We, however, profess that higher even than the happiness and justice of existence stands existence itself."[17] Such a statement, Benjamin claims, can only be true if it is read as ambiguous: "the non-existence of man is more terrible than the (admittedly subordinate) not-yet-attained condition of the just man."[18] What this means, however, is that man is never "mere life" (or "bare life" as the philosophical vocabulary would have it since Giorgio Agamben) but is fraught with a guilt that comes with life itself. This is a truth that casts a new light on the attacks of violence that so brutally escalated with the RAF. The motivation, as von Trotta's film shows, lies not in any utopian project but in an utterly violent relation to the law itself that can only be explained by the Benjaminian recourse to a notion of divinity. Divine law makes life itself fraught with a guilt that is too heavy a burden to bear for the female terrorist: "*Who is guilty? I am not guilty.*" The guilt of Marianne is disavowed, the guilt of Juliane incorporated in her work. In neither case should we understand the guilt as being formed merely through the historical events taking place in Germany through people such as their father. These events, rather, merge with the violence through which the law is incorporated in humanity and point to humans as something more than "bare life," as guilty through the very laws that make any promise of justice as a possibility. Marianne is obviously incarnating such a guilt but likewise Juliane. Juliane will leave her work, and all her former attachments, in order to unravel the cause behind Marianne's death. Her task is impossible. In the end, whether it was Marianne herself or the state that caused her death is not really the question. The death of the female terrorist incarnates the exertion of violence of the law itself, the law not only as divine, or as incarnating the contractual bond with the state, but rather as the terrifying intertwinement of both.

8

Rainer Werner Fassbinder
The Subject of Film

ANDREW J. MITCHELL

The Economy of Love 1:
Exploitation and the Free Market

Fassbinder's films are films of tenderness. This is obvious even to the casual viewer who is immersed in a world of characters living out the most fragile and delicate relationships, causing each other pain, providing each other succor. But these films are films of tenderness in another sense as well, for what Fassbinder's films present is film itself as the very medium of tenderness. For this to be the case, his characters cannot be the subjects of his films as long as we understand "subject" in its traditional philosophical sense as what underlies an existence (subject as substance). Instead, the term *subject* must be understood in the sense of a character's "subjection" to film or, and this is equally the case, its *exposure to world* (subject as interjection of world).

Fassbinder's world, however, is a world entirely given over to the free market. His characters are humiliated, beaten, and exploited by this world. And yet this is the only way that tenderness qua relation to world might be shown, along such a *via negativa* or, in other words, masochistically. The exposure and exploitation of tenderness is the single subject of Fassbinder's films: "The theme's remained the same, and always will remain the same: the manipulability, the exploitability of feelings within the system that we live in, and that at least one generation or more after us will certainly have to live in."[1]

The film *Fox and His Friends* expresses this in its German title, *Faust-recht der Freiheit. Faustrecht* is the right of the fist, the right bestowed by might. As the film shows, its freedom is the freedom to seize whatever lies within reach. Franz Biberkopf, a.k.a. Fox, fresh from winning the lottery, falls for a lover above his class, the snobbish Eugen. Fox does not worry that Eugen is with him solely for his money since, as he repeats in the film, Eugen "has enough himself." But the exploitation of the free market is not grounded in the satisfaction of needs. After two years of a lie, Eugen finally has drained Fox of his money. The film ends with Fox face down in a subway station, dead of a Valium overdose, with two small children rifling through his pockets, bobbing up and down like vultures on his corpse.

Because we are always in the world, exploitation is unavoidable: "I don't think anything's possible without venality. Some aspect of venality forms part of every opportunity to be happy."[2] Nevertheless, even in America, the land of the free market, and even in Hollywood, where the exploitation of film reaches its apogee, there is still a freedom to be found, as evinced by the émigré filmmaker Douglas Sirk: "For four years Douglas Sirk has been leaning on me to come to America. He says, 'The minute they want to make money off you, they give you the chance to do something so they can make money off you.' Whether that's freedom or not isn't the question. All I say is, I'd rather be unfree that way than imagine I was free here."[3]

There is no unalloyed happiness free of venality; the fist gets its hands on everything, but there is likewise no exploitation so complete as to preclude freedom; the fist can never grab enough. This is not the pure freedom of a subject, to be sure, but a mediated freedom, the freedom of film.

On Color

No color shines for itself. The shining of color is already its exposition to another. Exposure is exposure to color, whereby the world is visibly exposed. The tremendous amount of research that has gone into color, from coloration and mating in the animal kingdom to color and consumer preference in ours, can always succeed in finding a purpose for color or, at the very least, a reasonable explanation for it. These explanations only endear color all the more to us by demonstrating its inexplicability, in which case we could say that what shines in color is the end of explanation.

Color is not only a mark of distinction, a way for something to stand out, to scintillate, and to burn a hole straight to our eyes; it is likewise a way in which things are related to each other. Color is relational. There is no color particular to Fassbinder, but there is a relation of color that characterizes his films. His worlds are filtered worlds, where everything communicates with everything else colorfully. His colors attend a world in sympathy with itself, a world of tone. These films show us the media of the world, that through which and as which color shines.

Fassbinder colors the ordinary, a row of drinking cups at the hospital in *Ali: Fear Eats the Soul*, a cul de sac of parked cars in *Chinese Roulette*. Scenes such as these pass like the softest of fireworks across his films. But the softness of these surprises (and they are soft, even when garish as in *Lola*) attests again to their mediation. This medial space is one of entry and invitation, beckoning and shine. This medium is not something that intervenes between us and the colors' glow. It already fades into the brightness of those colors and continues to fade through us. The experience of color is the entry into film. The most utilitarian and familiar objects already furnish this medium.

Since color is felt intensity through a medium, Fassbinder's films in black and white are every bit as colored (and white, too, is a color). The black-and-white *Effi Briest* is almost a study in color through its motive use of fades to white. The double function that Fassbinder assigns to white through this technique holds for every color. On the one hand, color is an interruption: "These fades to white are used the way they are in a book, when you turn the page or when a new chapter begins, and the blank space creates a break"; on the other hand, color unites: "It also has a kind of cohesiveness, of course, because at a certain moment you get accustomed to the fades to white and then they don't strike the eye so much, but that's an effect we can't calculate in advance."[4] Fassbinder employs color precisely in this double manner, to interrupt and to cohere. These should not be understood as distinct occurrences, however; neither functions without the other but, instead, as complementary approaches to the mediacy of film.

The cohesive interruption of color draws us into film. Without being pinned down at the outskirts of a dualism (sensible / supersensible, subject / object), color is set free to shine. In this it burns all the brighter: "What happens is that the film becomes brighter, even though it doesn't actually become brighter, simply because you've got used to it. Those are effects we couldn't know ahead of time, because I've never seen a film with so many fades to white."[5]

Body, Meat, and Masochism

Sexual bodies; colored bodies; measured and crippled bodies; bitten bodies; organically sound, sexed bodies; and sex-changed bodies—Fassbinder's films are populated by bodies, something that cannot be said of every film or even of most. All of these bodies are on the market, to be sure, but Fassbinder stages the ways that these bodies remain incalculable. This does not keep them from being measured and weighed; on the contrary, the infinitude of these bodies is only displayed in being so assessed. Fassbinder's transsexual protagonist, Elvira, expresses the operative logic for both the body and Fassbinder's filming: "I invent the pains to find out what normal life's about. I'm not sure but maybe that's what people call masochism, although I don't believe it is." The infinitude of the body is nothing "in" the body but lies in the body's sensitivity to distance and difference. The infinite shows itself mediately in the tenderness of Fassbinder's characters within the free market.

This masochistic logic is carried to its extreme in the film *In a Year with Thirteen Moons*. Here the camera enters the slaughterhouse and saturates itself in the destruction of animal life as dictated by the consumer market. In her commentary on the film, Juliane Lorenz recalls that Fassbinder wore all white during the filming of this scene. The throats of the cows are slit, and the animals are drained of blood, decapitated, skinned and hoisted, then inspected, stamped, and certified. Elvira worked as a slaughterer, and she explains to Red Zora, in perfect accord with this masochistic logic, that slaughtering the animals is not acting against life. "It's life itself: the steaming blood, and death. That's what gives an animal's life meaning. And the smell when they know they're going to die and know that it's beautiful, and wait for it. Solitary and beautiful." Life is visceral and sensual, and therein lies its sense. Even in the slaughterhouse, where death is assured, even in a creature like a cow (and we should note how often someone is called "*blöde Kuh*" in these films), life exudes its sense in the unfurling of this phenomenal smell.

Elvira is no stranger to the subjection of meat. Her ex-lover Christoph berates her in just these terms: "You're a fat, revolting, superfluous lump of meat. And you know why? Because you have no will of your own, no initiative, no brain." Later, "It smells of putrefaction when you're around, of decay and death." From this standpoint the flesh is superfluous meat without will. The will bestows meaning, shapes meat into flesh. But the film shows us where this view leads when Elvira meets a man about to hang himself who uses this conception of the will to justify his act. The suicide is not opposed to life, he claims (reciting from section 69 of Schopenhauer's *The World as Will and Representation*); in fact, he "wants life and simply rejects the conditions under which he experiences it." In other words, the will must be sovereign and arbitrary or it cannot abide its conditions.

These conditions are the conditions of reality, and the suicide is unable to look beyond them. Nevertheless, reality is not an ultimate determination. As Soul Frieda explains, "No one falls for the fairy tale that there's a 'real life' in a 'real world' and that 'real life' is more important than loving." Loving finds within the limiting conditions of life not an end but an opening. Love transforms the body, locating life within its conditions but exuding it out beyond itself in the warmth and smell of life.

Frames, Arches, Balustrades, Halls

Characters in Fassbinder's films are not indifferent to their surroundings; they are involved in them. They are not separable and isolatable from them in the way that Descartes imagined the ego to be. Fassbinder's characters are essentially "surrounded." Architecture articulates character. Consequently, frames, arches, balustrades, halls, stairwells, awnings, and windows play a prominent role in these films. Quite often, Fassbinder's characters are in the other room or down the hall or up the stairs or inside a car that we view from without. We see them through the archway, down the hall, between balusts, through dirty rear windows, and so forth. Such views emphasize two seemingly opposed forces: distance and framing.

The architectural remarking of distance in these films should not be too quickly assimilated to a notion of "alienation," despite Fassbinder's own use of the term in his interviews. The aim of alienation is to interrupt the audience's identification with the characters onscreen. It seeks to provoke a brand of indifference in the spectator. But neither identification nor alienation allows for distance or the nearness that it brings. In the first instance, distance is swallowed up in the act of identification; in the second, indifference seals us off from the characters on film. The extreme sensitivity of Fassbinder's characters requires them to maintain a distance from the world if only in order to be nearer the world. The tenderness that determines them requires this distance for its sense. Fassbinder's characters are not diminished by distance, in other words, but revealed in it. Which is not to say that Fassbinder would show us various "sides" or "aspects" of his characters, as though a summation of these would deliver us the character in full. Characters are creatures of distance.

Around this metaphysical elusiveness of the subject at a distance, Fassbinder frames his characters in their architectural environs. We see character as part of a geometrical organization that bounds and hypostatizes it. Characters are surrounded by lines of relation and exclusion that define and condition the lives that they lead. These framed shots reveal the characters' bearing toward the formal relations in which they find themselves. Fassbinder's frames reveal his characters' relations to what we might term "orthogonal authority." Petra von Kant's assistant, Marlene, exists within such frames. Her actions are regulated by Petra's demands. The film ends with Petra approaching Marlene apart from this frame ("Tell me about your life"). Marlene's subsequent departure reveals her to be far from a passive victim of Petra. Even while remaining mute throughout the entire film, Marlene's departure proves that the frame's constraint is negotiable.

Complete definition by the frame is impossible. Fassbinder's framing of his characters draws attention to the frame itself and to what lies outside its bounds. We see what is omitted in the selection of a shot and that there is no complete or pure presence to be had on film. Since film is always framed and cut, what appears in the frame refers essentially beyond itself to what does not. What we see in the frame is thus not wholly unrelated to what we don't. With this, film projects itself beyond the edges of the screen.

Autopoiesis of the Subject

In *The Marriage of Maria Braun* Fassbinder's protagonist is a product of her own creation, literally picking herself up from the rubble of the war-torn world around her. Frau Braun successfully rises through the world of negotiation and contract. Her unflagging confidence refuses to let anyone else determine her fate ("Your time is up," says the prison guard in the visiting room; "On the contrary," affirms Maria). A self-proclaimed "specialist in the future," she looks beyond present circumstances in the envisioning of a new existence for herself: "Reality lags behind my consciousness." Maria's decisiveness and confidence is enough to inspire tears in the viewer. And yet the same refusal to allow others to determine her life condemns the marriage of the film's title to complete disaster. Without an outlet to the other, self-creation ultimately and explosively self-destructs.

Maria's self-creation transpires in the void left open by the absence of her husband, Hermann Braun, first believed killed in combat, later serving a prison term in taking the blame for Maria's accidental murder of a lover, and later, on his release, clandestinely departing for Australia to recreate himself as Maria's equal. This distance from her husband allows Maria to become who she is; her independence depends on his absence. With her husband out of the picture, Maria is free to take up with affluent lovers, like Karl Oswald, and to benefit from their generosity, all the while draping herself in a cloak of virtue. The independence that she cherishes is equally a renunciation of love. Her husband's absence allows her to never actually give herself to anyone. However remarkable this "fidelity," it makes for a shrewd policy of taking without giving that allows Maria to thrive in the world of business. "It's not a good time for feelings," she explains to her husband during visiting hours, "but that suits me. That way nothing really affects me."

With her husband's return from Australia as a self-made man, both he and Maria are ready to give, but they remain trapped within this same logic of nonaffection. They plan to draw up a contract whereby each will give all he or she owns to the other, though it remains a point of contention as to who will be the recipient; neither wishes to be. Their giving is again only another means of declaring their independence, a way, precisely, of not giving themselves.

Maria attempts to create a self independent of its conditions and impervious to the world outside it. But to be viable, any self of self-creation must recognize the self as no encapsulated thing easily extracted from its conditions but instead as integrated into a life exposed to others. Such a self gives itself to others and lets them be itself. Autopoiesis is always orexopoiesis, a creation of the contours of our world.

Maria's death occurs after the fraudulence of her attempt is exposed. First she discovers that Hermann had secretly agreed to leave his wife in the keeping of Oswald. For all her imperviousness Maria was still the object of a contract. Second, she is now a smoker. Cigarettes appear throughout the film as objects of craving and addiction—diners at the soup kitchen lunge at tossed-away butts, Maria's mother eagerly trades her jewelry for a few packs, the camera luxuriates in a close-up of a pack. It is no coincidence that Maria dies while attempting to light a cigarette at the stove. The subject cannot be kept from the world; any attempt to do so will only lead to its fatal explosion onto that world.

The Economy of Love 2: Matri-Parsi-Mony

In Fassbinder's films newlywed brides receive advice from their friends for maintaining proper relations with their husbands. It is the same piece of advice, whether from Sidonie in *The Bitter Tears of Petra von Kant* (offered as a corrective to Petra's stubborn independence) or from Marianne in *Martha* (offered to lessen the need for tranquilizers): give in now and receive more later. Marianne: "I've learned to agree with what my husband says, always. But when it comes to the crunch, I get my way. And Edgar doesn't even notice it." Sidonie: "Humility paid off. He thinks he's the boss. I let him think so, but in the end I get my way." The truth, however, is the reverse. These women give nothing, and what they get is not their own.

Sidonie and Marianne seek to gain from a relationship without risking their being in a relationship. Their policy of delayed gratification, while seemingly feasible, requires the wife to play solely the role of recipient. She withholds her opinion to receive from him his. Since the actions of one affect the other, this pretense of humility goads the husband to indulge all his worst and most tyrannical habits. The ploy of always giving in is actually a refusal to ever give oneself over to the relationship and the mediation of self that this entails. A policy of deferral would be sensible, though duplicitous and venal, assuming the human existed in isolation from others. Fassbinder's films give the lie to this assumption through a sustained assault on any attempt to exist for oneself, on one's own, or to get one's way. We are only ourselves insofar as those selves are already emptied out into the world and striated through a multitude of relationships. Sidonie and Marianne attempt to abstract themselves from this mediate space. They seek to get their way in spite of their husbands, as though they had a separate and inviolable identity somewhere outside of these relationships.

We exist in the midst of life and nowhere else. To withhold oneself from this is to destroy oneself, is to live while dead and to create the monster who feeds on your life, the husband, illustrated by the film *Martha*. As Martha consistently cedes to Helmut's demands and adheres to the advice of Marianne, Helmut becomes more and more of a sadist, sinking his teeth into Martha's neck during intercourse, and seizing increasing control over Martha's life (refusing to let her give, ridiculing her every idea) until finally she is paralyzed, confined to a wheelchair, and rendered completely dependent on Helmut.

Sidonie and Marianne try to live without giving. Even in "giving in" to their husbands they are ultimately taking orders. In the end, if they get their way, they only do so by having first created a vampiric husband as their master. Marianne's husband, Edgar, does not notice that she gets her way because she doesn't—she gets his. Without noticing it, Sidonie and Marianne get the way of the servant to the boss they create. What they have failed to give is what exceeds all giving, the refusal of giving that would disrupt the self-assurance of the subject and confront it with difference. They fail to enter the mediacy of relations, fail to love. Such dispossession is the only way that they could ever have room to receive—not in the future but now.

Glare and Refraction

The subject is never completely present. An infinite difference is harbored within it, or rather this difference splits it open. We are essentially open, not self-enclosed wholes. But openness cannot be thought in terms of presence and absence. Openness is never "fully" open, whatever that would mean. For an opening to be an opening, it can only be a "partial" opening. We exist neither at the pole of presence nor at that of absence, even in our death, but instead we exist mediately and exposedly. This "middle" that mediates us is not measured like a space of absence between present points. Nothing is present in Fassbinder's films, and everything is mediated. There is no outside to film, a point that glare makes evident.

Fassbinder shows us obstructed and obscured characters. He doggedly shoots his characters through screens, windows, glass, and mirrors, anywhere where he can show the medium glaring back at us. There are shots in *Fox and His Friends* where faces are entirely obscured by the glare on the windshield as a car drives down a tree-lined street. *Chinese Roulette* is likewise full of shots through windows, glass, and Plexiglas, and characters are seen from behind through the dirty rear window of a car. Often glare arises from the juxtaposition of one view on another, across the surface of a glass or a screen, in the difference between them. In all of these instances Fassbinder's filming illuminates the media of the everyday.

When asked about his tendency to focus on characters "indirectly," through mirror images and the like, Fassbinder replied, "First of all, you get a refraction that way."[6] This refraction is essential to presenting the truth of the character, not in the sense of a fidelity to what typically goes unremarked in our everyday doings, nor in order to more accurately depict these doings and show the overlooked mediation of our everyday perceptions, but truth in the sense of a filming of what is by no means present: the subject of the film. Refraction obliterates the undivided subject, but it also shows us a subject run through by mediation. The integrity of the character is disrupted by the colorful refraction of the world. We belong to that colorful world of film.

Refraction is not simply an interruption of character but a presentation of character beyond itself. The contours of the self vary widely from one moment to the next as that self falls into and out of the pull of the various relationships that lay claim to it. The glare that obscures the character reveals it in a new shape. Glare streaks through the characters in the film; it spreads over their faces and forms revealing whole new dimensions of character. Glare, too, is a relation to the world, even when at its most seemingly nonrelational or obscuring point. In disfiguring the human, Fassbinder reveals a whole other attribute of our existence, our integration with the world. This is neither a matter of thought or extension but of mediation and sense. Glare calls the subject back to the world and runs that world through the subject.

In short, there is nothing to film but glare. Characters do not exist outside the world but within it. In illuminating the medium, Fassbinder not only films its place between us; he welcomes us to this between.

Anxiety Waves

The anxiety that permeates Fassbinder's films does so by virtue of the medium itself. The separation of the subject from itself, its division at the point of its opening to the world, does not permit it to underlie a collection of attributes from the position of a substance. The subject is not substance in these films, and there is nothing beneath it on which it could rely. Anxiety, therefore, is not an internal condition of the subject but an effect in the world, a "special effect" of film.

In *Fear of Fear* this special effect rolls across the screen during Margot's attacks as waves of no determinate origin. This wavering of the world is neither a simple collapse of the world nor the obtruding presence of world. Instead, the world surges and resurges, appears to ebb and flow according to its own rhythm. By neither dissipating nor rigidifying, but wavering somewhere in between, the world opens itself to Margot during these attacks.

But Margot shuns this invitation, as shown by the way that she swims. As a swimmer, Margot is no stranger to fluidity, viscosity, mediation, and waves, but her swimming of late has attracted attention. Her neighbor, Karli, tells her at the pool, "That's not normal, back and forth like that, as fast as you can." Her husband repeats what he has heard about her: "You swim every day, tearing along like a madwoman." Margot struggles to escape the world by swimming, as she explains to Karli: "It helps me forget everything. Forget . . . everything."

In forgetting everything and forgoing the invitation of the world that waves to her, Margot estranges herself from sense. She is unable to express herself: "I can't explain it. I have anxiety. I know no word to express what I mean." And in the midst of a self-absorbed and largely indifferent husband, a daughter who is too young to understand her, a distrustful and prying family, and a doctor whose only interest is sexual gratification, there is no one to whom she can express herself even if she were able—except perhaps the town madman, Herr Bauer, who recognizes her problem at once: "You need someone with whom you can discuss it."

Margot is equally estranged from her body. She tries to find meaning in herself and on her own, by feeling herself—"As long as I can feel myself, I'm fine"—by hearing herself—"I want to hear myself scream to know I exist"—when precisely what is needed is to be felt or heard by another. When the autoaffection escalates to cutting, it is as though her body were acting on its own to force itself open to the world. Margot, of course, does not recognize this: "I simply wanted to feel the pain to take my mind off my anxiety." Margot cannot project her body beyond itself in any meaningful way; even her pain remains a selfish distraction from this.

It is not so much that Margot is unable to express herself as that she is unable to find herself in her expression, not so much that she is unable to feel herself as that she is unable to find herself in her open wounds. She does not know what to make of the face in the mirror: "So this is me? What is this me?" She tries to hold herself apart from the world, from who she is, as though the division of the self were to be understood as dividing two separate people, an in-itself and a for-itself, complete strangers to each other rather than (and contra this easy existentialism) the mediation of the subject into the world such that it might be buoyed by sense, something all good swimmers should know.

The Collapse of Independence

Independence fails in Fassbinder's films. We see characters who would be independent mistake lack of dependence for lack of relation, mistake dependence for passivity, and ultimately find that such a relationless, impassive life cannot be sustained. The attempt to live the independent, active life is played out in *The Bitter Tears of Petra von Kant*. When we first meet Petra von Kant, she is a successful designer, confident and in control, an impression created in no small part by the way she orders about her secretary, Marlene. But Petra's independence slowly reveals itself to be a denial of human passivity, a denial directly leading to her utter collapse in a nervous breakdown.

Petra's previous marriage crumbles as a result of this insistence on activity. She explains to her comfortably vapid friend Sidonie that she and her husband "wanted to decide everything anew, always be alert, always free." In such a relationship there is room for only one independent "individual." The other must be its object. And insofar as the individual is defined as purely active, this means that the other, qua individual, must be destroyed. Petra mistakes the opening of tenderness for sheer passivity. As she puts it, "You'd like to be tender, but again you have anxiety. You're afraid of losing points, of being the weaker one." This tenderless battle of individuals struggling to be the stronger party leads to sexual sadism and divorce. Petra's exit from the marriage, so surprising to Sidonie, is only another act of continuous "independence."

Independence is nothing solitary but an extreme narcissism in the midst of others (as the later film *Veronika Voss* makes clear). Like the narcissistic child, independence requires a supporting cast to keep it afloat. Consequently, immediately following her divorce, Petra hires the ever-silent and submissive Marlene as her personal secretary. Whereas Marlene is a willing accomplice to Petra's independency, Sidonie's unpolished friend Karin is not. Petra expects to be able to improve Karin in her own image and feed off of Karin's gratitude and praise. Such paternalism backfires, however, and Petra becomes increasingly needy of Karin. Karin returns to her husband, and Petra's downfall is assured.

Petra's dramatic collapse exposes the inner workings of the independent subject: Petra is the subject that needs to know ("I believe you love me, but I don't know"); the subject ever vigilant ("I haven't slept in so long"); the subject without regard ("What I've earned I'll smash as long as I like!"); and the self-deceived subject (with Karin throwing Petra's words back at her: "You were always talking about liberty. You always said: 'No obligations towards each other'"). Independence is dependency, and Petra utters the linchpin phrase of dependency as avowed in so many of Fassbinder's films: "I exist only for you."

In an interview Fassbinder notes that "there's a way of falling apart that can be productive," but such is not the case here.[7] Recovering from her breakdown, Petra now believes that "you have to learn to love without demanding." The opposite of an absolute position remains an absolute position, whereas what is needed is mediation. Petra cannot achieve this, but her secretary, Marlene, does in leaving Petra at the film's end. Marlene is the true subject of the film, for in her departure she shows that her submissiveness never attained the isolation and need of (in)dependence.

On Mirrors

In the mirror characters appear to themselves as they are, filmic. The "me" of the mirror appears as party to the refraction of mirrors, which is to say, it appears as interrupted. This interruption in the presence of the self to the self does away with any pretension to im-mediacy in the subject's relation to itself, for the "me" that appears on film is not a fully present object that the subject would have at its disposal. As a result, Fassbinder's films are not paradigmatically "existentialist" because the subject in the mirror is nothing that could be surmounted or overstepped by the freedom of a self-consciousness. The relation of the character to its mirror image is not that of a subject to what it "is not" nor even to what it "is in the mode of not being it." The character is an appearance on the screen (mirror), but it can be so only by virtue of this appearance being refracted. Just as the subject is nothing discrete but an opening onto the world of sense, the character on film opened as well. They meet because of this. Their identity is possible only as each is essentially out beyond itself and therefore capable of joining itself to itself (film is nothing but the bond between these two, the space of the colorful appearing of the world). The character is who it is as an appearance on film.

Mirror effects apply to actors, too. Actors "get closer to their own identity in contact with mirrors."[8] Identity is something that we approach. This relation could be said to make possible the actor's relation to his or her role, but it also means that the actor is identical to the role. If acting depends on a pure separation between actor and role, then there are no actors in Fassbinder's films. Everything is real because the real is the relational. "See, when they look at themselves while they're acting, they have a different attitude toward themselves, which I think is more concrete."[9] The hardness of concrete (the most Hegelian of all materials / media) arises from the fact that both the universal and the particular are mediated into it. What concretizes the actor before the mirror is the hard fact of identity; the actor is wholly exposed.

The character appears on film refracted, and the actor gains concretion, but the mediating effects of film apply just as much to the moviegoer. How does the viewer touch the film? Through the imagination. The film becomes a concrete reality once the viewer's imagination is mediated into it. The film becomes a mirror of the viewer. The imagination allows a meaning to be found in the film. Fassbinder: "Just as when you read, it's your imagination that turns the letters and sentences into a story, the same thing should happen with this film."[10] In reading, we take the individual letters and see them for their relation to a whole that is completely different from even the sum of all of them together. For this to happen with a film, the viewer would have to imagine the whole thing, be "invested" in it. In giving ourselves over to the film, we expose ourselves to the film's sense. Speaking of the relationships in his film *Ali: Fear Eats the Soul*, Fassbinder remarks that "the relationships are much more complex, I realize that. But it's my opinion that each viewer has to flesh them out with his own reality. And he has an opportunity to do that when a story's very simple."[11] The imagination fills out the film, and we are sensibly affected by it. We loan the relationships the flesh of our own reality, and in this way they become our own. We recognize ourselves in them.

The Economy of Love 3: Surplus and Return

Elvira gives herself wholly throughout *In a Year with Thirteen Moons*. Even her speech becomes frenetic, blathering, in the attempt to tell her whole story. Her misfortune is the impossibility of such a complete giving, but this misfortune allows her to give even more than she ever could have given were it possible to even once give completely. Toward the film's conclusion we hear her voice on a cassette recorder speak of her intentions in regard to her lover, Christoph, and she utters a truth not only of her own brief life but a truth of love in the time of film: "Giving him so much that he'd have some to give back to me. That may sound calculating, but it isn't. Maybe it's . . . what one calls love."

The prospect here is not for reflection. Elvira's problem is not one of determining how to receive more of herself back from the other. She is not seeking confirmation of herself, much less her own reflection multiplied. Insofar as this is love, something about which we can necessarily never be certain ("maybe" it is so), we will only understand love in film when we come to terms with this excess of "so much," the "*Übermaß*" of love and film.

Elvira's statement will be calculating only if the *Übermaß* (literally, what is beyond the measure) returns to the donor more of the same. The whole issue resides in the determination of this excess. To whom does it belong? Whom does it reach? While what lies beyond the limit or measure exceeds the recipient's ability to receive (and in this would lie the calculative hope of a return or reflection), it also exceeds the donor's ability to give. The excess is nothing at the donor's disposal. In giving to Christoph, Elvira's gift remains tied to her; she is the one who gave it. Elvira cannot give completely. In receiving this gift, Christoph is likewise unable to completely receive it. To do so would be to incorporate the gift to the point of obliterating its difference from the self. In assimilating the gift, Christoph would destroy its exteriority qua gift, that it came from elsewhere.

Casting giving in these terms makes it seem as though it took place from a donor to a recipient, each of whom stands outside the giving. Instead, the giving takes place "between" the two, first constituting them. The source and destination of the gift is this between. What eludes giving, rendering it impossible or incomplete, is precisely the presence of a donor and recipient. The donor cannot give completely but only because the donor is nothing objective that could be given. The recipient cannot receive completely, but only because the recipient is no encapsulated container. Each is already within the world of sense.

What, then, of love? Are we not already within this world of film? Have we not therefore already accepted the other's love? Obviously, this is not the case. Elvira's love is constantly refused, confused with calculation (Christoph: "You behave as if I had to pay off some huge debt"). If it were the case, we would ourselves completely belong to film, which would destroy it qua medium. We are not in the film but always entering it, always right on it but never in it.

But this does not prevent us from loving. It allows us to love all the more. The entry into love (our "falling" in love) is never complete. There is always more to give, even beyond ourselves. But there is also always more to be exploited and abused (as Elvira's life attests). Love is incomplete, though it is whole. Its excess lies in the giving, which ensures that love always "give back" and this whether accepted or refused.

Valium and Suicide

Valium is prescribed to patients who are determined to be "organically sound" by their doctors. It is prescribed for psychological conditions. Mental disturbances, due to heightened levels of stress, manifest themselves in bodily symptoms. In prescribing Valium, the aim is to break the connection between the worries of the mind and the victimized body. To do this, Valium targets the emotional centers of the brain. The soothing of emotion leads to the release of the body from the mind's grip. This relieves the body of the burden of signifying illness, to be sure, but it does so by depriving the body of emotional significance. By inhibiting the emotional openness of the subject, Valium aims at the "tenderness" of the patient, the sensible exposure of the body. The world wavers. Through a deadening of sentiment, Valium (and before it, morphine) restores for the independent subject an unsupportable and addictive calm (as Margot learns to say, "I have a deep depression and I need pills to pull out of it"). In Fassbinder's films, consequently, Valium functions as a substitute for love and a means for suicide. Valium unites love and suicide, for falling in love is the death of the individual. The dying and the falling each bid farewell to the isolated ego, one in willful destruction, the other in will-less surrender.

Desensitizing the emotional exteriority of the subject in order to restore it to a narcissistic position of independence is only a palliative, as Veronika Voss's doctor is no doubt aware: "I shouldn't prescribe you morphine, but someone to love you." Far from dampening the pathetico-emotional experience of the world, love allows for a doubling of it. Tenderness is exposed to the exposure of tenderness. Love locates the self outside of the self, driving it mad, out of its mind, and into the world where the lovers fall into each other. Love craves not: "I reject the craving to be loved, even though being loved might just be the most important thing in the world for me."[12] To crave and to need the other is to take oneself for incomplete (i.e., as completable in independence). Love neither completes nor needs.

Valium overdose is the most frequent means of suicide in Fassbinder's films, but we would be mistaken to consider suicide a selfish act of self-destruction. As Fassbinder explains, "Destruction isn't the opposite of what exists. Destruction is when this concept [of existence] no longer exists, when it doesn't have any meaning anymore. What people invent then—that would be exciting."[13] Destruction names the field between existence and nonexistence, a space of creation and invention. The suicide enters the film as one who will risk everything to escape the jungle of the free market: "This admirable jungle seems to have no way out, except through the decision in favor of death, except perhaps for the path . . . into madness. . . . But the 'land of madness' is like that of death: only possibly can they be adequate sources of hope."[14] Possibly suicide might be adequate to providing hope, nothing more than this. Such a suicide of possible hope is far from suicides in revolt against the conditions of existence. The suicide of possible hope suicides from "the courage to recognize a utopia and to open yourself up to it, however poor it may be."[15] The ego's self-destruction against all odds illuminates the courage of tenderness. Suicide achieves a sensitization to love. Fassbinder: "I hope I'll have the courage to choose one of those paths, and not to settle for the easy way out."[16]

The Invitation of Sense

The world beckons and invites us. It flashes with color and appeals to the tenderness of the body. But just as all the sense organs are distance organs and all action is action at a distance, so too does this invitation keep its distance, though we are receiving it. But it is nothing that we can ever completely receive, for it is always arriving and in this arriving inviting (this is the "projection" of film). The scene for the arriving of the invitation of sense is film.

The exposure of tenderness constitutive of the subject can only transpire mediately. For this openness empties the subject beyond itself but at the same time through itself. Everything is exposed. The opening of exposure is consequently no opening at all, as it is not where closedness leaves off. Exposure does not form a hole in a fabric such that the fabric would otherwise remain unaltered. If exposure is an opening, then it is only so because it opens everything everywhere. Even what is concealed appears in this opening, like shadows on the screen. The openness of the subject means that it cannot be localized to a body because this body is already surged through by the world. The subject so opened is inextricable from the world. As a result, the subject cannot be gathered up anywhere or located in any one place in order that it might be present to itself. It is already spilling into the world. The immediacy of self-presence is lost in this arriving.

Fassbinder films the invitation of the world in films that appeal to the tenderness of the viewer. When Fassbinder remarks that "it's pointless to make films for the public that the public can't feel involved in," the appeal is not to cater films to a public's sensibility, nor is it to make films from out of that same sensibility, but to approach the viewer sensibly.[17] The appeal will create a new feeling in the viewer, its organ: "My film isn't supposed to let feelings people already have be neutralized or soaked up; instead, the film should create new feelings."[18] These new feelings are sensitive to the distances of loving, the vulnerability of the body, the coloration of the world. They are feelings of sense, but insofar as the sensibility of sensation is something that the mind can only imagine, they are themselves imaginings. To feel differently is to imagine difference, and this is itself already revolutionary—not a revolution aiming to overturn, but as a remaining in motion, a moving into film.

Fassbinder speaks of filmmaking as a sensitizing process: "With the things you do, you try to sensitize your audience in a certain way to life and the world around them. That's a sensitizing process which you've put yourself through and now have to transfer to your audience—that's all it is."[19] The process is not the reproduction of personal experience, however: "As much as possible I want to avoid replaying my life. Do you understand what I mean?"[20] Instead, the "transfer" of sensation occurs in the feelings falling between the two parties. The transfer is a participation, though it must be acknowledged that if this were immediate, it would cancel film. "Participating—there I feel inhibited. It should be possible to participate in life indirectly—only as a mediator."[21] The invitation of sense cultivates new feelings, new articulations of tenderness. The subject opened and divided by tenderness lives the life of sense, mediated between the sensible and the supersensible on film. Fassbinder's films invite us to know ourselves as subjects of film in a world of sense.

9

Wim Wenders
The Role of Memory

JEFF MALPAS

The real storytellers and artists are places.

—*Wim Wenders*[1]

IN SPITE OF the evident attention given to the composition of sound in his films—he has, after all, worked closely with musicians such as Ry Cooder, Willie Nelson, Nick Cave, Daniel Lanois, and U2—the centrality of the image is a topic to which Wim Wenders has returned on numerous occasions in films, lectures, and conversations. In one respect this should be no surprise, for it is surely the image, or more specifically, the moving image, that is the essence of film. This is not to denigrate the role of sound but merely to acknowledge that, in film, sound works only in and through its relation to the image and to the succession of images. Yet it is not simply the centrality of the image to which Wenders draws attention but to the relation between the image and memory, as well as dream, between image and story, between image and place.

Responding to a question concerning the role of memory in his films, Wenders tells us that "every film starts off from memories, and every film is also a sum of many memories. Then again, every film creates memories."[2] The memory and the image are closely tied together: memory is frequently given in the form of the image, and the image also contains and gives rise to memory. Moreover, while memories are certainly not restricted to the visual alone,[3] the memories from which a film begins are surely for the most part, if not all (since one would not wish to dismiss the role of sound), the memories that are indeed given in the form of the remembered *image*. The idea of the film as beginning with memories, then, can itself be seen to reinforce the idea of the centrality of the image—in starting from memories, the film also starts from images. Wenders has also said that it is his conviction "that a film has to be preceded by a dream,"[4] and elsewhere that "a dream is made of images much more than of words. You SEE dreams."[5] The memory and the dream are often hard to disentangle—memory provides the stuff of dream, while dream can itself be the stuff of memory. It is the image that is common to both, however, and it is the image that each supplies as the stuff of film. The image at issue here, particularly inasmuch as it is *remembered*, cannot be any mere "representation," as if it were the flattened replica of something no longer present, but instead must carry the fullness, as well as the opacity, that typically comes with memory as such.[6] Moreover, while every film may start from a remembered image, or from a number of such images, the priority of the image at issue here does not derive from its being first in the succession of images that compose the film. Instead, the images from which the film starts are those images—those memories—from which the film can itself be said to arise, that stand at its heart and constitute its soul, but that may appear at any point in the succession of images.

The idea that every film begins with a remembered image (or is preceded by an image dreamt) is undoubtedly connected with Wenders's own beginnings in painting: "Let me go back to the very beginning," he says. "Once I was a painter. What interested me was space; I painted cityscapes and landscapes. I became a film-maker when I realized that I wasn't getting anywhere as a painter."[7] Moreover Wenders's involvement with painting, as well as with photography, is also evident in the often photographic or painterly composition and character of the scenes in his films. This is true of scenes in *Paris, Texas* (1984), as well as *Wings of Desire* (1987), but also of scenes in many of his other films. In *The End of Violence* (1997) the interplay between film and painting takes on a very specific form in Wenders's use of a version of Edward Hopper's *Nighthawks at the Diner* as the basis for a number of scenes. The connection with Hopper is particularly interesting, since one could say of many of Hopper's paintings, as Wenders does, that they also have a certain narrative, or even cinematic, quality: "An Edward Hopper painting is like the opening paragraph of a story. A car will drive up to a filling-station, and the driver will have a bullet in his belly. They are like the beginnings of American films."[8]

Wenders's own filmic techniques often draw attention to the scene *as* image, thereby also evoking the photograph or painting. Wenders will thus often shoot a scene in a way such that the camera dwells on the scene alone, leaving its image suspended on the screen, perhaps holding the shot after the action has passed or allowing the characters to appear as if they were incidental to the scene. In this way the image itself emerges as a distinct element in the film, not merely as one of a succession of images that constantly unfolds before our eyes but as a single constant appearance. Thus Wenders can say, while acknowledging the importance of the combination of images, the montage, that

> if each image couldn't be taken on its own terms and at its own worth, the sum of all of them would amount to nothing. . . . Each individual circumstance is so important to me that I'd happily see it by itself, and each image by itself. I think only if you give each image the right to be there for itself and tell its own story can you hope to be given the right by each image to place it in a larger sequence and make it part of some bigger whole.[9]

Once again, however, it is not the image as mere "representation" that appears here but the image in its fullness, its opacity, its reality—an image that does not somehow stand in for the world but rather opens it up. Wenders's films often appear as composed of just such distinct and distinctive images, with each image itself a memory and a source of memory.

This opening up of the world through the memory and the image occurs most directly and immediately through the way in which the image locates us, orients us, places us. The image thus "re-presents" a place or locale. In fact, if we turn our attention back to memory—that from which Wenders claims every film starts—then the sorts of images that are associated with memory are just those that are both placed and placing in this way,[10] while memory as such also seems to stand in a close relation to place. Perhaps nowhere is this relation made so evident as in the work of Marcel Proust, whose *In Search of Lost Time* (*A la recherche du temps perdu*) is a work dedicated to the exploration and recuperation of identity, lost in the inexorable passage of temporal succession, through the exploration and recuperation of the remembered places with which that identity is entwined, and through which it is articulated.[11] Indeed, not only are memories tied to places, but places are themselves haunted by memory. To return to a place is thus often to find oneself assailed by memories and emotions that may otherwise have remained hidden and obscure.

Memory—re-remembering—may thus be thought of as a form of "re-placing," a returning to some place that is no longer the place of our immediate location; similarly, to return to a place is also to be assailed by memory, to re-member. The role of memory, in one sense, is to effect such a return. It is no accident that *nostalgia*, which is literally, from the original Greek, a pain that comes from the unfulfilled desire to return to the place that is one's home, is so often associated with the experience of places and the memory of places. The close connection between memory and place may be thought to derive, in part, from the way in which places themselves serve to hold images, feelings, emotions, and experiences. It is this character of place that was the basis for the ancient "art of memory" that was employed, up until the time of the Renaissance, as a means to train memory through the association between certain places, located within a complex mental edifice (a "palace" or "cathedral" of memory), and particular images or ideas.[12]

Wenders's work provides us, of course, with some wonderful examples of the connection between memory and place—none better, perhaps, than *Wings of Desire*. Here is a film in which the leading character could almost be said to be the city itself—the original German release was titled *Der Himmel über Berlin* (*Sky/Heaven over Berlin*), and Wenders himself says that "the city called the film into being."[13] The role of Berlin in *Wings of Desire* is not as some sort of static backdrop to the film's narrative development. Wenders tells us that the film "isn't about Berlin because it's set there, but because it couldn't be set anywhere else."[14] The story of the film is, indeed, embedded in, and drawn from, the city, and in this sense the city itself substituted for the script that Wenders did not have—a "technique," if it can be called that, also exemplified in *Kings of the Road* (1976),[15] in which the places along the old border between East and West Germany provide much of the basis for the story. As *Wings of Desire* is drawn from the city, so is the sparse narrative structure of the film, which is constituted in terms of many different, if often minimal, narrative strands that themselves relate to the different locations through which the film moves and to which it so often returns: Potsdamer Platz, the public library, the Siegessäule Angel, the gutted building in which Peter Falk is filming, the vacant block on which the circus is set up, the bar in which Damiel and Marion meet. The multiple strands that make up the film's narrative come gradually to cluster around the strand that, over the course of the film, establishes itself as central, namely, the story of the angel-become-human, Damiel, and his relationship with the trapeze artist, Marion; in this way the various places through which the film moves also come to settle around the key places that figure in the relationship between Damiel and Marion. The integral relation between the city and the stories that make up the narrative structure of the film is such that Wenders can say of *Wings of Desire* that it is a film "driven" by place. In this respect the film stands in clear contrast to its Hollywood remake, *City of Angels* (1998, dir. Brad Silberling)—a film that, unlike *Wings of Desire*, is determined purely by story, not by place (and that also possesses, therefore, a much more traditional narrative structure), and in which the city that is referred to in the film's title, the City of Angels itself, Los Angeles, provides nothing more than a convenient location.[16]

In *Wings of Desire* the city of Berlin is constituted not only from its contemporary streets, buildings, and roads but also from the memories and images that are contained in those locations and structures. Indeed, it contains some of Wenders's own memories—for instance, the Renault 4 on which Marion sits in an early scene was the favorite car of Wenders's childhood; and Marion's caravan contains a photo of Wenders as a child, while the book that Homer examines in the library is Wenders's favorite (which also figures in *Notebook on Cities and Clothes*—1989), August Sander's *Man of the Twentieth Century*. Some of the early scenes in *Wings of Desire* are also interspersed with archival footage of Berlin during the war, and the memories recounted by Homer as he wanders through the derelict Potsdamer Platz are the memories of the actor himself, Curt Bois, who knew the prewar city. The Berlin that appears in *Wings of Desire* is thus imbued with memory and image—those of Wenders, and of Bois, of the characters within the film, of the paths and places of the city—it is itself made out of such memory and image.[17]

This is not to say, however, that the Berlin of *Wings of Desire* is *merely* an imagined or remembered city—as if this could be different from the real city. The city *is* its images and its memories as much as it *is* its buildings, its streets, its squares, and its people. Yet Berlin is also a city whose identity, and the memories and images that make up that identity, are, in many respects, as fragmented and broken as were its buildings and streets, as divided as was the city itself, at the time *Wings of Desire* was filmed. Part of the story of *Wings of Desire* concerns the experience of fragmentation, dislocation, and loss and the reconstitution of memory and of identity in the face of such fragmentation. Berlin appears, and appears as the city it is, in spite of the loss and destruction to which it has been subjected; the city continues to live, and the human beings who live within, whose lives it gathers together, continue to remember it, to imagine it, to reconstitute it—"We live in the cities / And the cities live in us."[18]

The loss, or perhaps better, the *questioning*, of memory and identity that appears as a theme in *Wings of Desire*, partly through the angel Damiel's own search for identity, and for human life, as well as through the loss, dislocation, and reconstitution of the city itself, is a recurrent element in many of Wenders's films, from his early works through to his most recent. Moreover, just as the issues of memory and identity that arise in *Wings of Desire* concern the city of Berlin no less than any of the characters found within that city, so too do memory and identity—as these figure elsewhere in Wenders's work, whether in *Kings of the Road*, *The American Friend* (1977), *Paris, Texas*, *The End of Violence*, or in almost any of his other films—relate not merely to the memories and identities of individual human beings but to the "memory" and, one might say, the "identity" of the world. What is at issue is a remembrance or imagining of the world, a reconstitution of the world, a return to the world. Thus Wenders can say of *Wings of Desire* that "I didn't just want to make a film about the place, Berlin. What I wanted to make was a film about people—people here in Berlin—that considered the one perennial question: how to live? / And so I have 'BERLIN' representing 'THE WORLD.'"[19]

It may, however, appear somewhat odd to talk of this apparent preoccupation with memory and image in terms of a return *to* the world or, as I have done above, as an *opening up* of the world, since it may well seem to lead in the exact opposite direction, *away* from the world, into what is indeed a form of nostalgia, a longing for what has been rather than what is, a preoccupation with what exists only *as image*, and *not* as reality. Such a view connects with a common tendency, within both European and American thought and culture, to treat memory and image as always somewhat removed from their objects, and thereby from the world, and so to view them as belonging to the life of the *subject* but not to the reality of *things*.

Yet the idea of the memory and the image as removed, or even abstracted, in this way is, arguably, itself somewhat removed from the actuality of human engagement in the world. The world in which we find ourselves is never presented other than as remembered and imagined. The world is given in and through the memory and the image, and the memory and the image are themselves part of the very fabric, the very substance, of the world—just as they are also constitutive of the fabric of a human life. It is, indeed, our memories, and the images that belong to them, that are the basic stuff of our identities as human beings, that inform our present and shape and direct our future. Without memory our lives are meaningless—are not lives at all—and we remain as mute and incapable as does Travis in the opening scenes of *Paris, Texas*, as he stumbles across the Texas desert landscape. The one thing Travis carries with him that provides him a sense of his own identity (as opposed to the merely nominal items of identity that enable those who find him to contact his brother), and by which he appears to define himself once he reenters the world of human discourse, is the image, the photograph, of a nondescript piece of land—"Paris, Texas. . . . That's where *I* began."[20]

The image and the memory to which it is related thus have the capacity to refer us back to ourselves, as well as back to the world, and to the things of the world. Yet the appearance of the image involves an inevitable doubling of that which is presented in the image with the image as such. The doubling that emerges here, the duplication that comes with the very appearance of the image, thus leads in two directions: back to that which is presented, and so back to the world, but also away from that which is presented, away from the world, and on toward a proliferation of images that is enabled by the image itself. One image leads on to many images, even when that multiplication is nothing more than the multiplication of the original image—duplicated by reflection, replication, reproduction. The proliferation of the image is, of course, assisted and promoted by the rise of a whole range of modern technologies, from the neon sign, the billboard, the newspaper, and magazine to film, television, video, and even inbuilt camera of the mobile phone. Moreover, just as the centrality of the image is a recurrent theme in Wenders's work, so too is the proliferation of the image—a proliferation that moves us away from the image as it refers us back to the world and on to the image as it connects with a multiplicity of other images. As Wenders puts it, it is a proliferation that takes us away from the "first hand" to a "second-hand" reality:

It's hard enough to experience anything at first hand anyway. Everywhere there are the pictures, the second-hand reality. And the pictures are proliferating with breathtaking speed. Nothing can stop them, no organization, no authority. . . . Images have distanced themselves more and more from reality, and have almost nothing to do with it now. Think back over the last ten or twenty years and the proliferation of images will make you quite dizzy.[21]

Film is itself, of course, one of the media that contributes to this proliferation, and Wenders's own movies often play with the image-proliferating effect of film. Thus Wenders frequently includes reproduced images within the scenes of his movies—advertising signs, cinematic projections, video or television pictures (for instance, in *Notebook on Cities and Clothes* Wenders places, within many of the shots, a small video screen playing images of the same or a similar scene); *Until the End of the World* (1991) takes the collection, duplication, and transmission of images, whether in relation to sight, memory, or dream (and the potentially dangerous consequences of such a project), as a central theme; Wenders's films also contain many direct references to film and the practices of film—*Kings of the Road* is an early example of this, and *Wings of Desire* and *The End of Violence* both use the device of a film within the film as an element within the structure of their narratives.

The idea that the reproduction of images by modern technologies is somehow problematic is not without precedent in modern aesthetic theory. Most famously, perhaps, it is a central theme in Walter Benjamin's "The Work of Art in the Age of Mechanical Reproduction," first published in German in 1936. Benjamin argues that modern techniques of reproduction, and the possibilities for the duplication of artworks that this allows, are destructive of the authentic presence of the artwork:

Even the most perfect reproduction of a work of art is lacking in one element: its presence in time and space, its unique existence at the place where it happens to be. . . . The situations into which the product of mechanical reproduction can be brought may not touch the actual work of art, yet the quality of its presence is always depreciated. This holds not only for the art work but also, for instance, for a landscape which passes in review before the spectator in a movie. . . .

One might subsume the eliminated element in the term "aura" and go on to say: that which withers in the age of mechanical reproduction is the aura of the work of art. . . . One might generalize by saying: the technique of reproduction detaches the reproduced object from the domain of tradition. By making many reproductions it substitutes a plurality of copies for a unique existence.[22]

The emphasis on the plurality of copies brought about by reproductive technique is important here, since it immediately connects with Wenders's emphasis on the proliferation of the image. It is also noteworthy that Benjamin takes as examples both the reproduction of the artwork and the representation of landscape in film—thus it seems that it is, indeed, the proliferation of the image that is at issue as much as it is the reproduction of the artwork in the image.

Film itself has a special role in Benjamin's account. The three tech-nologies that he specifically cites as playing key roles in the development of reproduction are lithography, photography, and film, and film he treats as the most powerful of these technologies. Moreover, Benjamin also devotes a significant portion of his discussion specifically to an examination of the structure of film, drawing a number of direct contrasts between film and painting:

Let us compare the screen on which a film unfolds with the canvas of a painting. The painting invites the spectator to contemplation; before it the spectator can abandon himself to his associations. Before the movie frame he cannot do so. No sooner has his eye grasped a scene than it is already changed. It cannot be arrested. Duhamel, who detests film and knows nothing of its significance, although something of its structure, notes this circumstance as follows: "I can no longer think what I want to think. My thoughts have been replaced by moving images."[23]

While there is much more to his argument (including a much more posi-tive appreciation of film and the image than may initially be apparent),[24] Benjamin seems to present film as placing us completely in the thrall of the image, compelled to move with it, and unable to contemplate what is presented to us or explore its own complex associations and intercon-nections—we are forced along in the train of images, along a path that is already determined for us and from which we cannot diverge. Thus while the painting makes available an open realm of possibilities, and thereby contains an essential indeterminacy, the film, so it would seem, carries a certain already determined direction, an already determined set of movements.

The problem to which reproduction appears to give rise, and which film may be taken to exemplify, is directly tied to the loss of the unique-ness of the object or work that is reproduced, and can be understood, in its simplest terms, therefore, as a threatened loss of identity. The repro-duction of the object involves a multiplication of the object that is also a reduction of the object to just that which is reproducible and repeat-able—to that which can be subject to, or graspable by, the techniques of reproduction. As a result, the object is severed from the space and time, the history, the place to which it originally belonged. Through reproduc-tion the original object is itself lost; indeed, the very distinction between object and reproduction ceases to matter, ceases even to be meaningful—there are, in a certain sense, only reproductions. In this way the reproduction ceases to refer us back to that which it reproduces, instead referring us onward to the multiplicity of reproductions of which it is a part. Thus Wenders can claim that amid the proliferation of images in the contemporary world, there is no longer any reality to which those images can be seen to relate, other, perhaps, than that of the constant play of images as such, no world other than the world of the image alone.

In *Until the End of the World* Wenders presents such a world of the image as itself having an intoxicating and addictive power. The characters of Sam and Clare are both infected by the "disease of images"[25] (elsewhere Wenders refers to the exposure to "the inflation of images" as "one of the worst diseases of our civilization"[26]), and in being so infected, in being so addicted, they cease to be able to function as human beings, withdrawing into a self-obsessive realm that is removed from the immediate place in which they remain situated—removed from the world in which they nevertheless remain embedded. This is the real danger of the proliferation of the image that is at stake here—a problem that goes beyond any loss of a sense of the authenticity of art alone. In the proliferation of the image, and the immersion in the realm of the image, we risk losing a sense of ourselves, of the world, and of the places within the world to which we never cease to belong, and of losing any sense of what these might be as properly distinct from the images of them or that may be generated in and through them. The proliferation of images generates a "virtual" world that is a part of the real world yet also, since it is a world specifically of *image*, not real. This virtual world is removed from the place of our ordinary embodied existence, yet it continues to depend on that embodied place—just as we continue to be anchored in the place of our immediate location—since the very possibility of the appearing of the image is dependent on the being located of the image and the one for whom the image appears as an image. Thus the image seems to take us away from where we are, yet the meaning of an image for us depends on our historical and cultural locatedness; its ability to move us depends on our affective orientation; its ability to be viewed depends on our being in a position for such viewing.

Talk of the "virtual" in relation to the image should be immediately suggestive, of course, of the apparent transformation of the world, and of our relation to it, through contemporary digital and virtual technologies. This transformation is often understood as having its most obvious effect in terms of a transformation of space and time, especially of space, and a related transformation in the human relation to place. It seems that in the world of the virtual, the digital, and the global place and places no longer matter, and instead every place becomes merely an interchangeable location within a homogeneous, flattened-out, space.[27] Within the contemporary film industry this reduction of place into mere "location" takes on a very real form as, under the influence of largely commercial imperatives, locations become nothing but the generic backdrops to increasingly formula-driven stories and action,[28] assuming prominence, if at all, only in terms of their commodified "touristic" or scenic value (as a *Sehenswürdigkeit*).

Yet if the proliferation of images does indeed present such a danger, and if, moreover, as Benjamin himself seems to suggest, film itself plays a role in this proliferation, then how can film offer any response to such proliferation that would not simply contribute, but would actually constitute a counter, to it? There seems no doubt that Wenders himself sees film as indeed having the potential to reestablish the reality of the image and in so doing to return us, by means of the image, to the world and the places within the world, to which we belong. To achieve this, even to attempt it, means standing that aspect of that duality of the image that leads back to that which is presented in the image, back to the world from which it comes, against the other aspect of the image that leads away from the world in the direction of the proliferation of images. It is to this former aspect, namely, that which leads back to what is presented, that Wenders can be taken as referring when he talks, as he does, of "the truth of images"[29] and when he also argues that film, in spite of the way it might also threaten the sense of reality and identity, may also have the power to enable its retrieval: "No other medium can treat the question of identity as searchingly or with as much justification as film. No other language is as capable of addressing itself to the physical reality of things. 'The possibility and the purpose of film is to show everything the way it is.' However exalted that sentence of Belá Balázs sounds, it's true."[30] The question remains, however, as to *how* film can do this—for clearly not all film is successful in attaining this end, and Wenders's own comments indicate that, even in his eyes, film also contributes, in fact, to an exactly opposite outcome.

In fact, Wenders is quite explicit about what he believes the solution here to be—a solution, moreover, that has already been implicit in much of the discussion so far. In *Until the End of the World* the character of Eugene (played by Sam Neill) tells us, in reference to the "disease of images" suffered by Clare (Solveig Dommartin), that "I didn't know the cure for the disease of images, but I believed in the magic and the healing power of words and of stories." Wenders himself comments that "Clare's sickness is a sickness of images, and she is healed by a much older and simpler art-form [than the art of film], by the art of storytelling,"[31] and he is also quite clear in acknowledging the role of story in his own filmmaking practice as an antidote to the loss of reality and identity that occurs through the proliferation or inflation of images (although it is something that he also acknowledges he had to learn). As Wenders puts it: "I found out that there was only one thing I was able to do to not let my images drown in the flood of all the others, and to not let them become the victims of the ongoing competitiveness and the overwhelming spirit of commercialization, and that was: *to tell a story.*"[32] The role of story and narrative has, in fact, stood in the background for a great deal of the discussion so far, without being explicitly taken up. For Wenders, however, the image and the story are closely connected. On the one hand, Wenders seems to treat certain images or kinds of images as themselves having a certain narrative possibility within them. Thus, referring to a novel by Emmanuel Bove and a book of reproductions of Hopper's paintings, Wenders writes that "these books remind me that the camera is capable of equally careful description, and that things can appear through it in a good light: the way they are. With these newly acquired images a new story can begin right away."[33] Yet he also says of the stories that appear in his films that "the stories . . . also work as a means of ordering the images," adding that "without stories, the images that interest me would threaten to lose themselves and seem purely arbitrary. For this reason, film stories are like routes."[34]

The idea that the story of a film may be like a "route" immediately picks up not only on the fact that so many of his movies have been, in one form or another, "road movies" but also on the role of place and places in his films—something evident not only in films such as *Kings of the Road* or *Wings of Desire* but throughout almost all of his works. Thus, when Wenders tells us, "My stories all begin from pictures," he goes on to say, as if it were the same thing, "My stories start with places, cities, landscapes and roads."[35] The stories that Wenders tells are the stories that are given in the images, in the pictures, but those images, those pictures, are themselves grounded in specific places, in particular spaces and times: "I could go on with the entire list of my films, proving to you that they all started like this: as a place *wanting* to be told, as a place *needing* to be told."[36] One might also say: as a place wanting, needing to be *shown*. The showing is, however, a showing that cannot occur other than in and through the *narrated* image; indeed, it is through its narrated character that the image is properly meaningful, that it carries the fullness and the opacity that makes it something other than a flattened-out "representation." In this respect the images of memory themselves have such fullness, and such opacity, precisely because of the narrational character that they also carry with them. The images of memory are like those Hopper paintings from which Wenders draws inspiration—they already carry stories within them, even though they are stories that still remain to be told (and so, too, are Hopper's paintings themselves like the images of memory).

Wenders's films attempt to slow down the production and proliferation of images through techniques that aim at allowing the object to appear in and through the image in a way that Benjamin argues is precisely what the mechanical reproduction of images destroys, namely, in terms of "its presence in time and space, its unique existence at the place it happens to be."[37] This means sometimes slowing down the movement of film, so that, contrary to Benjamin's description in which "no sooner has his eye grasped a scene than it is already changed," Wenders's films aim to retain the scene and the image within the succession of images so as to allow a certain presence to unfold before us. The way they do this is not merely through the use of certain shots or editing techniques (one such technique, as I noted above, is to allow the camera to linger over scenes, sometimes leaving a single scene to remain suspended in front of the camera in an almost meditative repose), but also through allowing the image to be retained in the succession of images through the *narration* of the image, through allowing the image to remain connected to the place, and to the world, by means of a narrative connection of images that always allows the possibility that more can emerge from the image. The image in Wenders's films is thus not flattened out into the merely reproducible but rather opens out into the uniqueness of the place, and of that which is present, in all the ambiguity of that presence, in the place.

If the role of memory in Wenders's films is, as he himself says, to provide that from which film starts, then the role of memory is only to be understood in terms of the intimate connection between memory and image and thence to identity, to story, to place, and to world. The role of memory in Wenders's films is not to take us away from the world into some form of narcissistic introspection, nor into any virtual world of multiplied and displaced images, but rather to return us to the places in which memory inheres, the places in and out of which identity is formed, the places in which the encounter with ourselves as well as others is possible. In this respect, too, Wenders's films can be seen as attempts to grapple with what is often seen as a characteristic feature of contemporary life: the apparent loss of a sense of identity, of a sense of reality, of a sense of place. Wenders's strategy has been to approach this problem not by rejecting the art and technology of film that seems to contribute to this loss and displacement but by making films that themselves open up to the world through the openness of the narrated image. In doing this, Wenders reminds us of the role of the image, as well as of memory, but he also draws attention to the importance of the stories that reside in places, of the life of places, and of the repose of human life in places.

Such a preoccupation with place, and the sense of place, is probably unsurprising for a German-born director who has spent so much of his life moving between the places of Europe and of America.[38] It is, however, a preoccupation that can be just as meaningful for those who remain "at home" as for those "on the road." It is also, perhaps, a preoccupation whose exploration is particularly well suited to the medium of film, since one way to think of film is as itself constituting a certain "memory" of place and of movement in place as recorded in light and sound; while all film, no matter whether "driven" by story or by place as such, depends crucially on place and location. Film always works *through* place (which is itself always more than any mere assemblage of landform or building, including, for instance, people and events), allowing the place to appear, no matter how imperfectly, and allowing us a certain entrance into that place. It is thus that film has the capacity to bring to light, and sometimes to rearticulate, our connection with place, with the world, and with ourselves.

10

Claire Denis
Icon of Ferocity

JEAN-LUC NANCY

Trouble Every Day

THE MAUVE IMPRINT of a bite mark on the young wife's shoulder: the outline of a mouth, a double arc, a teeth-mark, jaws open, lips retracted over hard enamel. Not the barely parted lips of the kiss on skin, but lips wide as when mouths kiss, only this time opened onto skin, and penetrating it: the kiss itself curled back, snarling, intensified, taken to its limits or beyond. A cruel kiss: a fleshly kiss (*cruor*: bleeding flesh). A young couple cuddles in an airplane: beginning of the film. Later we see this icon, without knowing when it was imprinted, similar to a tattoo or a brand made with the red-hot iron of ancient law.

What, therefore, is a kiss? Such is the question of Claire Denis's film. Or rather: what, therefore, is it to kiss? If it is to devour, that is one way of saying and thinking the kiss, which has long been accepted and reworked. It is an imaginative and metaphorical knot where folktales (Red Riding Hood, ogres), the fascination of cannibalism, the symbolism of Christian Communion and of the orgies of carnage of Dionysus, Osiris, and Actaeon, and furthermore ghouls, striges, vampires, werewolves, succubi, and incubi intertwine. This whole brood with a passion for flesh-eating lurks throughout the film. They are perfectly recalled, invoked, in a gesture made by Coré, the sick woman (if it need be put that way), standing on an embankment, shot from below and lifting up the shoulders of her coat to project for an instant the silhouette of Murnau's *Nosferatu*.

The expression that truly sums up the vampire is only made clear in the phrase "the kiss of the vampire." This is what is in question here, answering for a turnaround that is the result of our no longer living in an age of vampire stories: the kiss as vampire.

What is under consideration here is not any particular kiss. Rather, it is that the kiss, in essence, opens onto the bite and the taste for blood. And what is therefore also being considered is another well-known coupling, namely that, as they say, of Eros and Thanatos: not as a dialectic of opposites but as a mutual excitation and exasperation, each demanding the other to go further, to go to the very end, to lose itself absolutely.

.   .   .

What is under consideration is the kiss's relationship to sex: or more precisely that fucking, or "sex" if you prefer, is here part of the kiss, rather than the other way around.[1] Sex becomes a metonomy of the kiss [du baiser]: the latter being broader, more encompassing and more profound than sex. It must be understood that, here, the bite of the kiss devours the sexes (their organs), not in a castration but in an absorption that opens onto a sort of horrible sublimation: not that of a sex where a body comes to orgasm but that of an entire body where the sex bursts open and drenches itself with all the body's blood, with its life / its death and with what properly explodes it: which exposes it as composed of fragments, drops, streams and smears, clots and tatters that can never be restored to one form. The unbearable tearing of orgasm. It could be said that the whole story of the film is the allegory of this and that all the images of the film are its literality.

What is under consideration is the kiss that bites, but not as a kiss different from others: the kiss inasmuch as it bites, the kiss as the power of biting and of death, as a bringing-to-life / putting-to-death of the raw. This is why the young newlywed wife, the one who remains intact and from whom the terrible force turns bitterly, desperately away (without our being able to know what happens after the end of the film, back home), nonetheless carries the sign marking the passage from kiss to devourment, the bite mark, skin bitten to the point of bleeding, the icon of ferocity.

Intact, unpenetrated and unenjoyed, she is the virgin with the blood-flower on the skin (on it or under it? everything happens here via the skin), the blood à fleur de peau, just under the surface of the skin, or the skin blossoming with an imprint that at once signals both the passion and the self-restraint of the husband, who is inflamed by the kiss but also terrified at recognizing himself ready to ravage her ferociously. She remains intact, undecidably intact, on the edge of a return home that could either stop everything or make everything worse, although at the moment of departure she is wearing a pair of red and black leather gloves: a second, more striking flower, a second skin of blood that at the same time protects and exposes her for what she is, she as much as the others, that is, a body of blood (a living body is a body of blood: it doesn't have blood as one of its contents—it is its blood; it lives in it).

.   .   .

The kiss wants blood. The conventional image of the kiss is that of a mere skin-to-skin contact, lip touching lip, brushing not broaching the skin, and, when mouths are involved more intimately, exchanging not blood but breaths and salivas. Such is the image of the kiss or the kiss-image at the beginning of the film, as if quoting this cinematic imagery: the airplane, the honeymoon, the kiss, the languid or suave eroticism of a long-haul jetliner cabin at night. All the same, this quotation maintains a distance: the night outside takes the plane into the high-altitude cold and the din of jet engines; there is a sense of threat from somewhere. The question has already been slipped in silently: what, therefore, is this kiss? What does it want?

The film answers later with the bite mark, the icon of flesh on flesh. It answers that the kiss is the beginning of ferocity. Not for nothing does the kiss place its lips on the skin. The kiss does not just touch, or rather it takes touching to its very limits: when touching becomes burrowing, becomes touching underneath the skin, tearing out from it what it covers, what it protects and what it advertises, what it signals as the cover and the flood that it envelops.

The kiss of breaths mingles souls. The biting of blood explodes the soul: blood, life, spirit, desire, irrigation that brims over into the frantic irritation, the impossibility of putting an end to it, of going to the limit of the soul without completely losing oneself, scattered, gorged on this same blood. From start to finish everything is concerned with this soul, that is, with the form or concept of a body, but using this astounding enigma of a body that takes the form of its own explosion. Here the soul is the means of access to the act of devourment, and the act of devourment is the means of access to the soul: to the impalpable nature of the body, to its pervasive existence and to pure passion such as pure rage and pure devastation. A martyr of pleasure (*marturos* means witness).

.   .   .

This very access cannot but lead to ferocity, to the exasperation of broaching the skin. Touching desires to invade and is worn out by it; that's the truth of the matter. This truth is a singular monster, like all truths: it is at once true of the most tender kiss, as well as of the most horrendous slaughter; it is tenderness and cruelty combined in a fearsome chimera, exchanging their roles, almost like tender flesh (fresh raw meat) and the splendor of blood (*cruor*, blood spurting forth, versus *sanguis*, blood flowing in the organs).

Making holes in the skin, making skin: it is a film made entirely "on" skin. Literally: *pellicule expeausée.*[2] (*Pellicula*, little skin.) Not only does the skin come to the image in intense close-up, seen piecemeal or as great expanses, with different textures, moles and body hair, hollows and projections, navel, nipples, pubis, a body already dismembered by the image, carved up, broken into zones, a nape, a cheek, a stomach, but this skin is also everywhere in an image that comes out of a camera ferociously intent on laying hold of this fragile means of access to unrestricted power. It is also the image itself, the film, its skin, which caresses and kisses and rends its luminous chemistry in red and black, to the point where, when Coré, in a passion of ferocity, sets fire to the house, what we are presented with is the blazing not of any film set but of the film stock itself. Ferocity comes to the soul and to the image at the same time, to the substance of vision: to seeing as to living flesh, like flesh reanimated. Blood-filled eyes, eyes bloodshot and plunged into a place where nothing can be seen but unbearable and invisible excess, where cries and moans disgorge saturated color, the screen as a sponge.

(Of course all this abounds with artistry and technical mastery. But this is no ordinary trickery of the sort that permits the filming of a murder without one's actually committing it. It is instead the art of filming what is not a murder but the equivalent of the death at the heart of desire. This announces: I portray nothing; I am not what is called a "horror movie," which deals with representations, with images of violence that remain in the imaginary; rather I render visible that which is not able to be portrayed, what is not imaginary and belongs only to the deep structure, to the reality of the kiss, exasperation, exaltation, the welling-up and the expiring of orgasm—whose name signifies anger.)

·   ·   ·

The emblem of skin, of this taut, broken-open access to the bleeding soul, is the truck that the driver pulls up for what he thinks is a good score. Enormous and red, massive, powerful, filmed from behind as it reverses toward the girl, its hazard lights flashing like signals of desire, with its tightly stretched tarpaulin, the rear door advancing into our view, which it penetrates with its great size, forcing the camera to slide along its side, as the man gets down from his cab and approaches, trembling with desire, surprised, eager but vaguely uncertain, already delivered up, prey in the hands of what we do not yet know but which is already vaguely indicated by the reverse shot of the girl whose pout we are aware is not a gourmand's but a glutton's, and whose mouth waits to plump into blood-licking lips, intoxicating themselves in what they suck, the jaws of a ghoul that would grind the whole truck just to make its metallic paintwork spurt.

As it happens, the girl will do some painting later on in the film. On the wall of her room where she massacres the young man who comes searching for her—and who perhaps was in search of just that—we see painted improbable curves, like arches or vaults, like a gestural painting or some expressive abstract, a triple arcature repeatedly recalling the arc of the icon on the wife's shoulder, the bloody smearings transformed into a design both for a painting and a temple at the same time, like the plans for the nave of a shrine, a demoniacal iconostasis.

It is, therefore, a question of a ritual, just as the kiss is a ritual, and just as fucking, perhaps, is also a ritual. Giving a kiss, receiving it, making love—these are not merely acts; these are signs, propitiations, promises and prayers. These are acts at once endowed with a specific characteristic meaning, as well as that special signification that is unique to the act's execution, to its "performance." Sex is only a means to pleasure insofar as this pleasure brings about something very much unlike pleasure: a mystery, an order of the world.

Ritual in this sense is every act of art, and it is one of its measures. There is no art without ritual. Ritual is what is performed under its own pressure, even its own oppression. It is here that everything either becomes confounded or clear: at the point where the performance of the act is worth infinitely more than the act itself. Here the symbolic and the real intersect, but they also collide.

This singular collision, which is effectively that made by love, is what might be called the imaginary. Not in the vulgar sense of invented unreality but in the sense of the image made present. In the sense of the image presenting what it is.

. . .

Hence skin. The film films nothing but this. Tenderly, broodingly, attentively, relentlessly it makes images from skin: it does not merely show skin; it insinuates it into the overall image; it subtly confounds screen with skin; it *films* skin as if to film were to *spool*, to *filter*, or to *freeze*. It therefore also speaks of a bitten screen, a penetrated (*crevé*) screen. "To leap out from the screen" (*crever l'écran*), an old expression for conveying the exceptional quality of an actor's presence, a presence that transcends the flat image, tearing the screen as much forward (toward us) as backward, toward a background all the more deeply recessed because it is found nowhere else but in the image, even perhaps on the surface and skin of the image. Here the screen tears open in a wound running with blood. The image becomes an image of the image in tatters: no longer an image, no longer a figure, but the icon of an access to the unseen. The unseen, *sanguis*, the body's nutritive blood, life itself, its pulsing beneath the skin. Once the skin has been bitten *to the point of blood*, as one might say (both in the sense of "to a point of depth where there is blood" and "to the point of drawing blood"), the blood becomes *cruor*, blood spilt, a stream that no longer irrigates but spurts out like one or other of the sexual fluids, male or female come. Spilt blood of cruel sacrifice, an exposing to the world of raw life that is no longer there to support living but to permit access to more than life in a splash of blood, of sense, of presence.

Blood spilt, gushing, welling to the surface in the icon, brings to view what ought not to be seen except in the transparence of the skin overlying the blood vessels. It is the sight above all others that cannot be borne. "I do not want to see the blood," announces Lorca in his elegy for a matador killed in the bullring. Tauromachy, *erotomachia*, sacrifice, and sacred obliviousness. Suddenly a film is plunged, without any other pretext, into that perpetual story in film: the cinematic taste for blood, by which, doubtless, it also makes reference to painting and all its Christs and martyrs. Autoanalysis of the cinema as a locus both sacrificial and tragic (the one giving rise to the other), which generates the question: what comes after sacrifice, after tragedy, and after martyrdom? What follows when blood spilt no longer appears as crime and folly, while still spilling silently its blood's secret? Silently: the film is almost mute; when there is dialogue, it is often in English, and above all nothing is spoken of blood. But music has nothing to do with crime and folly: it follows the image in procession; it celebrates something.

.   .   .

The image itself bursts forth. It is not the image of a bursting of light; it makes of itself a bursting of light. It is physically, visually in the process of crashing onto, of breaking up on, the screen. There is no longer any screen; seeing and making seen are exhausted, saturated in one another and exalted. Doubtless, this process is frenzied, but its exaltation fades away in its own obscurity. There is no resolution, no ecstasy, no appeasement: only a loss of direction. There is crisis and reprise of the shriveling. This goes on relentlessly. *Trouble Every Day.*

Ferocity clings to flesh and burrows into it. It gets drunk on bleeding flesh, which it devours not to nourish but to spatter itself, to inundate itself, to anoint itself with it, to become in its own turn sticky liquid from underneath bitten skin spurted onto the skin of she who bites. From the skin of the dead man to the skin of the bite. To cover oneself on the outside with the warm and raw inside that the skin announces and envelops. This inside is the secret, the sealing of life within death by the fragility of skin, the sealing of the body within a cry, of sense within the blood. Ferocity wants this secret, which is nothing other, and contains nothing other, than the tearing apart of living integrity. This tearing apart is death, but it is also desire: it is a troubling, difficult approaching of the two. Ferocity is desire that wants to chew and suck the source of desire itself: not "pleasure" but fever and fury to the point of a death rattle, to the point of stupor.

Desire is this or it is nothing, exacerbated exasperation. The film constructs the exact allegory of this, which revolves around an axis of ambivalence. The ferocious truth of desire splits there into the symbolism of vampiric eroticism and the savagery of a rape that bites off the sex organs. It splits into mythology and malady (and, to take things further, perhaps also into the malady of mythology, and the mythology of malady). Into the mad woman who ends in flames and the obsessed man who never achieves any end. A woman and a man. A hyperbole and a monstrosity clinging to one another: the film dares to slip itself between them.

Between the two of them, their ambivalence figured in opposites:

the sorcerer and the innocent maiden. The manipulator of strange cultures and the young woman who stays on the edge of remaining a woman. Black male and white female. He in his helmet that reflects the lights of destiny, she in her shawl like a nun.

There is the grand allegory of insane fleshly desire and the suspicious fable of the sick brain—another piece of flesh that is raw, albeit drained of blood, cut into neat slices across its folds and fractal convolutions, with a strange brown color supposedly the result of some fixative agent. A brain like several slices of flan or even the repository of neuronal illnesses, perhaps genetic: this modern form of knowledge coupled with the reference to *Nosferatu* is a way of signaling the unknown, which grows in proportion to what becomes known.

Even less understood, if such a thing were possible, would be what the two boys were expecting to find in their neighbor's house and what the young chambermaid was expecting, too. Theirs are the skins offered up in sacrifice, the exposed skins (*peaux expeausées*): pelts and prey. Prey to ferocity, to desire and devourment, the one indistinguishable from the other, yet distinct, even opposites of each other given Shane's killing of Coré. He is trying to deliver himself from himself as from this ferocious otherness he contains within.

But there is no deliverance; all is sealed—the jetliner cabin at night, the boarded-up room, the battened shutters, sealed laboratory flasks, corridors and basements, glasshouse, laboratory, helmet, truck. One cannot escape, and everything begins over again—*Trouble Every Day*. This is not a sentencing; this is the ferocious obstinacy of an interrogation.

What hounds this ferocity is the truth of a body insofar as this body is only made from what is beyond its boundaries or rather is quite different from the ensemble of its organs and constituent parts, just as it is also quite different from its more or less pleasing form. The truth of a body is made apparent by its dismemberment, by its being torn limb from limb, by the welling up of blood from the skin: the skin, instead of being an envelope, becomes a surface to be opened up. The body wrenched apart offers up what there is of its interiority, of its depth and the secret of its life. Unity gives itself up to be broken down, letting out the infinitely fragile secret that the soul and the breath, desire, the passion of the unique and of the infinite are one and the same and have the same taste as the body that has been wrenched apart, the *membra disjecta* and their disjection itself exposed raw. In every sense, then, does the body experience the blowing of the soul: it is its breath, but it also blows the body out like a candle and likewise blows it apart.

Death and the kiss that bites appear to have in common the ability to arrive at the impossible place occupied by disjection, which is the conjunction—of a soul and a body or several bodies together, as a place of endless dividing up yet sharing. A body never stops developing and decomposing, being born and dying, configuring itself in the construction of an identity before reductively multiplying itself into zones of desire, pleasure, and pain, into pieces and fragments of pleasure, because orgasm is nothing else but the experience of explosion. Orgasm causes the explosion of its own image (the image of what is fitting and proper and the orgasm's own image).

Explosion: that which at once opens and closes to view. This film is an explosion. It takes the risk of going to the other side of film, of closing off to view while opening it up under the bite. The bite is the bite of the kiss, of love—one speaks of the bite of cold, of acid, or of flame. That which piercingly *rends*, as one used to say, which drives into the living flesh, in spasmodic repeated thrusting. The sort of love by which one is bitten (this is how ordinary language puts it). Not anatomical dissection, but the puncturing and plundering of living flesh toward something else besides death (though it may resemble this): toward a heartrending irradiation *rending* the heart of a tremor, *rending* the heart of a spasm that halts the blood and spills it. This, this thing or this beast, this tearing that transfixes, love, the transfixion or the transfusion of what—or who—could believe itself simply close by, the rupture of the specular and of the like image: the image in a blinding gush of blood.

Translated by Peter Enright

Reference Matter

Notes

Introduction

1. G.W.F. Hegel, *Philosophy of Right*, trans. T. M. Knox (Oxford: Clarendon, 1952), p. 12.

2. Siegfried Kracauer, *Nature of Film: The Redemption of Physical Reality* (London: Dobson, 1961), p. 301.

3. In the mid-1950s, while looking at documentary footage of a firing squad from the time of the Russian Revolution, Robert Warshow expresses an outrage that springs from what the camera shows but carries over into what the camera can be made to show and to represent. See Robert Warshow, "Re-Viewing the Russian Movies," in *The Immediate Experience* (New York: Atheneum, 1972), p. 280: "One need only think of what one of the great Russian directors might have done with a scene like this in order to appreciate how utterly vulgar art and belief can be, sometimes, when measured against the purity of a real event. There are innumerable examples of such vulgarity in the Russian cinema, moments when the director, taken up with his role as an artist who controls and interprets—few artists have put a higher value on that role than the early Soviet film directors—forgets what is really at stake and commits an offense against humanity." The traditional ethical imperative to break the spell of the way things are ("Do something!") is here rewritten for cinema so that what is required is instead to let things be.

4. Walter Benjamin, "The Work of Art in the Age of Mechanical Reproduction," in *Illuminations*, trans. Harry Zohn (London: Jonathan Cape, 1970), pp. 243–44.

5. Stanley Cavell, *The World Viewed: Reflections on the Ontology of Film* (Cambridge, MA: Harvard University Press, 1979), p. 214.

6. André Bazin, *What Is Cinema?* trans. Hugh Gray, vol. 1 (Berkeley: University of California Press, 1971), p. 99.

Chapter 1

1. Thanks to Benigno Trigo and Lisa Walsh for helpful conversations on these films.

2. This is according to the screenwriter, Joseph Stefano. See *The Making of "Psycho,"* dir. Laurent Bouzereau (Universal, 1997).

3. Ibid. Stefano says that Hitchcock used his television crew and insisted on a low-budget production to show what a "master" could do, since others had had box-office success with such pictures.

4. Jonathan Lake Crane, *Terror and Everyday Life: Singular Moments in the History of the Horror Film* (London: Sage, 1994), 10.

5. See Bouzereau, *The Making of Psycho*.

6. See Tom Cohen's remarks on Hitchcock's "zootropology," in *Hitchcock's Cryptonymies*, vol. 1, *Secret Agents* (Minneapolis: University of Minnesota Press, 2005), p. 64.

7. Michele Piso, "Mark's Marnie," in *A Hitchcock Reader*, ed. Marshall Deutelbaum and Leland Poaque (Ames: Iowa State University Press, 1986), p. 292.

8. Tania Modleski, *The Women Who Knew Too Much: Hitchcock and Feminist Theory* (New York: Routledge, 1988), p. 111.

9. Barbara Creed, *The Monstrous-Feminine: Film, Feminism, Psychoanalysis* (New York: Routledge, 1993), p. 142.

10. Raymond Bellour, *The Analysis of Film*, ed. Constance Penley (Bloomington: Indiana University Press, 2000), p. 246.

11. See ibid., p. 254.

12. Modleski, *The Women Who Knew Too Much*, pp. 102, 107.

13. Ibid., pp. 108–9; see also Julia Kristeva, *Powers of Horror: An Essay on Abjection*, trans. Leon Roudiez (New York: Columbia University Press, 1980), p. 3.

14. Modleski, *The Women Who Knew Too Much*, pp. 107–9; see also Kristeva, *Powers of Horror*.

15. See, e.g., Modleski, *The Women Who Knew Too Much*; E. Ann Kaplan, *Women and Film: Both Sides of the Camera* (New York: Routledge, 1990); and Creed, *The Monstrous-Feminine*.

16. Kristeva, *Powers of Horror*, pp. 12–13.

17. In *Hitchcock's Cryptonymies* Tom Cohen remarks on what he calls the "Mar-inflected" names in Hitchcock's films: *"mer," "mère,"* and *"merde"* or "sea," "mother," and "shit" (1:97).

18. In Bouzereau's documentary on the making of *Psycho*, Janet Leigh says that what attracted her to the film was that at first it seemed like a film about a woman choosing between two men, Sam and Norman; and the suspense revolves around which one she would choose.

19. Jacqueline Rose, "Paranoia and the Film System," *Screen* 17, no. 4 (1976–77): 97.

20. Sidney Gottlieb, ed., *Alfred Hitchcock: Interviews* (Jackson: University Press of Mississippi, 2003), p. 50.

21. Tom Cohen discusses Hitchcock's images of various sorts of bombs, particularly time bombs, which Cohen associates with Hitchcock's style itself. See Cohen, *Hitchcock's Cryptonymies*, vol. 1; and Tom Cohen, *Hitchcock's Cryptonymies*, vol. 2, *War Machines* (Minneapolis: University of Minnesota Press, 2005).

22. Gottlieb, *Alfred Hitchcock: Interviews*, p. 57.

23. Ibid., p. 102.

24. Ibid., p. 61.

25. Modleski, *The Women Who Knew Too Much*, pp. 101–14.

26. E. Ann Kaplan, *Motherhood and Representation: The Mother in Popular Culture and Melodrama* (New York: Routledge, 1992), p. 121.

27. See, e.g., Piso, "Mark's Marnie"; Robert Kapsis, "The Historical Reception of Hitchcock's *Marnie*," *Journal of Film and Video* 40, no. 3 (summer 1988): 46–63; Kaplan, *Motherhood and Representation*; Mary Lucretia Knapp, "The Queer Voice in *Marnie*," *Cinema Journal* 32 (1993): 6–23.

28. Robin Wood, *Hitchcock's Films* (South Brunswick, NJ: A. S. Barnes, 1977), p. 135.

29. For a discussion of Scottie (James Stewart) in *Vertigo* as investigating female sexuality, see Modleski, *The Women Who Knew Too Much*; and Kelly Oliver and Benigno Trigo, *Noir Anxiety* (Minneapolis: University of Minnesota Press, 2002). Even Mitch, the lawyer in *The Birds*, interrogates Melanie about her sexual desires, especially why she came up to Bodega Bay—insisting it was to see him—and what she was doing nude in a fountain in Rome.

30. Bellour, *The Analysis of Film*, pp. 28–68, 217–37, 238–61.

31. Knapp, "The Queer Voice in *Marnie*," pp. 13–14.

Chapter 2

1. This essay first appeared in German under the title "'Dieser verrueckte Visconti' oder Einsichten in Fleisch und Blut," in *Zwischen Ding und Zeichen*, ed. C. Voss and G. Koch (Paderborn: Wilhelm Fink, 2005), pp. 38–49.

2. Theodor W. Adorno, *Negative Dialectics*, trans. E. B. Ashton (London: Routledge and Kegan Paul, 1973), p. 57.

3. Hans-Erich Nossack, *Die Tagebücher, 1943–1977*, vol. 1 (Frankfurt am Main: Suhrkamp, 1997), p. 445.

4. "But the voice, my dearest, / does not answer to my thought."

5. Everything, oh everything in this moment
speaks to me of the fire that you feel:
I read it in your glances,
in your soft tenderness.

6. G.W.F. Hegel, *Aesthetics*, trans. T. M. Knox (Oxford: Clarendon, 1975), p. 153.

7. Stanley Cavell, *The World Viewed* (Cambridge, MA: Harvard University Press, 1979), p. xiii.

8. Ibid., p. 31.

9. Ibid., p. 149.

10. See Alexander García Düttmann, "Separated from Proust," *Angelaki: Journal of the Theoretical Humanities* 9, no. 3 (Dec. 2004): 89–90.

11. Gilles Deleuze, *Cinema 2: The Time-Image*, trans. Hugh Tomlinson and Robert Galeta (Minneapolis: University of Minnesota Press, 1991), p. 94.

12. Cavell, *The World Viewed*, p. 177.

13. Rinaldo Ricci, quoted in "Crocache dal set," in Leonardo de Franceschi, *Il film "Lo straniero" di L. Visconti: Dalla pagina allo schermo* (Venice: Marsilio, 1999), pp. 148–49: "As usual, Visconti's work was meticulous with regards to scouting locations, casting minor roles such as the man with the dog, casting all those roles connected with the machinery of the court and which were filled only after an extended and exhausting search in Algiers."

14. Luchino Visconti, *"Lo straniero,"* *L'Europeo*, Feb. 16, 1967; repr. in De Franceschi, *Il film "Lo straniero" di L. Visconti*, p. 131.

15. Rosa Luxemburg, "Possibilismus oder Opportunismus," in *Sächsische Arbeiter-zeitung*, Sep. 30, 1898.

16. Luchino Visconti, "Vent'anni di teatro," in Lino Miccichè, *Luchino Visconti: Un profilo critico* (Venice: Marsilio, 1996), p. 117.

17. Luchino Visconti, "Tradizione ed invenzione," in Lino Miccichè, *Luchino Visconti: Un profilo critico* (Venice: Marsilio, 1996), p. 97.

18. Gaia Servadio, *Luchino Visconti: A Biography* (New York: Franklin Watts, 1983), p. 188.

19. Deleuze, *Cinema 2*, p. 4. In the 1930s Visconti translated into Italian the novel *Adrienne Mesurat*. Every now and then he wanted to make it into the subject of a film. Its author, Julien Green, has recourse to a "visionary gaze."

20. Deleuze, *Cinema 2*, p. 20.

21. Youssef Ishaghpour, *Visconti: Le sens et l'image* (Paris: Editions de La Différence, 1984), p. 93. Suzanne Liandrat-Guiges endeavors to demonstrate that the "amassing" of things and quotations undertaken by Visconti gives rise to an "animated sculpture." "Hermeneutic activity" is unable to transform this sculpture into a recognizable, uniform figure. See Suzanne Liandrat-Guiges, "Aria di tomba," in *Visconti a Volterra: La genesi di Vaghe stelle dell'Orsa*, ed. Veronica Pravadelli (Turin: Lindau, 2000), p. 37.

22. Cf. Federica Mazzochi, *"La locandiera" di Goldoni per Luchino Visconti* (Pisa: Edizioni ETS, 2003), esp. pp. 21–23. Mazzochi underlines the "visionary" aspect as well, when she writes that there is always an image that appears and imposes itself, forming in its distinctness the starting point for Visconti's labors (p. 19).

23. Roland Barthes, "La locandiera," in *Ecrits sur le théâtre*, ed. Jean-Loup Rivière (Paris: Seuil, 2002), p. 198.

24. Luchino Visconti, "Cinema antropomorfico," in Lino Miccichè, *Luchino Visconti: Un profilo critico* (Venice: Marsilio, 1996), p. 101.

25. Marc Recha, "Mi escena: Un día fantástico," *El Cultural*, Nov. 20, 2003.

26. Servadio, *Luchino Visconti*, p. 181.

Chapter 3

1. The preeminent status of the aesthetic technique could be put in terms of the historical account of the declining significance of the arts in the era of their aesthetic autonomy that Hegel gives in his lectures on aesthetics, but this would miss some of the peculiarities of cinema given that its status as an art emerges after its origins in folk art and that it does arguably claim the status of a public need that Hegel describes as lost to

art in the modern era of art's autonomy. For a discussion of the folk art origins of cinema, see Erwin Panofsky, "Style and Medium in the Motion Pictures," in *Three Essays on Style*, ed. Irving Levin (Cambridge, MA: MIT Press, 1995), pp. 91–129. For Hegel's account of the declining relation of art to the purpose of the presentation of the absolute and the emerging significance of technique as the context for the self-reflection of autonomous art, see G.W.F. Hegel, *Aesthetics: Lectures on Fine Art*, trans. T. M. Knox, vol. 1 (Oxford: Clarendon Press, 1998), p. 80.

In "Style and Medium in the Motion Pictures" Panofsky argues that the unique feature of film is that it starts with the "objects that constitute the physical world" (p. 122). Whereas other representational arts impose an idea on shapeless matter, Panofsky writes, cinema cannot "prestylize reality." Its challenge is to exercise technique in such a way that "the result has style." The earlier representational arts conform "to an idealistic conception of the world. . . . They start with an idea to be projected into shapeless matter and not with the objects that constitute the physical world." In contrast, in the movies "justice" is done "to the materialistic interpretation of the universe which . . . pervades contemporary civilization" (p. 122). Panofsky's view that film aims to stylize elements of the material world is interesting to consider from the perspective of Antonioni's cinema. On the one hand, it is difficult to claim that Antonioni's films refrain in any absolute way from the prestylization of reality (with the additions of color, say, in *Il deserto rosso* and *Blow-Up*, or, in an even more minimal sense, the use of settings that conform to prestylization, such as the use of Gaudí's Casa Mila apartments in *The Passenger*). But in the sense that Panofsky uses this category to differentiate film from theater, there is a qualitative difference between these aesthetic devices and the sin of "prestylization." It is amusing, however, that Antonioni glosses Carlo Ponti's [his producer's] eventual rejection of a project to be set in the jungle as motivated by the fear that Antonioni would either "never leave the jungle or that [he] . . . would start painting it." See Antonioni's comments on such prestylization in Michelangelo Antonioni, *The Architecture of Vision: Writings and Interviews on Cinema*, ed. Carlo di Carlo and Giorgio Tinazzi, American edition by Marga Cottino-Jones (New York: Marsilio, 1996), p. 46; his discussion of Ponti and the jungle is on p. 169.

2. In this sense the debates over Antonioni's relation with neorealism and the citation of his early film *Il grido* miss the crucial point about the emphasis in his films on the exploration of cinematic elements. Bazin emphasizes the formal aesthetic criteria of neorealism over its social content. See André Bazin, *What Is Cinema?* trans. Hugh Gray, vol. 2 (Berkeley: University of California Press, 2005), pp. 16–40. See also Deleuze's critique of Bazin. Deleuze describes not a tension between form and content in relation to the treatment or depiction of "the real" but a problem "at the level of the 'mental,' in terms of thought" (Gilles Deleuze, *Cinema 2: The Time-Image*, trans. Hugh Tomlinson and Robert Galeta [Minneapolis: University of Minnesota Press, 2003], p. 1). See Deleuze's further development of this point in ibid., pp. 5–6. I discuss Deleuze's approach in note 3.

3. It is worth noting some features of Deleuze's approach to cinema and the perspective this approach opens for the treatment of Antonioni's films: Deleuze describes postwar cinema as bringing into form a different type of image: a pure optical-sound image. From

this development results not a confusion between the subjective and the objective and the imaginary and the real but the presentation of their fundamental indiscernibility. Cinema's "powers of the false," which Deleuze praises, emerge from the "camera-consciousness" that documents "any place whatevers" instead of the "sensory-motor 'motivating' situations" of characters. The characters in postwar cinema are now "found . . . in a state of strolling, of sauntering or of rambling which defined pure optical and sound situations. The action-image then tended to shatter, whilst the determinate locations were blurred, letting any-spaces-whatever rise up where the modern affects of fear, detachment, but also freshness, extreme speed and interminable waiting were developing" (Gilles Deleuze, *Cinema 1: The Movement-Image*, trans. Hugh Tomlinson and Barbara Habberjam [Minneapolis: University of Minnesota Press, 1989], pp. 120–21). It is the loosening of the sensorimotor linkage in postwar cinema that allows time to rise "up to the surface of the screen" and the presentation of time in its pure state also means that time no longer derives from movement but "gives rise to false movements. Hence the importance of false continuity in modern cinema: the images are no longer linked by rational cuts and continuity but are relinked by means of false continuity and irrational cuts. Even the body is no longer exactly what moves; subject of movement or the instrument of action, it becomes rather the developer [*révélateur*] of time, it shows time through its tirednesses and waitings (Antonioni)" (Gilles Deleuze, "Preface to the English Edition," in *Cinema 2*, p. xi). I think it is important to put Deleuze's account of postwar cinema, and specifically his thesis regarding the new ways time is shown in the medium of film, in the context of his broader interest in philosophical and scientific reversals of the subordination of time by movement. This broader interest is visible in the cinema books in the importance given to Henri Bergson.

Panofsky is less accommodating to experimentation in film than Deleuze because he attaches to the status of film as a mass medium the virtue of communicable meaning, and thus effectivity, virtues that he opposes to avant-garde cinema (Panofsky, *Three Essays on Style*, p. 120).

4. By "sensible" here I mean accessible to experience.

5. Peter Brunette describes the narrative of this film as "reticent," as if Antonioni were deliberately coy in the information he gives his audience. See Peter Brunette, *The Films of Michelangelo Antonioni* (Cambridge, UK: Cambridge University Press, 1998), p. 176, nn. 7–8.

6. These scenes include further context for the difficulties in Locke's marriage and a dispute in his relation with the girl. I discuss them further in note 17.

7. Musical tracks are used in two places in the film: once when Locke is driving through a tree-lined grove, and the girl sits facing the back of the car; and a second time for the concluding credits. Other music in the film is indigenous to scenes, such as the piped music coming from outside the hotel after Locke discovers Robertson's body. Although the music in the final scene for the concluding credits is that of a guitar player in the hotel, its prominence over all other auditory traces distinguishes it from the other localized examples of music. Antonioni described the genre of the suspense thriller as "banal" and "not what interested [him]" in *The Passenger* (see Antonioni, *The Architecture of Vision*, p. 346).

8. This is not to say that these codes do not appear in this film. The relationship between Rachel Locke and her lover has some of the signal features of "sick Eros," such as the violent drive for possession, but this feature occupies only one scene in the film; and at least in the studio version Locke's own relation with the girl is free of the malignancy of this disease, and their sexual relationship is implied, not shown by Antonioni. The treatment of the theme of "sick Eros" leads Deleuze to describe Antonioni as a great Nietzschean symptomatologist (see Deleuze, *Cinema 2*, p. 8).

9. The term is from Marc Augé, *An Anthropology for Contemporaneous Worlds*, trans. Amy Jacobs (Stanford, CA: Stanford University Press, 1999).

10. In his "Age of the World Picture" Heidegger uses the phrase "moral aesthetic anthropology" to emphasize the way that the moral attitude depends on an aesthetic form: "Humanism, therefore, in the more strict historiographical sense, is nothing but a moral-aesthetic anthropology" ("The Age of the World Picture," in *The Question Concerning Technology and Other Essays*, trans. W. Lovitt [New York: Harper and Row, 1977], p. 133). For Heidegger's critique of "values" see his lectures on Nietzsche, esp. *Nietzsche*, vol. 1, *The Will to Power as Art*; and *Nietzsche*, vol. 2, *The Eternal Recurrence of the Same*, both vols. trans. David Farrell Krell (San Francisco: Harper and Row, 1979).

11. Reprinted in *L'avventura*, ed. Seymour Chatman and Guido Fink (Brunswick, NJ: Rutgers University Press, 1989), pp. 177–79. It is possible to extend Antonioni's critique of this myth to the use of cinema to render such codes legible or to confront them. Indeed it is important to be wary of the inflation of such awareness into the status of a myth regarding the political significance of the arts on account of the fact that they render social codes in rebellious or critical terms.

12. For this reason, as Peter Brunette notes, the slower integration of women in the professions in Italy gives them a central role in the works set by Antonioni in the Italy of the 1960s, a role in which they offer a perspective distanced from and implicitly critical of many of his male characters. See Brunette, *The Films of Michelangelo Antonioni*, pp. 8–10, 42–46, 103–4.

13. Indeed, Antonioni later described how he was interested in this film in looking at places, such as the desert, in which a nonhistorical existence could be found (see Antonioni, *The Architecture of Vision*, p. 183). It is clear that the political drama in the film runs counter to this aspiration, or at least shows the imposition of the historical mode of existence in the West and its traits, such as the technological framing of experience all over the globe. Put more boldly, the film does not open with a contrast between the nonmodernized desert culture and the expectations of the Westerner. The guns that run the guerrilla war, the cigarettes that have the status of a currency, the evidence of Western education in the proliferation of the colonial language, and finally the fact that politics is played in an international theater are all signs of the permeability of these worlds.

14. According to Antonioni there are two documentaries in this film: Locke's documentary on Africa and Antonioni's documentary on Locke (see Antonioni, *The Architecture of Vision*, p. 335). We might add that the footage in the film of Locke's interviews and his footage of an execution also present us with a picture of Locke's life prior to his "project."

15. William Arrowsmith's description of this politicized context as an arms runner supplying rebels opposed to the "legitimate government" is difficult to understand. Among the many scenes that belie the title of "legitimacy" are those that sketch the brutality of the covert operation against the rebels conducted in the theater of European countries, as well as the execution scene in Africa, and, finally, Locke's weak interview with the ruler of this country on the status of the rebels is used by Antonioni to underscore the tensions between Locke and his wife, who is appalled at the reporter's polite interview of a tyrant and dismayed at his rejoinder that he is playing a game and abiding by its rules. Most of Antonioni's films include scenes of games, although Antonioni's scene of a game was cut from the final rushes of *L'avventura*. Is the game in *The Passenger* Locke's profession? Or is it the way that he plays at another man's identity? Clearly his commitment to the latter increases when the girl is included in the game. Arrowsmith's discussion of *The Passenger* is in William Arrowsmith, *Antonioni: The Poet of Images* (Oxford: Oxford University Press, 1995), pp. 146–71.

16. This distinction between moral belief and the rule-bound existence of the journalist differentiates him from the dualism treated in Antonioni's earlier films in which two different times—the past beliefs and the present context—are at odds with each other.

17. The title *The Passenger* loses the sense of the modern professionalization of the West that the original title evokes, although it does suggest the uncommitted disposition of the journalist. This is not the place to go into the complex story that affected the screening of this film and the rights over its distribution; however, suffice it to note that Antonioni cut back his original version by nearly two hours, and the rights to an amended version integrating three scenes missing from the studio release is held by Jack Nicholson. It is significant to note that these scenes would have given more context to the motivation of the Nicholson character—showing him back at the London house looking at a note left for his wife by her lover and also showing discord between him and the girl. Such discord is important in the film given that it becomes her project that Locke become Robertson or, put in more impersonal terms, that an observer become a committed actor. It is also the prospect of such a transition that interests his wife. Brunette discusses these scenes in *The Films of Michelangelo Antonioni* (pp. 135–36).

18. The place of time in Niklas Luhmann's work has a number of dimensions. Here I draw simply on his view of time as a resource for the reduction of complexity. Luhmann also discusses time from the perspective of the genesis and management of systems. See his discussion of time and events in Niklas Luhmann, *Social Systems*, trans. John Bednarz Jr., with Dirk Baecker (Stanford, CA: Stanford University Press, 1995), p. 287. This perspective is quite distinct from Deleuze's interest in the ways modern cinema makes perceptible the element of time as distinct from anything "in" time. For Deleuze, "what is specific to the image, as soon as it is creative, is to make perceptible, to make visible, relationships of time which cannot be seen in the represented object and do not allow themselves to be reduced to the present" (Deleuze, *Cinema 2*, p. xii).

19. This theme is approached from a different angle in Jarmusch's *Ghost Dog: The Way of the Samurai*.

20. It is interesting to consider what place political events occupy in this aesthetic/ formal cinema. The main characters in *Blow-Up* and *The Passenger* explicitly use such "events" to give an aesthetic structure to their projects. In the cases of the documentary that Locke is making about Africa, which needs something "extra" (something he hopes to find with the guerrillas), and the book of photography that the photographer is splicing with pictures from a doss-house, politics plays the formal, aesthetic role of an aestheticized relation to time structured by the goal of avoiding boredom.

21. As Wittgenstein put it: some things cannot be said but "only shown"; and cinema, we may add, is merely one venue for such "showing." See Ludwig Wittgenstein, *Tractatus Logico-Philosophicus*, trans. D. F. Pears and B. F. McGuinness, rev. ed. (London: Routledge, 1974), 4.1212, p. 31.

22. I do not want to rehearse here the reflections on cinema's proficiency in depicting time. On this point see Panofsky, *Three Essays on Style*, p. 96; and Deleuze, *Cinema 2*, esp. pp. 34–44.

Chapter 4

1. This chapter is reprinted with the publisher's kind permission from Michael J. Shapiro, *Deforming American Political Thought: Ethnicity, Facticity, and Genre* (Lexington: University Press of Kentucky, 2006), pp. 65–104. The quotation is from Miriam Hansen's introduction to Siegfried Kracauer's *Theory of Film* (Princeton, NJ: Princeton University Press, 1997), p. x.

2. Jacques Rancière, "The Politics of Aesthetics," http://theater.kein.org/node/99 (accessed Nov. 7, 2007).

3. Quoted in David Sterritt, "Director Builds Metaphor for Jazz in *Kansas City*," in *Robert Altman: Interviews*, ed. David Sterritt (Jackson: University Press of Mississippi, 2000), p. 213.

4. Sterritt's observation in ibid., p. 212.

5. The quotation is from Eric Sundquist, *Cultural Contexts for Ralph Ellison's "Invisible Man"* (Boston: Bedford Books, 1995), p. 11. Sundquist is one among many who have recognized Ellison's aesthetic strategy. See also, e.g., Horace A. Porter, *Jazz Country: Ralph Ellison in America* (Iowa City: University of Iowa Press, 2001), where Porter writes about "*Invisible Man* as Jazz Text" (pp. 72–91).

6. Sundquist, *Cultural Contexts for Ralph Ellison's "Invisible Man,"* p. 11.

7. See Jacques Rancière, *The Politics of Aesthetics*, trans. Gabriel Rockhill (New York: Continuum, 2004), pp. 23–24. The quoted remarks are part of the political sense Rancière ascribes to the novels of Virginia Woolf, which he sees as more political than those of Emile Zola. Although Zola's novels are more explicit social epics, according to Rancière they are less attentive to micropolitical levels of dissensus.

8. Ibid., p. 24.

9. The quotations are from Mary Ann Doane, *The Emergence of Cinematic Time* (Cambridge, MA: Harvard University Press, 2002), p. 194.

10. Connie Byrne and William O. Lopez, "*Nashville*," in *Robert Altman: Interviews*, ed. David Sterritt (Jackson: University Press of Mississippi, 2000), p. 20.

11. The quotation is from Krin Gabbard's review of the film: "Kansas City," *American Historical Review* 102, no. 4 (Oct. 1997): 1274–75.

12. The quotations are from Altman's response to David Breskin's query, "Do you think there's a politics to your styles, to the style itself?" (David Breskin, *Inner Views: Filmmakers in Conversation* [New York: Da Capo, 1997], p. 287).

13. Gilles Deleuze, *Francis Bacon: The Logic of Sensation*, trans. Daniel W. Smith (Minneapolis: University of Minnesota Press, 2003), p. 71.

14. Ibid., pp. 71–72.

15. "McCabe and Mrs. Miller," www.wordlookup.net/mc/mccabe-and-mrs.-miller .html (accessed Sep. 19, 2007).

16. Virginia Wright Wexman, "The Family on the Land: Race and Nationhood in Silent Westerns," in *The Birth of Whiteness*, ed. Daniel Bernardi (New Brunswick, NJ: Rutgers University Press, 1996), p. 131.

17. For this version of the typical strong stranger who must remain outside of society see Will Wright's structuralist reading of classic westerns in his *Six Guns and Society* (Berkeley: University of California Press, 1975).

18. Susan Armitage, Elizabeth Jameson, and Joan Jensen, "The New Western History: Another Perspective," *Journal of the West* 32, no. 3 (1993): 5–6.

19. Graham Fuller, "Altman on Altman," in *Robert Altman: Interviews*, ed. David Sterritt (Jackson: University Press of Mississippi, 2000), p. 195.

20. Deleuze, *Francis Bacon*, p. 14.

21. Ibid., p. 6.

22. The convenient albeit partial review is a quotation from Pam Cook, "Women and the Western," in *The Western Reader*, ed. Jim Kitses and Greg Rickman (New York: Limelight, 1999), pp. 293–94.

23. See Gilles Deleuze, *Cinema 1* (Minneapolis: University of Minnesota Press, 1986), pp. 87–88.

24. See Noel Burch, "Spatial and Temporal Articulations," in *Theory of Film Practice*, trans. Helen Lane (New York: Praeger, 1973), p. 17.

25. Quoted in Bruce Williamson, "Altman," in *Robert Altman: Interviews*, ed. David Sterritt (Jackson: University Press of Mississippi, 2000), pp. 38–39.

26. Fuller, "Altman on Altman," p. 198.

27. The idea that the gun is "the moral center of the Western," is expressed in Robert Warshow, "Movie Chronicle: The Westerner," in *The Western Reader*, ed. Jim Kitses and Greg Rickman (New York: Limelight, 1999), p. 37.

28. Alan Nadel, *Containment Culture: American Narratives, Postmodernism, and the Atomic Age* (Durham, NC: Duke University Press, 1995), p. 195.

29. Fuller, "Altman on Altman," p. 198.

30. Quoted in Harry Kloman and Lloyd Michaels, with Virginia Wright Wexman, "A Foolish Optimist," in *Robert Altman: Interviews*, ed. David Sterritt (Jackson: University Press of Mississippi, 2000), p. 113.

31. Gene M. Bernstein, "Robert Altman's *Buffalo Bill and the Indians or Sitting Bull's History Lesson*: A Self-Portrait in Celluloid," *Journal of Popular Culture* 13, no. 1 (summer 1979): 17.

32. Among the most effective recent treatments is Vincent Amiel's *Le corps au cinéma: Keaton, Bresson, Cassavetes* (Paris: Presses Universitaires de France, 1998).

33. Ibid., p. 2.

34. Ibid.

35. Jerome Game, "Cinematic Bodies," *Studies in French Cinema* 1, no. 1 (2001): 50–51. Game is examining Amiel's approach to the cinematographic body.

Chapter 5

1. Marvin D'Lugo, *The Films of Carlos Saura: The Practice of Seeing* (Princeton, NJ: Princeton University Press, 1991), p. 140.

2. *Carlos Saura: Interviews*, ed. Linda M. Willem (Jackson: University Press of Mississippi, 2003), p. 50.

3. D'Lugo discusses the role of the song and the ending of *Cría cuervos* in terms of "the possibility of growth," which marks a critical difference from Saura's previous film, *Cousin Angelica*. See D'Lugo, *The Films of Carlos Saura*, pp. 136–38.

4. Martin Heidegger, *Being and Time*, trans. John Macquarrie and Edward Robinson (New York: Harper and Row, 1962), pp. 349–50.

5. Ibid., p. 279.

6. Martin Heidegger, *The Fundamental Concepts of Metaphysics: World, Finitude, Solitude*, trans. William McNeill and Nicholas Walker (Bloomington: Indiana University Press, 1995), p. 363.

7. Ibid., p. 364.

8. "Because in each case existence is only as factically thrown, historiology will disclose the quiet force of the possible [*stille Kraft des Möglichen*] with greater penetration the more simply and the more concretely having-been-in-the-world is understood in terms of possibility, and 'only' presented as such" (Heidegger, *Being and Time*, p. 446).

9. Ibid., p. 447.

10. Martin Heidegger, "Letter on 'Humanism,'" in *Basic Writings*, trans. and ed. David Farrell Krell (New York: HarperCollins, 1977, 1993), p. 220; I have changed the word *power* to *force* in this quote to make clear that Heidegger quotes his phrase from *Being and Time* cited before.

11. Heidegger, *Basic Writings*, p. 220.

12. Martin Heidegger, "The Origin of the Work of Art," in *Basic Writings*, trans. and ed. David Farrell Krell (New York: HarperCollins, 1977, 1993), p. 179.

13. Giorgio Agamben, *The Man Without Content*, trans. Georgia Albert (Stanford, CA: Stanford University Press, 1999), p. 99.

14. Ibid., p. 101.

Chapter 6

1. Glauber Rocha, interview by Gary Crowdus and William Starr, trans. Ruth McCormick and Susan Hertelendy, in *Art, Politics, Cinema: The Cineaste Interviews*, ed. Dan Georgakas and Lenny Rubenstein (London: Pluto, 1985), p. 14.

2. Glauber Rocha, "Eztetyka da fome," in Sylvie Pierre, *Glauber Rocha: Textos e entrevistas com Glauber Rocha*, trans. Eleonora Bottmann (Campinas, Brazil: Papirus, 1996), p. 125. Unless otherwise specified, all translations are my own.

3. Glauber Rocha, *Revisão crítica do cinema brasileiro* (São Paulo: Cosac and Naify, 2003), p. 66. In 2007 the World Cinema Foundation released a restored *Limite*.

4. Carlos Heitor Cony, quoted in João Carlos Teixeira Gomes, *Glauber Rocha: Esse vulcão* (Rio de Janeiro: Nova Fronteira, 1997), p. xxi.

5. René Gardies, *Glauber Rocha* (Paris: Seghers, 1974), p. 63.

6. Glauber Rocha, "Eztetyka do sonho," in Sylvie Pierre, *Glauber Rocha: Textos e entrevistas com Glauber Rocha*, trans. Eleonora Bottmann (Campinas: Papirus, 1996), p. 135.

7. Glauber Rocha, "From the Drought to the Palm Trees," trans. Robert Stam and Burnes Hollyman, in *Brazilian Cinema*, ed. Randal Johnson and Robert Stam (New York: Columbia University Press, 1995), p. 89.

8. Gilles Deleuze, *Cinema 2: The Time-Image*, trans. Hugh Tomlinson and Robert Galeta (Minneapolis: University of Minnesota Press, 1991), p. 220.

9. Gardies, *Glauber Rocha*, p. 121.

10. For the critic Jean-Claude Bernardet there is a "brutal shock" in *Land in Anguish* when the camera passes from the people gathered at Vieira's rally to the actors claiming to speak in the role of the people. See his letter of July 21, 1967, to Rocha, included in Glauber Rocha, *Cartas ao mundo*, ed. Ivana Bentes (São Paulo: Companhia das Letras, 1997), p. 287. In a detailed and insightful response Bernardet carries his objections to the film through to a critique of the prevailing political conditions: the question of how to reach the public artistically is simultaneously the question of how to politicize the masses.

11. Glauber Rocha, "The Tricontinental Filmmaker: That Is Called the Dawn," trans. Burnes Hollyman and Robert Stam in *Brazilian Cinema*, ed. Randal Johnson and Robert Stam (New York: Columbia University Press, 1995), p. 78.

12. Witold Gombrowicz, *Diary*, trans. Lillian Vallee, vol. 1 (Evanston, IL: Northwestern University Press, 1988), p. 69.

13. See Hannah Arendt, *Lectures on Kant's Political Philosophy*, ed. Ronald Beiner (Chicago: University of Chicago Press, 1982), p. 61: "Since Kant did not write his political philosophy, the best way to find out what he thought about this matter is to turn to his 'Critique of Aesthetic Judgment.'" What Kant has to say about aesthetic judgment does not need to be loaded down with reservations and qualifications in order to be applied meaningfully to politics. Arendt's great insight is weakened if it is taken up in terms of the question of determining the limits of the analogy. The political truth of Kant's reflections on aesthetic judgment is that unless aesthetic judgment escapes its segregation in the delimited realm of aesthetic phenomena to deploy itself in and as the political, it cannot properly be that which Kant says it is.

14. Cf. Cornelius Castoriadis, "The Greek Polis and the Creation of Democracy," in *Philosophy, Politics, Autonomy*, ed. David Ames Curtis (Oxford: Oxford University Press, 1991), pp. 122–23. In his interpretation of the Funeral Oration of Pericles, Castoriadis draws out the links between the decision-making processes of politics and what is called beautiful.

15. Jean-François Lyotard, *Peregrinations: Law, Form, Event* (New York: Columbia University Press, 1988), p. 38.

16. Immanuel Kant, *Critique of the Power of Judgment*, trans. Paul Guyer and Eric Matthews (Cambridge, UK: Cambridge University Press, 2000), p. 229.

17. See James H. Johnson, "Revolutionary Audiences and the Impossible Imperatives of Fraternity," in *Re-creating Authority in Revolutionary France*, ed. Bryant T. Ragan Jr. and Elizabeth A. Williams (New Brunswick, NJ: Rutgers University Press, 1992), pp. 57–78. Illustrating how in the early 1790s in France the stage was no longer considered a realm set apart for aesthetic contemplation, Johnson discusses the arrests and confinements of actors identified with their aristocratic roles.

18. Rocha, "The Tricontinental Filmmaker," p. 77.

19. Hannah Arendt, *The Human Condition* (Chicago: University of Chicago Press, 1998), p. 173.

20. Among the insights of Kant's third *Critique* is the thesis that instrumental rationality (as a species of teleology) and the appreciation of the beautiful share a basis in the faculty of judgment. For neither instrumental rationality nor the appreciation of the beautiful does the question of what an object objectively is exhaust the subject's relation to the object, yet by inquiring into the use of the object for the empirical or empirically modeled desires of the subject, instrumental rationality does not come up against the a priori (i.e., nonactual) character of the subject.

21. For a recent example see Humberto Alves Silva Júnior, "Glauber Rocha: Arte, cultura e política," in *O olho da história* 12, no. 9 (Dec. 2006): 6.

22. Ismail Xavier, *Sertão Mar: Glauber Rocha e a estética da fome* (São Paulo: Editora Brasiliense, 1983), pp. 121–23.

23. Frantz Fanon, *The Wretched of the Earth*, trans. Constance Farrington (Harmondsworth, UK: Penguin, 1967), pp. 244, 250.

24. Raquel Gerber, "Glauber Rocha: Uma Obra Pessoal," in *Glauber Rocha*, ed. Jean-Claude Bernardet and Paulo Emílio Salles Gomes (São Paulo: Paz e Terra, 1991), p. 37.

Chapter 7

1. This has been pointed out by Stefan Aust in his history of the Baader Meinhof group. Aust suggests that the reference to Melville was made to imply that members of the group saw themselves as heroes, risking their lives in the face of the Leviathan. See Stefan Aust, *Der Baader-Meinhof-Komplex* (Hamburg: Hoffmann und Campe, 1997), p. 289.

2. Thomas Hobbes, *Leviathan*, ed. Richard Tuck (Cambridge, UK: Cambridge University Press, 1996), p. 9.

3. For historical details on France see Ieme van der Poel, *Une révolution de la pensée: Maoïsme et féminisme à travers: "Tel quel," "Les temps modernes," et "Esprit"* (Amsterdam: Rodopi, 1992).

4. The novel was called *Kärlek med förhinder* [*Love with a Hindrance*], by fictive author Per A. Rosenberg (Lund, Sweden: Bo Cavefors, 1978). The same press also published *Ulrike Meinhofs förbjudna tankesätt* [*The Forbidden Thoughts of Ulrike Meinhof*] in 1977.

5. See Thomas Elsaesser, "Margarethe von Trotta: German Sisters—Divided Daughters," in *New German Cinema* (London: Macmillan, 1989), pp. 232–38.

6. See E. Ann Kaplan, "Female Politics in the Symbolic Realm: Von Trotta's *Marianne and Juliane* (*The German Sisters*) (1981)," in *Women and Film: Both Sides of the Camera* (London: Routledge, 1983), pp. 104–13. The relation between the sisters is the key to understanding the function of the law in the film and the processes of identification undergone by the sisters:

> This doubling [of the sisters] is not a mere externalization of an inner split (as was the case in the German Romantic *Doppelgänger*); nor is it intended simply to show the different possibilities for women struggling to find themselves in an alien, male-dominated realm. It functions rather on an altogether more complex level, revealing, first, the strong attraction that women feel for qualities in other women that they themselves do not possess; second, the difficulty women have in establishing boundaries between self and Other; and finally, the jealousy and competition among women that socialization in patriarchy makes inevitable. Sometimes, the doubling takes place on the imaginary / symbolic axis, one of the pairs functioning smoothly in the public sphere, while the other seems to desire regression to the presymbolic and repetition of the merged phase of early mother-child relating. (Kaplan, "Female Politics in the Symbolic Realm," p. 107)

See also "Discourses of Terrorism, Feminism, and the Family in von Trotta's *Marianne and Juliane*," *Persistence of Vision* 1, no. 2 (spring 1985): 61–68; repr. in *Women and Film*, ed. Janet Todd (New York: Holmes and Meier, 1988), pp. 258–70. For a reading of von Trotta's film in relation to the RAF, see Lisa Di Caprio, "Baader-Meinhof Fictionalized: *Marianne and Juliane* / The German Sisters," *Jump Cut* 29 (1984).

7. Hobbes, *Leviathan*, p. 120.

8. Ibid., p. 100.

9. Arendt explains Luxemburg's antinationalism not as a disavowal of German culture but rather as stemming from the fact that the Jews of Europe were the first Europeans, identifying not with one single nation but with European commonality and languages. See Hannah Arendt, *Men in Dark Times* (London: Harvest, 1968), p. 42.

10. See Julia Kristeva, "Women's Time," in *The Kristeva Reader*, ed. Toril Moi (Oxford: Blackwell, 1986), pp. 187–213.

11. Reason's imposition of freedom, Hegel has shown, is doomed to fail. There is no space for political terrorism; the introduction of the force of negativity makes any such actions not only vile but intrusive. Terror is the face of death encountered in absolute freedom, a moment in which death has no significance "for what is negated is the empty point of the absolutely free self" (G.W.F. Hegel, *Phenomenology of Spirit*, trans. A. V. Miller [Oxford: Oxford University Press, 1977], p. 590). Thus, one cannot simply realize freedom in terms of an abstraction or of a form of self-consciousness that remains abstract in itself; such realization of the absolute turns from the positive realization of thought to the negative differentiation of substance. Absolute freedom, therefore, shudders at the terror provoked by its own realization and turns to a production of differences that one may, perhaps, call a fear of death or self-annihilation. The movement of negation can

never complete itself as absolute freedom. What happens is rather the transformation of culture and ethical life.

12. See Jürgen Habermas, "Yet Again: German Identity—A Unified Nation of Angry DM-Burghers," in *When the Wall Came Down*, ed. Harold James and Marla Stone (London: Routledge, 1992), pp. 86–102.

13. Giovanna Borradori, *Philosophy in a Time of Terror: Dialogues with Jürgen Habermas and Jacques Derrida* (Chicago: University of Chicago Press, 2003), pp. 41–43.

14. Walter Benjamin, "Critique of Violence," in *Reflections: Essays, Aphorisms, Autobiographical Writings*, ed. Peter Demetz, trans. Edmund Jephcott (New York: Schocken Books, 1986), p. 287.

15. Ibid., p. 239.

16. Jacques Derrida, "Force of Law: The 'Mystical Foundations of Authority,'" trans. Mary Quaintance in *Cardozo Law Review* 11, nos. 5–6 (July/Aug. 1990): 1033.

17. Benjamin, "Critique of Violence," p. 251.

18. Ibid.

Chapter 8

1. "'I've changed along with the characters in my films': A Discussion with Hella Schlumberger About Work and Love, the Exploitability of Feelings, and the Longing for Utopia," in Rainer Werner Fassbinder, *The Anarchy of the Imagination: Interviews, Essays, Notes*, ed. Michael Töteberg and Leo A. Lensing, trans. Krishna Winston (Baltimore: Johns Hopkins University Press, 1992), p. 28. All notes are drawn from this volume.

2. "'I'm a romantic anarchist': A Discussion with Frank Ripploh About *Veronika Voss* and *Querelle*," p. 68.

3. "'I'd rather be a streetsweeper in Mexico than a filmmaker in Germany': A Conversation with *Der Spiegel* About the Politics of German Film and Fassbinder's Announcement That He Intended to Leave the Country," p. 141.

4. "'Images the moviegoer can fill with his own imagination': A Conversation with Kraft Wetzel About *Effi Briest*," p. 151.

5. Ibid.

6. Ibid.

7. "'I make films out of personal involvement, and for no other reason': A Discussion with Hans Günther Pflaum About *Berlin Alexanderplatz* and *Lili Marleen*," p. 46.

8. "'Images the moviegoer can fill with his own imagination,'" p. 151.

9. Ibid.

10. Ibid., p. 150.

11. "'At some point films have to stop being films': A Conversation with Hans Günther Pflaum About *Fear Eats the Soul*," p. 11.

12. "Hanna Schygulla—Not a Star, Just a Vulnerable Human Being like the Rest of Us: Disorderly Thoughts About an Interesting Woman," p. 209.

13. "'Of despair, and the courage to recognize a utopia and to open yourself up to it': Two Monologues and a Text on *Despair*," p. 174.

14. Ibid.

15. Ibid., p. 176.

16. Ibid., p. 175.

17. "'Images the moviegoer can fill with his own imagination,'" p. 158.

18. "'The kind of rage I feel': A Conversation with Joachim von Mengershausen About *Love Is Colder Than Death*," p. 7.

19. "'Reacting to What You Experience': Ernst Burkel Talks with Douglas Sirk and Rainer Werner Fassbinder," p. 44.

20. "'I've changed along with the characters in my films,'" p. 24.

21. "'Reacting to What You Experience,'" p. 44.

Chapter 9

1. "In Defense of Places," *Director's Guild of America Magazine* 28, no. 4 (2003): www .dga.org./news/v28_4/craft_wendersplaces.php3. Wenders makes a similar comment in *Once: Pictures and Stories* (Munich: Schirmer/ Mosel and DAP/ Distributed Art Publishers, 2001), p. 13: "I firmly believe in the story-building power of landscapes. . . . Landscapes can be leading characters themselves and the people in them the extras."

2. Wim Wenders, "Film Thieves," in *Wim Wenders: On Film: Essays and Conversations* (London: Faber and Faber, 2001), p. 194.

3. Moreover, while memory may most often, at least for the sighted, be heavily oriented to vision, it is often other senses, especially taste and smell (as Proust's work famously demonstrates), that are the triggers for the recall of memory.

4. Wim Wenders, "The Art of Seeing," in *Wim Wenders: On Film: Essays and Conversations*, p. 297.

5. Wim Wenders, "The American Dream," in *Wim Wenders: On Film: Essays and Conversations*, p. 129.

6. Or, to be more precise, that comes with experiential memory—it is not, of course, something normally associated with what we may call informational or ideational memory.

7. Wim Wenders, "Impossible Stories," in *Wim Wenders: On Film: Essays and Conversations*, p. 210. Elsewhere Wenders writes, "The first films I made were like paintings sustained over a certain length of time. I had more painter models than directors" (Wim Wenders, "The Truth of Images," in *Wim Wenders: On Film: Essays and Conversations*, p. 324).

8. Wim Wenders, "A Step Ahead of the Times," in *Wim Wenders: On Film: Essays and Conversations*, p. 419.

9. Wenders, "The Truth of Images," pp. 326–27.

10. Once again, the connection is with experiential memory, not the memory of information or idea.

11. See my discussion of Proust in Jeff Malpas, *Place and Experience: A Philosophical Topography* (Cambridge, UK: Cambridge University Press, 1999), pp. 157–91.

12. See Frances A. Yates, *The Art of Memory* (Chicago: University of Chicago Press, 1974).

13. Wenders, "The Truth of Images," p. 330. Wenders does say, however, in the commentary included as part of the DVD version of the film, that he prefers the English title.

14. Wim Wenders, "An Attempted Description of an Indescribable Film," in *Wim Wenders: On Film: Essays and Conversations*, p. 233.

15. The more evocative German title is *Im Lauf der Zeit* (*In the Course of Time*).

16. See Wenders, "In Defense of Places."

17. The film now also constitutes, of course, a memory of the city as it no longer is, since many of the locations Wenders used, Potsdamer Platz, for instance, have been redeveloped, and the city is no longer divided as it was when the film was shot. As Wenders comments, "The whole film suddenly turned into an archive for things that aren't around anymore" (Wenders, "A Step Ahead of the Times," p. 419).

18. *Notebook on Cities and Clothes*—see the English commentary as given in *Wim Wenders: On Film: Essays and Conversations*, p. 363 (the title of the film is given here as *Notebook on Clothes and Cities*).

19. Wenders, "An Attempted Description of an Indescribable Film," p. 233.

20. Travis's comment to his brother in *Paris, Texas*.

21. Wim Wenders, "Talk About Germany," in *Wim Wenders: On Film: Essays and Conversations*, p. 442; see also Wenders's English commentary in *Notebook on Clothes and Cities* (in *Wim Wenders: On Film: Essays and Conversations*, pp. 363–74).

22. Walter Benjamin, "The Work of Art in the Age of Mechanical Reproduction," in *Illuminations*, ed. Hannah Arendt (New York: Schocken Books, 1969), pp. 220, 221.

23. Ibid., p. 238. The embedded reference is to Georges Duhanel, *Scènes de la vie future* (Paris: A. Fayard, 1930), p. 52.

24. In fact, Benjamin sees film and photography as both having the power to reawaken our sense of what is given in the image. Benjamin's analysis, then, does not stop with the recognition of a certain loss through reproductive proliferation—see my "Heidegger in Benjamin's City," *Journal of Architecture*, 12. no. 5 (Nov. 2007): 489–97, for a further exploration of the possibility that the proliferation of images may actually lead us back to a sense of the presence of things. Moreover, as I argue here, Wenders's work can be seen as constituting a response to the apparent problem posed by the proliferation of images in a way that seeks to use the technologies that contribute to such proliferation so as to return us to a sense of the things as such and the places in which those things are to be found. In this latter respect Wenders could be seen to follow a path that is itself indicated in Benjamin's own work.

25. The phrase is from *Until the End of the World*, but see also Wenders, "The Truth of Images," p. 340.

26. Wenders, "The Truth of Images," p. 327.

27. Of course, just as the proliferation of images remains dependent on place even as it also displaces, so contemporary digital and virtual technologies remain bound to place even as they tend toward its apparent obliteration. The tension at issue here is something that I have discussed in a range of contexts elsewhere. See, e.g., Jeff Malpas, "Acting at a Distance and Knowing from Afar: Agency and Knowledge on the World Wide Web," in *The Robot in the Garden*, ed. Ken Goldberg (Cambridge, MA: MIT Press, 2000), pp. 114–20; Jeff Malpas, "Cultural Heritage in the Age of New Media," in *New Heritage: New Media and Cultural Heritage*, ed. Yehuda Kalay, Thomas Kvan, and Jane Affleck

(London: Routledge, 2007), pp. 19–24 (this essay also takes Benjamin's essay as a key source for the issues under discussion); and Jeff Malpas, *Heidegger's Topology* (Cambridge, MA: MIT Press, 2006), pp. 293–97.

28. See Wenders, "In Defense of Places."

29. See Wenders, "The Truth of Images," pp. 324–29.

30. Wim Wenders, "The American Friend," in *Wim Wenders: On Film: Essays and Conversations*, p. 177.

31. Wenders "The Truth of Images," p. 340.

32. Wim Wenders, "Urban Landscape from the Point of View of Images," in *Wim Wenders: On Film: Essays and Conversations*, p. 379.

33. Wim Wenders, "Reverse Angle," in *Wim Wenders: On Film: Essays and Conversations*, p. 180.

34. Wenders, "Impossible Stories," p. 213.

35. Ibid., pp. 210, 211.

36. Wenders, "In Defense of Places."

37. My reading of "The Work of Art in the Age of Mechanical Reproduction" shifts the discussion away from Benjamin's focus on the work of art and on to the image, and, consistent with this, my reading of Wenders is not focused on film as art but on film in its relation to the image. Wenders does not aim at restoring, through film, the "aura" of the artwork or at establishing a certain "aura" for filmic works in particular. Instead, his work shows that the image may serve to return us to that from which it comes rather than taking us perpetually farther away from it.

38. There are, of course, a number of issues that could be explored here, not only in terms of Wenders's own biography (and on this matter see his talk, given in the München-er Kammerspiel, on Nov. 10, 1991, entitled "Talk About Germany," in *Wim Wenders: On Film: Essays and Conversations*, pp. 434–44) but also relating to the history of German film over the last fifty years or more. Indeed, a range of issues lie just beneath the surface of the discussion here (including, for instance, German cinematic realism) and deserve further exploration. Wenders's work provides a fertile ground for such discussions, although they are discussions that must be left for another time.

Chapter 10

1. As Nancy's wordplay on *baiser* (to kiss / to fuck) is difficult to render meaningfully into English, I have had to compromise. The original reads: "*Il s'agit du baiser, ou de baiser: mais très précisément en sorte que baiser, ici, ou si l'on veut 'le sexe,' est rapporté au baiser, plutôt que l'inverse.*"—Trans.

2. This play on words (italicized) makes use of the homophonic *po* and *peau*. Placing *peau* (skin) in what would normally be *pellicule exposée* (exposed film) highlights not only some of Nancy's points about the integral relationship between film and skin but also actually figures the distinction between exterior and interior that he discusses: a word representing something exterior (skin) hidden inside a word that actually means "to discover what is within."—Trans.

Index